vocalarts
workbookanddvd

A practical course for achieving clarity
and expression with your voice

DAVID CAREY AND REBECCA CLARK CAREY

methuen | drama

To our parents, who gave us our voices:
Brian and Elna Carey
and
Owen and Barbara Clark

Acknowledgements

We would like to warmly thank the following: Cicely Berry, Jane Boston, and Yvonne Burgess for their insightful comments on our manuscript; Robert Cohen, Barbara Houseman, Gillyanne Kayes, and Miriam Rabkin for their generous advice and support; Stephen Ambrose for his diligence and talent in translating our ideas into line drawings; and Matt Bannister, Annie Hemingway and Peter Todd for their skilled contributions to the DVD.

We would also like to wholeheartedly acknowledge the contribution that our teachers and our students through the years have made to our understanding of voice. In particular, David would like to thank all his past students of the Voice Studies course at the Central School of Speech and Drama.

Finally, thanks to all at A&C Black, particularly Jenny Ridout and Katie Taylor for their support and enthusiasm for this project.

First published 2008

Methuen Drama
A & C Black Publishers Limited
38 Soho Square
London W1D 3HB
www.acblack.com

ISBN 978-0-7136-8824-5

A CIP catalogue record for this book is available from the British Library.

This book is produced using paper that is made from wood grown in managed, sustainable forests. It is natural, renewable and recyclable. The logging and manufacturing processes conform to the environmental regulations of the country of origin.

Typeset in 10/14pt Glasgow XL

Printed and bound at Caligraving Ltd, Thetford, Norfolk

Forewords

This book is valuable both for the voice teacher and for the student working on his/her own voice - for, in a very comprehensive way, it brings together all the factors which are needed to find one's own authentic voice.

I find the book both refreshing and remarkable since it teaches, not by telling you what to do, but rather by first making the reader aware of their own personal bodily responses to breathing, tension, resonance etc., and to the whole process of making sound in their everyday life. In a most imaginative, and often humorous, way, it arouses our curiosity as to how we each make sound and speech in the variable circumstances of our lives. With this enhanced awareness of our own habits, it then instructs us, through very clear and specific exercises, how to build on this knowledge by managing our tensions and developing our breathing potential; the exercises are always an exploration.

The message that underpins the work is that good breathing not only produces a good voice, but also feeds the actor in their exploration of character, and in the truth of that character. In other words, to breathe deeply is to think deeply.

Cicely Berry

Each time we speak, we reveal our nationality, disposition, attitudes, background, idiosyncrasies, familial traits and mannerisms. We carry our lives and childhoods in our voice and this is an important part of the armoury of any artist or any person who wishes to be heard.

Voice is about connecting both our primitive thoughts and our sophisticated ones to a mechanism that can communicate. Having 'a voice in the world', whatever that world is, is the gift we inherit and one we can develop. Voice holds our self-esteem, confidence, comfort and control. It is a physical activity: we 'draw breath' and speak. Without it, as Winnie in Beckett's *Happy Days* says, there is 'Nothing to break the silence of this place.'

Voice is about not having to live in the silence of the lonely imagination, instead sharing our thoughts and sculpting sound so that not only is meaning conveyed, but also the essence of who we are. It is about our possibility. So there is not a person on the planet who will not benefit from making sure that their voice is being true to its master, the inner self.

For actors, of course, vocal skill is crucial - not just for serving personal expression, but also for serving the play we are releasing. It is also crucial to be able to sustain vocal energy over a prolonged time so that neither mood nor fatigue can shake our abilities. It was in this context that I first met David Carey at the Royal Shakespeare Company, when he came quietly into a rehearsal room to observe rehearsals with Cicely Berry, the transformative voice coach of the previous generation. That was about 25 years ago, since when he has had many individual sessions with many actors, and has always been sympathetic to the myriad problems that strike each performer. In this book he and his fellow writer, Rebecca Carey, draw on their unique experience as voice teachers to give us valuable insight into the process of developing the actor's voice.

The actor's voice is always being tampered with, even as it tries to be the most 'normal'. It is the tool that, along with the spectacular truths held in poetic language, is one of the most distinguishing aspects of our humanity-driven trade. We need voices to be able to perform better than our natures and yet to reveal our natures. We are asked to be the conduits of big thoughts – bigger than normal conversational usage – and so voice work is as much about tuning into our own possibilities as it is about gaining vocal skill. It also has a philosophical dimension and, through it, we open up the possibilities for the listener to be touched more profoundly.

Recently, I performed in Epidaurus, the ancient Greek amphitheatre. A terror of a lifetime to act to 5000 people, out of doors, and not to have a microphone! I was struck that our colleagues in ancient Greece were undertaking the same activity 2400 years ago. How did they cope with vocal challenges? I was reminded of the exercises, some of which are presented in this book, the power of breath, the necessary relaxation and heightened awareness of thought and feeling. All this as true then as now. Technology enhances volume, but only we ourselves can enhance the power of concentrated thought, the distillation of which is carried in the miraculous journey from breath to rhythm. I feel that by reading this book, we start this journey into the air and into ourselves.

Only in testing variation can the actor reach for the heights needed to be a conduit for what is demanded by complicated texts. Acting is the art of transforming both the ordinary and the extraordinary so that it can be heard in a poetic way, so that it lodges in the listener's mind and haunts them after the event. Actors must develop the voice so that when we have the thought in mind we can communicate it with real 'depth charge'.

For each new generation of theatre practitioners the style of that delivery must change, but not the fact of it. Here we have writers who are offering important insights to us all in a way that our new ears can hear, so that our new voices can speak. Employing contemporary media and tried-and-true training, they present concrete, practical information and in an imaginative way. Using the exercises in this book, one is put in touch with the self-empowering aspect of voice, the chance to extend and expand our range. That is a great gift, to be empowered with old knowledge so one may be more fully in the present. Ultimately this is what *Vocal Arts* offers to actors, students, teachers and any kind of speaker: not just the means to develop technical skill, but also a process to enable fuller expression of the self in the moment of speech.

Fiona Shaw

Introduction

The Vocal Arts Workbook **and you**

When we think about the arts, most of us think about music, painting, sculpture, literature, dance, drama – all acts of expression which speak to the human condition and which have been given form through the creative application of skill. Speaking can also be considered a form of art – we have chosen to call this the **Vocal Arts**. The vocal arts are so commonly practised, though, that sometimes we forget how powerful they can be. The voice and the words we speak are fundamentally a product of our whole selves – our thoughts, our feelings, our body and our soul – and so have the potential to affect us deeply as both speakers and listeners. To develop our vocal artistry is to develop our ability to affect and contribute to our common human experience.

This book will help anyone interested in developing his or her vocal artistry. Whether you use your voice professionally or are just interested in improving how you speak, you can benefit from exploring **The Vocal Arts Workbook and DVD**. Working with this text and DVD will help you to use your voice so that it fully and accurately represents your intentions – just as the writer uses words or the dancer, the body. It will give you the skill to express yourself with greater ease and success, so that you communicate thoughts and feelings with the precision and authority of an artist.

If you are a student of the performing arts, and especially of acting, this book is most particularly for you. In it, we will often refer to the demands of performance and the training that you will undergo in a drama programme. This is an arena in which vocal skills will be of enormous importance to you. Many drama students find that the work they do on freeing and developing their voices is the linchpin of their training. And even if you never aspire to act professionally, the work can open the door to your expressive potential as a human being.

This publication is also intended for use by drama teachers who would like to introduce voice into their curriculum, or to support the voice teaching they are already doing. We believe that exploring, exercising and playing with the voice can be an exciting component of studying drama at any level. There are, of course, a number of excellent books available on voice, and we will refer to them often. However, as far as we are aware, very few of them specifically address teaching and learning voice in an educational context. This book is designed to help fill that void. It can be used as the basis for a designated, year-long voice class or as a starting point to integrate 20–30 minutes of voice work per session into an acting class; Appendix 2 at the back of the book outlines a couple of suggested curricula that could be used for different periods of instruction. Additionally, it can be used by movement teachers who want to integrate vocal expression into their work, or as an intensive unit on voice within a directing programme. And, although we are focusing on the spoken voice, many of the exercises can be adapted by singing teachers for individuals and groups. We expect too that this book will be a helpful resource for experienced voice teachers and their students.

Learning and teaching *Vocal Arts*

Successful application of the knowledge and exercises involved in voice work depends on many of the same factors that underpin any successful learning and teaching. Work on the voice, in particular, is work on the self, and learners need to feel that they are free to work without fear of judgement.

An inquisitive spirit that is open to play and discovery is also vital in voice work. Often we are our own worst enemies when it comes to vocal expression; we judge, censor and constrict ourselves. As you do the practical work, it's important to give yourself permission to do things and make sounds that are unexpected and unfamiliar. Allow yourself to explore beyond how you usually use your voice and, more significantly, how you feel you 'should' use your voice. Actively seek to discover and *enjoy* possibilities in your voice, your body and yourself that you may not have experienced before.

It is important too that you be attentive to the work; it never proceeds the same way twice, and you may make different discoveries doing the same exercise from one day to the next if you pay close attention. You must be willing to persevere with exercises when dynamic change is happening, and to see it through. You also need to accept the fact that not every exercise will produce discernable results every time. If something isn't working for you right now, put it aside and come back to it later.

This work requires both a sense of discipline and a sense of play. It demands the ability to improvise – to run with something that is yielding results or to adjust something that is not. And it requires sensitivity to the unfolding of individual growth. None of these are things that we can provide in a book. However, the work also requires structure, which is something we can.

The Vocal Arts Workbook: an overview

This book is divided into five chapters, each of which addresses one of the fundamental principles of vocal expression. **Relaxation, Release and Alignment** focuses on preparing you physically for work on the voice; **Breath and Voice – Connect** focuses on establishing the essential relationship between your breath and your voice. **Breath and Voice – Supply and Support** looks at developing that relationship so your breath can become fully responsive to the demands of performance; and **Resonance and Range** explores how the pitch and resonance of your voice can respond more expressively to your intentions. Finally, **Articulation and Muscularity** focuses on increasing the effectiveness of your engagement with muscular articulation. Each chapter lays a foundation for the work that follows. However, since dividing the voice into categories is inherently artificial, we suggest that you first take a quick read of the whole book in order to get an idea of how the work hangs together and where it is going. Then, usually, it will make sense to go through the book chapter by chapter, although there may be moments when it will be appropriate to return to earlier exercises to reinforce or rediscover basic principles. You may also find that a topic which appears later in the book becomes a pressing issue in the work you are doing; should that happen, turn to whatever section is useful to you and make the most of it. There is a progression that the training usually follows, and some parts of the process will only make sense when others are in place first – but no two learners will develop in exactly the same way, so please consider our outline to be your servant, not your master.

Each chapter consists of several sections: *Framework; Exploration; Exercises; Follow-up; Suggested texts;* and *Further reading.* In general, we directly address you, the learner, throughout the book; however, we also provide Teaching Tips which give specific notes for teachers. Here is a full account of each of the chapter sections.

Framework

Each chapter begins with a *Framework* section, offering an introduction to the topic at hand and our approach to it. This includes a description of the relevant basic anatomy. An understanding of vocal anatomy is not a prerequisite for good vocal use; in fact, much of our work employs images that have little to do with precise anatomical function. Nevertheless, we have found that having some knowledge of what is actually happening in your body can give you a framework for understanding what you experience in exercises. This is useful because it demystifies the process; you can appreciate that the vocal growth you undergo is not the result of magic but of specific changes in muscle use – and that which is specific is repeatable. Ideally, intellectual insight and physical experience can work together to help you translate your discoveries into new habits. You may find it useful to review the framework material from time to time as you progress, in order to deepen your understanding of the work.

In the *Framework* section, we also discuss the role that the topic of that chapter plays in overall effective use of the voice. In addition, for those of you who are studying voice as part of a drama course, we occasionally touch on the connection between this work and the actor's task in general. This can help you to see where you can apply principles you've learned in voice class to the work you are doing in other areas, or vice versa.

> **Teaching tip**
> You may find it valuable to have students read through the *Framework* section before beginning extensive work on a chapter. Alternatively, you may prefer to have them experience some of the exercises first and then delve into how and why they work.

Exploration

The *Exploration* section of each chapter serves two functions. The first is to give you a sense of where you are starting from in relation to the work of that particular chapter. Understanding how you usually do things will help you begin to explore new patterns of behaviour. It will also help you to recognise when your habits start to change. The second function is to encourage you to think about the issues surrounding your voice in ordinary usage. To develop your skill fully, you need to cultivate awareness of your voice not only as a student in the classroom but also, if you're an actor, in rehearsal and performance; and, as a human being, in daily life. The exercises in this section help you to do this.

Teaching tip

We suggest that one or more of the explorations be undertaken in the week before work in that chapter is to begin.

Exercises

Vocal Arts is a practical discipline, so the bulk of this book is devoted to practical exercises. The exercises in each chapter are grouped under headings; beneath each heading there may be several exercises which focus on developing the same skill. This is important because people respond differently to different exercises on different days. You shouldn't panic if you don't 'get it' on the first try of every exercise; by coming at each element of voice production through a couple of exercises, eventually you will find a way to move beyond old habits into a new experience. With a bit of diligent practice, fresh patterns can become new, subconscious habits.

We often use images in conjunction with exercises because many of the muscles that are associated with the voice are not easy to control directly. Engaging the imagination provides a holistic approach that helps the muscles respond more fully. For example, simply giving yourself the mental command 'Let go' for a tightly clenched jaw will only help it to release so far. Gently massaging the muscles will encourage further release – but visualising the jaw softening and opening as you massage will help even more. To get the full benefit of all the exercises, therefore, it is important that you engage your imagination as well as your effort.

The exercises are sometimes very physical and can involve work on the floor, so we would advise you to wear clothing that is casual and easy to move in; tracksuit bottoms and t-shirts are usually good. If you are working in a class, however, your clothes should not be too baggy, as your teacher needs to be able to observe how you are breathing and using your body in the exercises.

Although this book is designed particularly with new students in mind, it can be used at any level. We have not divided the work into categories of 'beginning' or 'advanced', because even the most experienced learner can benefit from a re-exploration of fundamental exercises, and a novice can make discoveries by engaging in more sophisticated work from time to time. What advances in this work is less the exercises themselves, and more how much the learner can discover in them.

Teaching tip

If you are teaching from this book, it will help the students immeasurably if you either demonstrate each exercise first, or do it along with them. You may choose to have students read the exercises before class so that they have an idea of what steps they will be following. It can also be good for them to read or re-read the exercises after class as a way of reinforcing the experience.

For each of the exercises, we give an estimated time. This is an approximation of how long it takes to actually do the exercise; it does not include the time you might take to explain or demonstrate beforehand or discuss afterwards – which may be as long as the exercise itself. Some exercises may take less or more time depending on the size of the group.

In the early stages of the work, we suggest that you explore each exercise in a section. As the class progresses through a chapter, we recommend that you devote some time in each session to reviewing at least a few of the earlier exercises in that chapter. As you move on through the book, it is also a good idea to use some exercises from previous chapters as a warm-up for each session.

Follow-up

We recommend that you keep a journal as you work through this book, as it can be a very effective way of sharpening your awareness of what your voice and body are doing. As you consider what you have experienced, you can also gain greater insight into which exercises had particular value for you and how you might re-create the positive results. Much of the *Follow-up* section of each chapter is devoted to questions intended to stimulate detailed observation and encourage reflection on the work. More free-form notes on your own impressions and experiences are useful as well.

The *Follow-up* exercises are designed primarily to help you make the connection between vocal use in class and vocal use outside of class. They are usually very simple, but are nonetheless a key component in overall development. To help you maintain your growth after you have completed the course, we've included a vocal workout in Appendix 1.

Teaching tip

In addition to assigning *Follow-up* work, we would encourage you to make time at the end of every class for a brief discussion of discoveries, observations and questions. We have found that these conversations can be very effective in helping students become aware of what they have learned during the session.

Suggested texts

The primary purpose of vocal expression is to communicate your thoughts and feelings through language, so we believe that it is important to engage your voice with language throughout your training. For that reason, at the end of chapters 2 through to 5 we have included a section of text-based exercises. Most of these exercises do not focus on any particular passages of text, but rather on applying the specific skills developed in that chapter to the act of speaking. The material you choose to work with in those exercises is up to you; we do, however, give some suggestions at the end of each chapter of texts that we feel lend themselves well to the exercises described. We have mainly chosen poetic texts because we have found that poetry has focus, specificity and economy – qualities that are very useful for facilitating good vocal practice. Furthermore, working with poetry allows you to become involved in a heightened act of communication without having to worry about characterisation, given circumstances, objectives or other issues associated with dramatic text. We would encourage you to explore other poems also, particularly those from different historical periods and with different cultural perspectives. We have found that when you get away from your own rhythms, syntax and vocabulary, you often find it easier to get away from old vocal habits as well. In Appendix 3, we provide a list of recommended anthologies and websites where you should be able to find the texts we suggest and many other excellent poems.

Further reading

We would never try to pretend that this book comprehensively covers every voice issue, so we have included suggestions for further reading on every topic. As mentioned previously, there are many excellent resources available, and we encourage you to use whatever speaks to you in your teaching and learning. The vocal development of every individual will progress uniquely, and you may find that the work of different teachers will be of use to you at different stages in your journey. We believe that the more you read and experience, the more clearly you will be able to define what works for you as either a learner or a teacher of voice. Our work is profoundly indebted to many outstanding practitioners who have taught and inspired us, and, in Appendix 4, we give a more detailed overview of those experiences and individuals that have shaped our approach to voice work. In particular, we'd like to acknowledge the profound influence that Cicely Berry and Kristin Linklater have had on the teaching of voice in the 20th and 21st centuries.

The Vocal Arts DVD

Many of the exercises we use can be hard to describe: physical postures can be difficult to capture in words, and qualities of sound even more so. The companion DVD to this book gives a brief demonstration of those exercises that we feel can be best understood when they are seen and/or heard. It is designed to supplement the workbook, not to provide independent vocal training. The demonstrations are not intended to show perfect technique, but to give you an idea of what the exercise looks like in practice. The exercises that appear on the DVD are marked in the book with a ☺. If you are teaching from this book, you may want to watch those exercises on the DVD before introducing them in class. Your students may also find it beneficial to use the DVD to review the exercises after class. If you are working from the book on your own, you should watch each exercise as you come to it in the book, then pause the machine and try it. You can then return to the DVD to review as needed. What you will see are demonstrations of the essential points. In most instances, when you perform the exercise by following the instructions in the workbook, they will take longer: for example, if an exercise involves several repetitions, we have generally shown just the initial cycle of movement or sound. Once you have an image of how the exercise works, you can proceed to explore it more fully yourself.

Working with *The Vocal Arts Workbook and DVD*

In order to use the voice as effectively as possible, most people will need to adopt new patterns of muscle use. Our habits of muscular behaviour are developed over many months or even years (think of how long it takes a child to learn to walk upright, or ride a bicycle, or tie shoelaces). These habits are not necessarily wrong, but they may remain unquestioned unless we are injured or are required to learn a new task or improve a skill. Vocal habits are no different, and are usually so ingrained as to be considered normal by most of us. But these apparently normal habits can restrict our effectiveness as expressive human beings. Often they involve an inefficient or inappropriate use of muscles; that is, we may habitually – 'normally' – engage muscles inappropriate for the task when we speak, and/or we may use inappropriate levels of muscular activity (too much or too little effort). This applies both to the specific muscles of voice and speech and to the general muscles of our physical framework which support and interact with the voice. The exercises in this book are designed to encourage the effective engagement of the appropriate muscles for the production of voice. In order for this to happen, you must first free yourself of restrictive tensions which keep you locked in old, inefficient patterns. You can then experience a new pattern – one which will allow you to express yourself with greater ease, range and precision.

Changing muscular habits may cause aches and pains to occur in the first instance, or may disrupt patterns of behaviour that developed in order to compensate for illness, physical injury or disability. We offer the following general advice on health and safety at this point, but will also draw attention to specific exercises in the text where caution might need to be applied.

If you are in a voice class and feel temporarily unwell for any reason, let your teacher know. He or she may suggest that you sit the work out or ask you to engage with the work to the best of your ability at that time. Do not push yourself to extremes or undertake anything that does not feel safe in your weakened state. Your first responsibility is to preserve your own health – not to please the teacher!

With regard to 'aches and pains', learn to distinguish between the dull ache of muscles that have been exercised and the sharp pain of physical injury. Muscles that are not used to performing a particular function will ache when they are first asked to engage in an appropriate way, or may feel sore the next day – this is a

Contents

Forewords

This book is valuable both for the voice teacher and for the student working on his/her own voice – for, in a very comprehensive way, it brings together all the factors which are needed to find one's own authentic voice.

I find the book both refreshing and remarkable since it teaches, not by telling you what to do, but rather by first making the reader aware of their own personal bodily responses to breathing, tension, resonance etc., and to the whole process of making sound in their everyday life. In a most imaginative, and often humorous, way, it arouses our curiosity as to how we each make sound and speech in the variable circumstances of our lives. With this enhanced awareness of our own habits, it then instructs us, through very clear and specific exercises, how to build on this knowledge by managing our tensions and developing our breathing potential; the exercises are always an exploration.

The message that underpins the work is that good breathing not only produces a good voice, but also feeds the actor in their exploration of character, and in the truth of that character. In other words, to breathe deeply is to think deeply.

Cicely Berry

Each time we speak, we reveal our nationality, disposition, attitudes, background, idiosyncrasies, familial traits and mannerisms. We carry our lives and childhoods in our voice and this is an important part of the armoury of any artist or any person who wishes to be heard.

Voice is about connecting both our primitive thoughts and our sophisticated ones to a mechanism that can communicate. Having 'a voice in the world', whatever that world is, is the gift we inherit and one we can develop. Voice holds our self-esteem, confidence, comfort and control. It is a physical activity: we 'draw breath' and speak. Without it, as Winnie in Beckett's *Happy Days* says, there is 'Nothing to break the silence of this place.'

Voice is about not having to live in the silence of the lonely imagination, instead sharing our thoughts and sculpting sound so that not only is meaning conveyed, but also the essence of who we are. It is about our possibility. So there is not a person on the planet who will not benefit from making sure that their voice is being true to its master, the inner self.

For actors, of course, vocal skill is crucial – not just for serving personal expression, but also for serving the play we are releasing. It is also crucial to be able to sustain vocal energy over a prolonged time so that neither mood nor fatigue can shake our abilities. It was in this context that I first met David Carey at the Royal Shakespeare Company, when

1 Relaxation, Release, Alignment

Framework

Until the body has achieved a certain degree of relaxation, release and align-ment, full vocal potential cannot be realised. The initial stage of voice work is, therefore, a kind of *via negativa*; it is about releasing habitual tensions from the body in order to develop the effective engagement of the appropriate muscles. Although the voice is created by the movement of the breath through the vocal folds, tension in an area as remote as the feet can affect the quality of the tone that is produced. Through the work of this chapter, it is possible to develop a greater awareness of habitual tensions, to learn to release them, and then to engage the appropriate muscles effectively.

In theory, it's not hard to grasp that physical tension is undesirable. We all know how uncomfortable we feel and how disadvantaged we are in situations that make us tense – when the shoulders tighten, the jaw clenches, the breathing becomes shallow and the stomach churns. But even though there are physical tensions that we associate with stress and long to be rid of, there are also physical tensions that we associate with passion, commitment, and intensity; and, frankly, on some level we cherish and nurture them. Often, the more physic-ally worked up actors get, the more they feel that they are really connecting. The muscles, however, make no distinction: tension is tension, and tension very often gets in the way of effective performance.

Of course, a certain amount of muscular activity is necessary just to sit upright; complete relaxation would be an absurdity. The key question is whether or not the muscles are engaged in a way that is appropriate to the task at hand. Muscles either engage (contract) or disengage (relax). The word 'tension' is used to describe a muscular contraction that is either unrelated to the task (e.g. squinting your eyes to pick up something heavy) or is inappropriately strong. A boxer throwing a punch generates a tremendous amount of energy through the strong engagement of certain muscles – but an excess of contraction in those or the surrounding muscles will actually block that energy and could cause the boxer injury. An actor playing a scene of high intensity likewise needs to engage strongly – not only physically, but also mentally and emotionally. While excess muscular contraction may make a person *feel* even more engaged, in fact it will block their expressive energy by impeding their ability to communicate. An actor's job is to communicate: powerful communication happens when energy flows through a channel (physical, vocal, emotional, mental) that is open, responsive, and free.

Of course, just as it is possible to confuse tension with passion and intensity, it is also possible to confuse disengagement with ease and naturalness. For example, it is fashionable today to appear 'cool', to seem laid-back and at ease. In vocal terms this is often characterised by insufficient engagement of the muscles of respiration and articulation in conjunction with tension in the larynx and jaw. The resulting sound feels relaxed, but is actually under-energised. Should an untrained person be required to energise their 'cool' voice, it is likely that they would do so not by activating the habitually relaxed muscles of breathing and articulation, but by increasing muscular activity in the jaw and larynx – thus producing a very tense, blocked sound. Muscles which are insufficiently engaged are often described as 'lazy'; we prefer to use the words 'sluggish' or 'lethargic', as these do not imply a deliberate indolence.

Habitual lethargy is no more the same thing as true relaxation than tension is the same thing as purposeful engagement. The relaxation and release that we will work to achieve come not from tuning out, but from focused attention. In fact, disengaging the mind during a relaxation exercise – allowing the attention to wander – will probably cause the body to settle even more deeply into its usual tension patterns. It's perfectly possible to lie flat on the floor for half an hour (and even fall asleep) with a tight lower back, locked ankles, and a bunched tongue root; and then to rise groggy, stiff, and no more released, but with the illusion that one has 'relaxed' simply because one has had a little lie down. Releasing unnecessary tension requires a dynamic, heightened awareness, and you will need to engage actively with the exercises and images in this section of the book. An effective relaxation session will leave you feeling more, not less, energised. A performer who is appropriately relaxed on stage, who has successfully freed themselves from habitual tensions and excessive effort, will have tremendous energy, liveliness, and an easy connection to even the most intense aspects of their character's experiences.

The tensions that are the most inhibiting to the actor's power of expressivity are often those of which he or she is least aware. Where do these tensions come from? Babies and young children are usually geniuses at employing the exact amount of muscular effort necessary to get the job done. Their bodies tend to be free and beautifully aligned. We use the word 'alignment' to refer to that posture which is most physiologically efficient – that is, the posture which requires the least amount of muscular activity to stay upright. It involves what Alexander Technique teacher Glynn Macdonald calls the 'dynamic relationship between head, neck and torso' (1998:39).

To see healthy children aged two or three walking, crouching, running or simply sitting on a stool is to observe creatures that have an intuitive awareness of good, physiologically efficient posture: they are in balance; their centre of gravity is stable in their pelvis; and their head/neck/torso relationship is in dynamic alignment. But over time – under the influence of various elements of their environment, such as diet, emotional or physical distress, or the myriad unconscious choices of lifestyle and culture that children and adolescents will make as their bodies and minds grow – the instinctive awareness of the healthy body can become numbed. A broken ankle at age six may heal within a couple of months, but the tilt of the pelvis that comes from favouring one leg over the other may remain for many years. The desire to hold a folder over her developing breasts may fade as a young woman moves through adolescence, but the slight inward curve of the shoulders may remain. Stubbed toes teach us not to swing our legs so freely. Being teased about being tall teaches us to slouch. Trying to see over crowds if we're short teaches us to crane our necks. Fashion magazines teach us to hold in our stomachs and thrust our hips forwards. The body is a sponge; it absorbs all these influences and holds on to them for a very, very long time. As a result, we can literally become ignorant of the knowledge our bodies were born with: knowledge of how the body feels when it is balanced; knowledge of where our centre of gravity is; and knowledge of how the spine works to support and sustain the dynamic relationship between the head, neck and torso. This kinaesthetic knowledge is vital for the Vocal Arts.

Without kinaesthetic knowledge, our bodies may become stuck in postural habits that can restrict our vocal and physical expressivity. Being off-balance causes muscles to become tense and unresponsive. Thankfully, though, if we listen to our body we can become re-sensitised to the messages it is giving us, and we can reinforce our instinctive knowledge with more conscious awareness. A number of body practices can achieve this reawakening, but our experience has led us to use a combination of Alexander Technique, Chi Kung (or Qi Gong) and Yoga.

Alexander Technique is a programme of physical and mental training created by the Australian actor and voice teacher, F M Alexander. It is founded in the principle that the way in which we use our body affects the way in which it functions. By focusing on simple activities like standing, sitting and breathing, Alexander Technique encourages conscious awareness of muscular tensions and behavioural habits in order to develop an improved use of our body. **Chi Kung** is a Chinese system of exercises designed to unblock energy within our bodies and to develop 'internal strength' (Chuen, 1991). Again, through using simple activities like standing, breathing and stretching, it encourages the release of mental and physical tensions in order to increase the healthy functioning of mind and body. **Yoga** is an Indian system of exercise and meditation which was originally designed to achieve spiritual union with the Absolute. Today, particularly in the West, its focus on postural stretches and breathing is often used to reduce stress and improve physical and mental fitness. These and other practices help attune us to what has been called our 'sixth sense' – proprioception, or the kinaesthetic awareness of our body's state of balance, its posture and the muscular activity we use to move through space. As we learn to listen to this kinaesthetic sense, we can become aware of how the head can balance on top of the spine, how the whole body can be aligned to achieve a sense of ease and energy, and how we can use muscles efficiently to enhance our movement potential.

Of particular importance for our vocal practice is the **spine**. The spine consists of four main sections, all of which are intimately related to areas of the body responsible for producing the voice. These comprise the seven cervical vertebrae which make up the neck and which connect with the voice and speech organs in the head, throat and larynx; the 12 thoracic vertebrae to which the ribs attach, and which are thus connected to the lungs and respiratory muscles in the chest; the five lumbar vertebrae in the small of the back to which respiratory muscles of the diaphragm and abdomen attach; and the five fused vertebrae of the sacrum

– the base of the spine – which attaches to the pelvis and so relates to the deep breathing muscles of the abdomen and the pelvic floor. These four sections (plus the coccyx, our vestigial tailbone) create a sequence of gentle curves in the spine that make a dynamic whole (see Fig. 1). Distortions of these curves, however, will have an immediate effect on the voice. Too pronounced a curve in the lumbar area, for example, or a collapse in the thoracic vertebrae will affect the management and capacity of breathing. Likewise, if the neck is twisted or shortened, the functioning of the vocal muscles in the larynx will be impaired and the size and shape of the vocal resonators in the throat and head will be diminished.

Efficient alignment of the spine, or good posture, may feel odd to you at first. However, as Kristin Linklater has pointed out in her seminal book *Freeing the Natural Voice* (1976, revised 2006), what feels *familiar* may not actually be what is *natural* – that is, what your body would do if it had not been subjected to stress, strain, and bad habit. Give your new stance a chance; live in it for awhile, even if it initially feels funny. Our

Cervical curve

Thoracic curve

Lumbar curve

Sacrum
Coccyx

Fig. 1 The Spine and Physiologically Efficient Posture

bodies are smart, and, if you help it along, yours will quickly come to recognise how efficient good posture is and employ it more regularly.

Good posture can also make you feel vulnerable. Many postural habits are acquired in response to self-consciousness – about being short, being tall, having large breasts, having small breasts, being overweight, being underweight, having big bottoms, having scrawny bottoms, etc. So raising your head or letting your abdominal muscles relax or bringing your shoulders back may make you feel very exposed. It's okay to feel that way, but it's also important that you have the courage to stick with it. If you're training to be an actor, in particular, you have to be available to the demands of your role – and you can't be available if you are trying to hide your bottom by tilting your pelvis forwards.

Of course, very few characters that you'll be called upon to play will naturally have perfect alignment. Although years of Alexander Technique lessons may not be part of your character's history, starting with a body that is balanced and aligned will give you a sense of physical presence, power, grace and stature that will come in handy when portraying a wide range of characters. It will also benefit you in your everyday life. Of course, there are characters with bodies that have been pushed and pulled out of alignment in the course of their lives. Your job is not only to embody another's experience, but also to communicate it – so you must find a physical characterisation that allows you to do both effectively. If you have found, through work on relaxation, release and alignment, how to open your back to get in the breath you need to support your voice, you can access that extra reserve when you are playing a character who has a caved-in chest and slumped shoulders. If, however, your back is habitually locked and you then add the caved chest and slumped shoulders of your character, you are going to be hard pressed to support a voice that can carry a full range of thoughts and experiences to the back row night after night. The ability to move from an aligned, neutral posture into a physical character choice (rather than 'pasting' that character choice on top of your own, ingrained physical habits) not only allows you to transform more fully, it also enables you to use your voice to communicate more effectively.

Because the patterns of muscular tension that stand between you and optimal alignment are acquired unconsciously and over time, they can become very deeply entrenched, so that work on releasing them is never really finished. Our approach to this is also eclectic: progress can be made through actively stretching and manipulating the muscles; through direct, conscious instruction to release; and through focus on images to which the muscles can sometimes respond more profoundly.

On any given day, with any given student, any one of these methods may prove to be more or less effective. It is essential, however, that all of the exercises be entered into with a spirit of active curiosity. Passively going through the motions will bring very limited benefits; likewise, harsh self-judgement can impede progress.

The learning cycle begins when we move from unconscious incompetence (habitually using muscles in a way that is inefficient without realising it), to conscious incompetence (gaining an awareness of the inefficient pattern). From there we can work our way to conscious competence (introducing a new use of the muscles through exercise and focused attention), and finally to unconscious competence (using the muscles in a more efficient way without having to think about it). It is pointless – in fact it may be destructive – to berate ourselves for not being at a different stage in the cycle, for it is impossible to get where we want to be without developing a calm, detailed awareness of where we are.

Exploration

In the morning, identify three times during the day when you are likely to be under moderate stress – for example, driving to school and looking for parking; presenting a monologue in class; trying to get all your emails answered during your lunch break, etc. Write the following in your journal and plan to have it at hand at each of these times:

Feet	Abdominal muscles
Ankles	Upper back
Knees	Chest
Thighs	Shoulders
Pelvis	Neck
Buttocks	Jaw
Lower back	Eyes and forehead

During the three activities, or as soon after as you can, take a couple of moments to focus your awareness on each of these areas of your body. Make a note of any area in which you feel tight, locked, collapsed, off balance, or achy. Then, at the end of the day, look at your list and see if there is a pattern of tension tending to settle in certain parts of your body. Pick the three areas where you most consistently felt tight or experienced the greatest degree of discomfort.

Focus your attention on the first of these three areas. See if you can double the amount of tension, stiffness, or discomfort in that part of your body, and notice any changes that this creates in other parts of your body. Try to take a very deep breath (as if you were at the doctor's with a stethoscope on your back) and notice where in your body the breath fills and where it feels blocked. Go back to the original degree of tension and observe the same things. See if you can halve the amount of tension and make the same observations. Repeat the process with the other two areas, making notes throughout. Write your observations in your journal and discuss them in class.

Exercises

> **Teaching tip**
>
> The exercises in this section are organised under four headings: *Stretching*, *Floor Work*, *Roll-ups* and *Keeping It Loose*. Initial class sessions could begin with the swinging exercise described below, 20–35 star jumps, walking or running through the room making eye contact, or a quick game of some kind of tag to ensure that students are beginning with an engaged rather than a lethargic energy. Either some stretching or a floor work exercise or both could follow. Next, some attention could be given to the spine with a selection from the roll-up exercises. By the third or fourth session, some of the early breath awareness exercises from the next chapter could be introduced, as well as some work from *Keeping It Loose*.

Stretching

A word here about stretching. At the beginning of the course, you should give your instructor – either verbally or in writing – a brief history of any injuries and/or significant illnesses you may have. If there are any serious injuries – to the back in particular – the instructor should discuss with you any treatment and instructions you have been given and any adjustments you may need to make. We give some guidelines below, but if at any point a stretch seems likely to exacerbate an injury, you should simply sit it out. It can also be useful for the instructor to do a brief check-in at the beginning of each class to see how people are feeling. Someone who has strained a muscle or sprained a joint may want to sit out certain stretches or exercises; someone who has a bad cold may need to do some of the floor work lying on their side so that they can breathe more easily – and all participants should be encouraged to be responsible for looking after themselves. You also need to learn to listen to your body and distinguish between the ache or discomfort that comes from stretching deeply or engaging strongly in a strenuous exercise, and the pain that comes when a weak or injured muscle is being pushed too far. There is no shame in backing away from something that you genuinely feel may be injurious.

A bit of cardiovascular exercise before stretching can effectively warm up the muscles. We find the following swinging exercise particularly useful:

⊙ Swinging – torso and legs (2 minutes)

Skip the second part of this exercise if you have problems with your knees.

1. Begin by standing with feet parallel, about hip-width apart, knees soft, and arms to the side.

   Start by swinging your arms gently from side to side. Try to keep the rest of your body still without freezing or locking anywhere.

   Let your waist join in the swing, twisting from side to side, but keep your hips still. This is a particularly good point in the exercise to feel a stretch in your ribs and back.

   Let your hips join the swing.

   Widen your stance and let the momentum of the swing pull your heels up off the ground.

2. Widen your stance again and bend your knees in a little lunge as you swing from side to side.

   Deepen the lunge until finally you are touching the ground with your hand on either side. Continue this for at least six lunges.

   Continue to lunge, but not all the way to the ground.

   Let go of the lunge and simply swing from side to side.

   Let your feet be still on the ground as you swing.

   Let your hips be still as you swing from your waist.

   Let your waist be still as you swing from your shoulders.

   Let everything be still except the breath.

In this exercise and all the following stretching exercises, KEEP BREATHING.

Teaching tip

Regarding the opening stance, 'soft knees' may be a concept that is difficult for students to grasp initially. Have them tighten their thighs and reach down to touch their kneecaps to feel what tight knees feel like. Then have them bend their knees and touch their kneecaps so they can feel that bent knees are not the same as soft knees. Then have them stand with just a bit of give in the knees and with relaxed thighs. Ask them if they can then move their kneecaps slightly from side to side with their hands. This is 'soft knees'. You may need to demonstrate and/or help individual students to find this stance.

🎧 Granny Dance – arms and torso (1 minute)

Begin standing with feet parallel, about hip-width apart, knees soft, and arms to the side.

Raise your left arm; at the same time, bend your left knee and raise the foot up onto the toe. Then push your heel down to the floor as you press the palm of your hand up towards the ceiling.

Repeat on the right, and then alternate sides four or five times.

Tilt your torso forwards about 30 degrees and continue stretching from side to side four or five times.

Tilt your torso forwards another 30 degrees and stretch; then tilt another 30 degrees, so that your chest and arms are parallel to the ground, and continue stretching from side to side four or five times.

Tilt towards the ground another 30 degrees and stretch, and finally come to a roll-down position and reach for the ground as you stretch from side to side.

Partnered Stretches – upper back and torso (about 2 minutes each)

🎧 I. Find a partner who is somewhere in the neighbourhood of your height.

Stand facing your partner with your feet close together; leave about 4–5 inches between your toes and theirs.

Clasp each other's wrists.

Slowly lean away from each other, keeping your bottom in line with your body.

You will be holding up your partner; the stretch is actually easier if you can trust your partner and not try to take their weight without giving yours.

Let your shoulders be pulled forwards, and feel the stretch across your upper back.

Hold the stretch for 30 or 40 seconds, and then both bend your knees and lower your bottoms to the floor until you are sitting.

Taking each other's weight again, stand back up together and then gradually come out of the backwards lean and balance on your own two feet.

Repeat a couple of times.

II. Stand side by side with your partner, with your feet close to each other and close to your partner's feet.

Hold hands.

Lift your other arm up over your head. Your arm should be next to your ear – not in front of or behind it.

Grasp wrists with your partner above your heads.

Lean your hips out away from your partner, taking each other's weight as you do so.

You should feel a nice stretch along your side. Hold it for 30–40 seconds, and then return to standing.

Repeat on the other side.

Teaching tip

It can be interesting to have the students do the first stretch once to get the hang of it, and then do it again noticing what they are doing with their breathing. Many will find that they are holding their breath. Ask them to repeat the exercise while consciously engaging their breathing – keeping it moving all through the exercise. Many will find that this makes the movements of the stretch much easier.

Shoulder Stretches (1–2 minutes each)

Begin standing with feet parallel, about hip-width apart, knees soft, and arms to the side.

I. Stretch your arms out straight in front of you with the palms facing up, and cross one over the other at the elbow.

Bend both arms. The elbow of the arm on top should be peeking out over the bottom elbow.

Try to touch your palms together – you may only get the fingers of one hand touching the palm of the other, which is fine.

Lift that whole tangle of arms up in front of your face as far as it will go and hold for about a minute (see Fig. 2).

Focus on the sensation of releasing and opening in the shoulders and upper back.

This is also a particularly good position for feeling your breath drop all the way to your pelvic bowl.

Repeat with the other arm on top.

Fig. 2 Shoulder Stretch

11

II. Stretch the right arm across your chest. Use the left forearm to pull the right upper arm in even closer to the chest.

Hold the position for about a minute.

Remember to keep breathing and focusing on the opening of the right shoulder blade.

Repeat on the other side.

III. Clasp your hands together behind your back, arms straight.

Roll one shoulder back, and then the other.

Try to lift your hands as far up and away from your back as you can.

Hold the position for about a minute, breathing fully all the time.

Neck Stretches

I. (3–4 minutes)

Begin standing with feet parallel, about hip-width apart, knees soft, and arms to the side.

Let your head drop forwards. We'll call this position 6:00.

Roll your head around so that the right ear is over the right shoulder and you are facing straight ahead, pointing your face neither to the ceiling nor the floor. We'll call this 3:00.

Roll your head around to the other side so that the left ear is over the left shoulder and you are facing straight ahead, pointing your face neither to the ceiling nor the floor. We'll call this 9:00.

Return your head to 6:00 and then roll it gently between 5:00 and 7:00, feeling the specific stretch of the muscles at the back of the neck and down into the shoulders.

Expand the rolling motion between 4:00 and 8:00 for about 30 seconds, and then expand it again so that you are rolling your head from 3:00 on one side to 9:00 on the other. Continue for about 30 seconds.

Bring your head to a rest at 3:00. Be sure that your ear is over your shoulder and your face is pointing straight ahead, not up or down. Check that your body has not been pulled to the right and you are still standing straight.

Take your right hand – the one that your head is nearest to – and rest it over your head. There's no need to pull on the head, just let the weight of the arm rest there. Imagine that you are carrying a heavy weight in the other hand. This heaviness will increase the stretch along your neck. Keep breathing and hold for 30-40 seconds.

Drop the heavy weight, drop your right hand, and let your head roll back around through 6:00 to 9:00. Repeat the stretch on this side.

Let your head roll back around to 6:00. Lace your fingers together and drape your hands over the 'fat' part of the back of your head (known anatomically as your occipital bone). Let your elbows fall down towards the floor rather than holding them out towards the walls. There's no need to pull on the head; just let the weight of the arms rest there.

This is a particularly good position to feel the ribs opening to the breath through your back. Focus on your breathing and hold the stretch for about a minute.

Let your arms drop and allow your head to float up. Register the feeling of release in the neck.

Teaching Tip:
In the 3:00 and 9:00 positions, it can be hard for students to sense if their faces are indeed pointed straight ahead. It is worth taking the time to help them make any necessary adjustments. In rolling between 5:00 & 7:00 and 4:00 & 8:00, the motion is **not** that of shaking the head 'no'; it is that of moving the ear towards the shoulder.

II. (about 2 minutes)
Begin standing with feet parallel, about hip-width apart, knees soft, and arms to the side.

Position your head so that your gaze is straight out to the horizon, not tilted to the ceiling or the floor.

Grab a little bit of hair at the crown of your head (just where the top of your head is about to slope down and become the back of your head) and give it a little tug. This will help you lengthen the neck. Imagine both your shoulders and your jaw falling down away from your head. Let go of the hair.

Keeping your neck long and your gaze at the horizon, rotate your head around so that you are looking over your left shoulder.

Place the flat of your left hand against the right side of your face. Try to push your head to the right, but resist the movement with your hand.

Don't let the effort of pushing creep into your jaw or shoulders.

Hold for about 30 seconds, and **keep breathing**.

Release the pressure, rotate the head around to the right, and repeat on the other side.

Register the feeling of release in the neck.

Halloween Cat – spine stretch (1–2 minutes)

Get down onto your hands and knees, with your back parallel to the ground and flat like a table.

Curl your tailbone down towards the floor, which will cause your back to arch up towards the ceiling, like a Halloween cat.

Hold the stretch for a moment, but keep the breath moving.

Then, slowly rotate your tailbone so that it points up to the ceiling, which will cause your back to sink down towards the floor, like a broken-down old horse. Your face will naturally lift up, but don't lift it so far that the back of your neck collapses.

Hold the stretch for a moment, but keep the breath moving.

Repeat the movement between the Halloween cat and the broken-down old horse two or three times.

Hip Sequence (5–7 minutes)

Do this exercise carefully, or make adjustments if you have problems with your knees.

1. Place your left foot a good metre in front of the right. The toes of your left foot point forwards, and those of the right point out at a 45-degree angle.

   Roll down over your left leg and hold the ankle.

   In this position, imagine that you have an inflatable air cushion in each of your hip sockets. Take a good, deep breath, and imagine the breath filling those cushions. Release the breath and repeat the breathing cycle two more times.

2. Roll back up, pivot your back foot so that the toes are pointing forwards, and bend your front knee so that you are in a slight lunge. You will come up onto the toes of your back foot. Don't bend your front knee so far that you can't see your toes.

   Bring your arms up over your head with the palms facing each other. Try to lift your fingers another quarter-inch and drop your shoulders another half-inch.

   In this position, imagine that you have inflatable air cushions on either side of your torso, running from your armpit to the bottom of your ribs. Take a good, deep breath, and imagine the breath filling those cushions, expanding your ribcage to the sides. Release the breath and repeat twice.

3. Bring your arms down and gently lower yourself down to the floor, folding your left leg in front of you and stretching your right leg straight behind you. You should be sitting up off the floor – a bit like doing the splits, but with your front leg bent under you.

   In this position, imagine that you have inflatable air cushions on both sides of your lower back/upper bottom area. Take a good, deep breath, and imagine the breath filling those cushions. Release the breath and repeat twice.

4. Bend your right leg behind you as you sit down on the floor, keeping your left leg bent in front of you. You should be sitting up, not resting on your hand.

   In this position, imagine that your breath can drop straight down to your pelvic bowl. Breathing in your own time, close your eyes and take a moment to focus on simply 'being in your body'.

5. Swing your right leg out from behind, and place your right foot in front of your left knee. Hug your right knee to your chest with your left arm, and look over your right shoulder.

   In this position, imagine that you have an inflatable air cushion on either side of your upper back. Take a good, deep breath, and imagine the breath filling those cushions. Release the breath and repeat twice.

   Unfold yourself and repeat the sequence on the other side – starting with your right foot in front.

Sun Salutation – all-over body stretch (5–7 minutes)

If you have problems with your back, you may need to skip step four.

We've encountered several versions of this traditional Yoga exercise. If you know another version that works for you, use it. Breathing should be strongly engaged, even blown out on the out-breath.

1. Begin standing with feet parallel, about hip-width apart, knees soft, and arms to your side.

   On the in-breath, lift your arms out to your side and up until they are over your head, palms facing in. Think of your shoulder blades travelling down your back as your arms go up.

   On the out-breath, reach forwards, tilting from your hips until your back and arms are parallel to the floor and flat like a table, and then continue down until your fingers are brushing the floor.

   On the in-breath, hold your calves and pull your chest in to your knees.

2. On the out-breath, step your left leg back and bend your right knee, bringing yourself into a lunge. Keep your chest up and open.

   Hold this position on the in-breath.

3. On the out-breath, place your hands flat on the floor and bring your right foot back to join your left. Your body should be flat like a board, as if you were doing push-ups. Avoid sinking between your shoulders and tilting your chin upwards.

   Hold this position on the in-breath.

4. On the out-breath, bring your knees to the floor and pull your hips back so they are over your ankles. Push your upper body forwards, running your nose along the ground, and then push your hands against the floor to lift your upper chest. Keep your shoulders back and down.

   Hold yourself in this position on the in-breath.

5. On the out-breath, curl your toes under and push your bottom up into the air so your body is in the shape of an upside-down 'V'.

   Hold this position on the in-breath.

6. On the out-breath, bring your left foot forwards into a lunge. Keep your chest up and open.

   Hold this position on the in-breath.

7. On the out-breath, bring your right foot forwards to join your left so that you are in a roll-down position.

   Hold the position on the in-breath.

8. On the out-breath, keep your knees loose as you roll back up to standing.

9. On the in-breath, lift your arms out to the side and up until they are over your head, palms facing in. Think of your shoulder blades travelling down your back as your arms go up.

   On the out-breath, lower your arms.

   Repeat once, and then repeat twice on the other side, moving your right leg into the lunges.

Teaching tip

Talk through the actions of the sun salutation while demonstrating once with the students just watching. Also talk them through the actions as you do the four repetitions with them. Model strongly engaged breathing. Many students will raise their bottoms in the air during the pose, in which their bodies should be flat like a board; they will need to be reminded not to do so.

Floor work

Much of the early work on relaxation, release and alignment is done on the floor. This allows you to observe how your body feels and how your breathing functions when almost all muscular engagement, including that necessary to sit or stand, is stripped away. You can then work on re-introducing only that engagement which is necessary to the task at hand.

For most exercises, you can work in supine – on your back with your legs stretched out in front of you and the toes falling away from each other; or in semi-supine – with feet flat on the floor and knees pointing up to the ceiling. In either position, the arms should be to the sides with the shoulders falling towards the floor. This should cause the palms of the hands to open to the ceiling.

Many people will feel most comfortable with a folded scarf or thin book under the head to keep the neck long. The chin should not, however, be forced down towards the chest.

Spending time on the floor can get chilly, so you are advised to put on sweaters and socks before you begin.

If you have back problems that make it difficult or uncomfortable for you to lie on your back, you can do these exercises lying on your side instead. Change the side that you are lying on from time to time.

Calm focus should reign in the room during floor work. In general, you shouldn't speak during the exercises unless something occurs which demands the instructor's attention.

We start with three visualisation exercises, which can be used interchangeably.

Visualisations (7–10 minutes each)

I Start in supine or semi-supine. Imagine lying on the soft, warm sand of a tropical beach. You are under the shade of a palm tree, but as time passes, the shadow will move, and your body will progressively be exposed to the direct sunlight.

First imagine the sun warming your toes. Focus on the image of the toes loosening and softening.

Imagine the sun then shining on your feet and any tension there melting away.

Proceed, step by step, through the following sequence, at each point imagining the warmth of the sun melting any tension:

Ankles	Shoulders
Shins and calves	Upper arms
Knees	Lower arms
Thighs	Hands
Pelvis	Neck
Lower abdomen and back	Face
Ribs	Scalp
Chest and upper back	

When you are finished, stretch and wiggle on the floor, then return to supine and notice your breathing – how often it comes, where it moves in your torso, and how much effort goes into it.

II. You've probably come across bean-bag chairs – or at least bean bags. For this exercise, begin (in supine or semi-supine) by imagining that you are a bean-bag person and that you are stuffed to the point of almost bursting with little styrofoam balls. You do not need to put any additional tension into your muscles to achieve this state – it describes where you are when you first lie down.

Imagine that there is a seam in your foot and that a small hole opens up in that seam. This will allow a few of those styrofoam balls to escape. As they fall out of the open seam, the balls that are left in the foot are less tightly packed; they begin to shift as more of them start to pour out of the hole. Gradually, imagine the foot emptying, which allows the balls packed into the ankle to shift and loosen and begin to escape too.

Focus on the image of the emptying proceeding up the lower legs, knees, thighs, and pelvis.

Imagine a hole opening along a seam in the lower back and the flow of balls proceeding from there to the lower abdomen, ribs, upper back, and chest.

Imagine small holes opening up at the tips of the fingers and the balls draining from the hands, the forearms, the upper arms and the shoulders.

Imagine an opening in the back of the neck and picture the neck, jaw and face softening as all the balls from the head roll away.

When you are finished, stretch and wiggle on the floor; then return to supine and notice your breathing – how often it comes, where it moves in your torso, and how much effort goes into it.

III Begin in supine. Imagine that your legs are becoming very heavy. Consciously relinquish to the floor all responsibility for 'holding' your heavy legs in any way.

Imagine the arms and shoulders becoming very heavy. Give them also entirely to the floor.

Visualise the face, jaw, and entire head becoming very heavy. Imagine that if the floor were a mat, your head would be sinking into it another half-inch – you don't need to press your head down to do this; just focus on its great weight.

Move slowly into semi-supine.

Now turn your attention to your pelvis. Imagine that, as it is (no need to introduce any additional tension), it is a big slab of butter that has been in the freezer. Because it's frozen, it is hard and brittle. Imagine taking this 'butter pelvis' out of the freezer into a warm room, and visualise it gradually softening, becoming by degrees more yielding and pliable until finally it begins to spread a bit on the floor under its own weight, as a large block of butter will do on a warm surface.

Concentrate for a moment on that picture of the hips melting and widening along the floor.

Next, imagine that your shoulder girdle is also a slab of butter that has been in the freezer. Imagine it too coming into a warm room and progressively softening and then widening.

Turn your attention to your spine.

Feel each distinct bump of your spine along the floor, and imagine the separate vertebrae in the areas that are not against the floor, i.e. the lower back and the neck.

In your mind's eye, picture a small sac between each vertebra (these small sacs do, in fact, exist, but function quite differently from what we will imagine).

Imagine that with every breath you take, a tiny puff of air fills each of these sacs. The filling of the sacs will cause your spine to lengthen, imperceptibly, along the floor. You don't have to pull your spine in any way to make this happen – just work the image.

On the out-breath, imagine the little sacs emptying of air, but the spine staying long against the floor.

Repeat for six or seven breath cycles.

When you are finished, stretch and wiggle on the floor, then return to semi-supine and reconnect to the sense of width across the pelvis and shoulders and length along the floor.

Teaching tip

When leading visualisation exercises, it is important to use a tone of voice that is soothing but not narcotic. Walking around the room can help you keep up your own energy and volume. Give each portion of the exercise the time that it needs to develop, but keep the overall pace moving. Avoid long periods of silence. Remind the students that meaningful release requires an active mental engagement with the exercise, and that relaxation means freeing the body's potential energy – not falling asleep! It may help some students to work with their eyes open: if possible, dim the lights so that they don't have to squint against the glare.

Even with the best of intentions, however, it is not uncommon for students to fall asleep. If you notice that a student has done so, simply standing next to them may prompt them to rouse. If this doesn't work, placing a hand on their shoulder will usually do the trick. Avoid calling attention to sleeping students – the less self-conscious they feel about it, the more quickly they will be able to refocus their attention on the exercise.

Some students may find visualisation disturbing – the images used may seem illogical or may have negative connotations. A simple alternative is the following exercise:

Tension and Release (5–7 minutes)

Start in supine or semi-supine.

Put as much tension in the feet as possible – clench them tight, tight, tight for five seconds, then release on an out-breath. You may notice, as you tighten them, that tension creeps into other parts of your body as well – for example, the lower back. Try to keep all other areas as soft and loose as possible and focus on tensing in the feet alone.

Repeat in the following sequence:

Ankles	Shoulders
Shins and calves	Upper arms
Knees	Lower arms
Thighs	Hands
Pelvis	Neck
Buttocks	Jaw
Lower abdomen and back	Face
Ribs	Scalp
Chest and upper back	

When you are finished, stretch and wiggle on the floor, then return to supine and notice your breathing – how often it comes, where it moves in your torso, and how much effort goes into it.

The following exercise is very useful after you have begun to experience some release on your own. Working with a partner increases both awareness of one's own tensions and sensitivity to another's process.

☺ Partnered Manipulations (15–20 minutes per partner):

Each student should get a partner (if there is an odd number, the instructor can pair with a student).

1. Partner A, lie on the floor in supine.

    Partner B, sit next to one of A's legs.

    Partner B, take A's leg at the calf and lift it a few inches off the ground, gently jiggling it, if necessary, until partner A has given you as much of the full weight of the leg as s/he is able. Partner A, try not to 'help' in holding that leg up!

    Partner B, rest A's leg on your own knee.

    Gently hold A's foot and begin to point and flex it.

    Partner A, send images of softness and looseness to the ankle joint, as well as the mental message 'Let go'.

    EVERYBODY KEEP BREATHING

    As the joint loosens, partner B can begin making circles or figure 8s with A's foot and wiggling it gently.

    Ankles can take a while to warm up, so don't rush it.

    B, don't get caught in the same pattern of motion or A may begin to unconsciously help you. Surprise A with unexpected (but not sudden or jarring) movements.

2. Next, partner B kneel next to your partner's knee, facing his or her feet.

    B, lift and support A's thigh with your arm, allowing his or her knee to bend and lower leg to dangle.

    Still holding the thigh upright, move the lower leg through the knee's range of motion. Note that the knee joint moves primarily up and down – do not try to force it to go side to side.

    If A tries to help or resists the movement of the lower leg, B can lightly jiggle the leg through the point of resistance, or quietly say 'Let go'.

    EVERYBODY KEEP BREATHING

3. After a minute or two, B – still holding onto A's leg with the knee bent – swivel around so that you are facing A's face.

    B, you can then hold onto the lower leg and manipulate the hip joint by moving the knee away from the body, across the body, up towards the chest and down towards the ground. You can also rotate the leg within the hip socket.

    If there are any areas in the range of motion that feel tight, gently work through them until A is able to let go.

    After a couple of minutes, straighten A's leg, and, still holding on to the lower leg, gently lean back, stretching the leg away from the body in a direction parallel to the floor.

Accepting no help, return the leg to the floor.

4. Repeat with the other leg.

5. Next, sit beside one of A's arms.

Take A's arm at the wrist and lift it a few inches off the ground, gently jiggling it, if necessary, until partner A has given over as much of the full weight of the arm as s/he is able. Partner A, try not to help in holding that arm!

B, rest A's arm on your own knee.

Gently move A's hand back and forth and, as the wrist joint begins to soften, in small circles.

Don't get caught in the same pattern of motion or A may begin to unconsciously help you. Surprise him or her with unexpected (but not sudden or jarring) movements.

EVERYBODY KEEP BREATHING

6. Next, work on moving the forearm through the elbow's range of motion.

After a minute or two, hold on to the upper arm and move it through the shoulder's range of motion, which is wide and should be thoroughly explored.

7. After a couple of minutes, straighten A's arm, and, still holding on to the upper arm, gently lean back, stretching the arm away from the body in a direction parallel to the floor.

Accepting no help, return the arm to the floor.

8. Repeat with the other arm.

9. B, next sit directly above A's head.

Remove any scarves or books and slide your fingers under A's head, cradling it without, initially, lifting it off the floor. A, deepen your breathing while giving the weight of your head to your partner.

B, when you feel A's head start to get heavier, rock it from side to side in a 'no' movement.

When the neck is free, B can then lift the head slightly in a 'yes' nod and move it in circles or figure 8s.

A, begin to breathe out on a 'fffff' sound. Then turn it into a 'vvvv' sound. Finally try humming a bit. Notice if creating sound makes it harder or easier for you to really let go of your neck.

After a couple of minutes, B gently return A's head to the floor.

10. A, now take a moment to scan through your body and notice how it is feeling, particularly in those areas where you had previously identified tension.

A, try to take a very deep breath (as if you were at the doctor's with a stethoscope on your back) and notice where in your body the breath fills and where it feels blocked.

Everybody take a stretch and a wiggle as the A partners slowly bring themselves back to sitting up.

Switch over and repeat, with A taking B's role.

A, as you now work, see how much you can preserve the physical sensation of release and relaxation you found through having just done the exercise. Remember to keep breathing and use minimal effort to get the job done.

Teaching tip

This work requires a good level of trust between the students, so monitor to make sure that students are all using slow, gentle movements when performing the manipulations. If there are any students who may be uncomfortable with touching or being touched by a member of the opposite sex, you may want to have the whole class work with same-sex partners.

Discourage chatting and giggling, although some students may be ticklish and should be supportively coached to try to breathe through the impulse to laugh. Some students cannot resist telling their partners that they are tense in particular areas. Such observations can be counter-productive, however, and may increase tension. Monitor the class dynamic and, if necessary, remind them that this is a non-verbal exercise. All students will need to be reminded to keep breathing throughout the exercise. Note that this is an exercise that can be extended into further breathing or voicing when the students are ready.

Roll-ups

Lovely as work on the floor can be, it's not where you're going to do most of your talking. In order for the release and relaxation work to benefit you when you are upright, attention must be paid to the method of getting up off the floor and into a standing position. The movement from a dropped-over position, or roll down (where you are standing on your legs but your torso and head are still hanging down), to a fully upright position is called a roll-up. This process of standing up may seem like something that is far too simple to require practice, but, as with anything, our habitual way of doing it may not be the one that best serves us. Patient engagement with the exercises may lead you to some surprising discoveries about your own body.

In particular, efficient rolling up can help you come to an aligned stance in which your postural muscles are engaged only to the extent necessary, leaving the body freer to respond to breath and movement impulses and to support your voice. The work of rolling up is the work of 'finding your spine' – finding that sense of physical centring which gives you both strength and dynamic energy.

If you are in an acting training programme, it may feel that you spend inordinate amounts of time rolling up and down your spine, which can make it tempting to take a mental vacation and do it on automatic pilot. The roll-up will really only help you find a balanced, aligned posture, however, if it is done with focused awareness. The discipline of learning to listen to your body – being aware of its specific movements and working with ease, efficiency and precision every time you do something as fundamental as rolling up your spine – is ultimately the core work of acting: learning to be in the moment. Ideally, every time you do a roll-up, your dynamic awareness of your spine will help you to engage both your physical and your mental energies.

Whenever you complete a roll-up, take a moment to check that you are balanced on your feet. As far as possible, your weight should be neither too far forwards nor too far back, and should be evenly distributed in both legs. Take a moment just now to stand up and think about your feet. Each foot has three points designed to bear your weight: one at the heel, and two on the ball of your foot just behind your big and little toes. When you are standing upright, imagine your weight being distributed evenly across these three tripod points in each foot. Now make sure that your ankles, knees and hips are not stiff or braced. Pay attention to your pelvis also: imagine the shape that your pelvis makes is like a bowl and see it filled with water. If you shift your weight over to one leg or the other, the water will spill out of the opposite side of the bowl. Similarly, if you tip your pelvis too far forwards or back, the water will spill out the other side. Think of keeping the water in your pelvic bowl smooth and even. Tell yourself that your back is long and wide; that your shoulders are loose and low; that your neck is long and free; that your head is facing forwards and the crown of your head is going up; and, most importantly, that you are breathing fully. Well done! You are beginning to experience your aligned posture. Keep returning to these directions at the end of each roll-up exercise.

Getting Off the Floor and the Everyday Roll-up (1–2 minutes)

In supine, take a little stretch and wiggle to get some energy moving through your body, and then roll over onto your stomach.

Draw your knees under you so that your bottom is over your heels. Stretch your arms out in front of you and let your head hang down towards the ground. This Yoga position goes under various names – child's pose, folded leaf; we call it prayer pose.

Imagine that your face is heavy and your jaw is hanging down towards the floor.

See if you can walk your fingers out another inch in front of you. Then see if you can leave them there and sink your bottom a bit closer to your heels.

Take a couple of nice, deep breaths, and feel your back opening.

Now, curl your toes under and push yourself back into a squat.

Let your knees spread open as wide as possible.

Let your arms rest outside of your knees.

Your head may be hanging all the way down to the floor; if it is, lift and lengthen your neck so that your head is in line with your spine.

In this position, start to bounce on your toes a bit (unless you have trouble with your knees).

With each bounce, imagine your spine – from the base of your skull to the tip of your tailbone – getting a little bit longer. Do this for 10 or so bounces.

Then, with each bounce, imagine that your hips are getting a little bit wider. Do this for 10 or so bounces.

Finally, with each bounce imagine that your shoulders are getting a little bit wider. Do this for 10 or so bounces.

Stop bouncing, and raise your tailbone up into the air – think of it as floating its way up. Leave your upper body hanging forwards; this is a roll-down position.

Check that your knees are loose.

On the roll-up, imagine that your tailbone is getting heavy and that it is the sinking of the tailbone that causes the rest of the spine to unfurl, like a leaf. Think of the back lengthening and widening as you build each vertebra on top of the other, leaving the head and neck till last.

Finally roll up the neck, thinking of unfurling it too into length. Imagine a surge of energy running between your shoulder blades and up your neck. You should be able to rise up onto your toes without shifting your weight.

Return to your alignment directions.

Whenever you get up off the floor, go through this process of rolling onto your stomach and moving from prayer pose through the squat into a roll-down. Do the bounces too, if they are helpful. Always finish by returning to the alignment directions.

The Wall Roll-up (about 1 minute)

Position yourself so that you are in the roll-down position with your bottom against the wall.

You're going to take a nice, slow roll-up to standing. As you do so, try to place each vertebra against the wall as it builds on top of the one beneath it. Keep breathing throughout.

To get the lower back vertebrae against the wall, you will probably have to start with your feet fairly far away from the wall and a good bit of bend in your knees. Feel free to shuffle your feet towards or away from the wall as you go, and adjust the degree of bend in your knees.

As you move through your mid-back into rolling up your upper back, you will probably find that your lower back, in the lumbar curve, peels away from the wall. This is fine, but do try to keep the sacrum (the bony plate at the base of the spine) flat to the wall.

Don't try to force the vertebrae in the neck against the wall; do find a position for your head against the wall in which the nose is pointing neither up nor down.

When you have completed the roll-up, take a good, deep breath and feel your back spreading softly against the wall.

Roll back down, trying to peel each vertebra away from the wall, one by one.

Repeat a couple of times, being sure to breathe at all times.

Step away from the wall and rock gently back and forth on your feet to find the point where you feel most balanced. You should be able to rise up onto your toes without shifting your weight. Return to your alignment directions.

◉ The Zipper (1–2 minutes)

For this exercise you will need a partner who is somewhere in the neighbourhood of your height. Once you are both in a roll-down, position yourself so that your bottom is against your partner's bottom.

Together, you're both going to take a nice, slow roll-up to standing. As you do so, try to bring each vertebra of your spines together one at a time. Imagine that the vertebrae joining are like the teeth of a zipper coming together. Keep breathing throughout.

To get the lowest vertebrae to touch, you will probably have to start with your feet fairly far away from each other and a good bit of bend in your knees. Feel free to shuffle your feet towards or away from each other, and adjust the degree of bend in your knees as you proceed.

As you move through your mid-back into rolling up your upper back, you will probably find that your lower backs, in the lumbar curve, peel away from each other. This is fine, but do try to keep your sacrums flat against each other.

When you have completed the roll-up, take a good, deep breath and feel your back spreading softly against your partner's.

Roll back down, trying to peel each vertebra away from your partner's, one by one, like the teeth of a zipper coming away from each other. Again, you may find that you need to shuffle your feet a bit on the way down, which is fine.

Repeat a couple of times, being sure to breathe at all times.

Step away from your partner and rock gently back and forth on your feet to find the point at which you feel most balanced. You should be able to rise up onto your toes without shifting your weight. Return to your alignment directions.

Teaching tip

This exercise allows you to see particularly clearly which students have a tendency to roll up by lifting the back straight up or in two sections, rather than moving through all the articulations of the spine. The sacrum is, of course, fused and moves as a plate, and there are several vertebrae in the lumbar curve that do move together, but otherwise the students' spines should meet point by point. If this is not happening, they may simply be standing too close together and need to adjust the distance between their feet as they go. They may also need to think of softening their ankles, knees and/or hips. If they are still having trouble finding that sense of 'zipping up' vertebra by vertebra, you can place your hand flat between their sacrums and instruct them to squeeze your pinkie between their spines, moving it up as they go.

With this and the following partnered exercises, if there are any students who may be uncomfortable with touching or being touched by a member of the opposite sex, you may want to have the whole class work with same-sex partners.

Let Your Fingers Do the Walking (about 2 minutes per partner)

Find a partner who is somewhere in the neighbourhood of your height.

Partner A, roll down.

.Partner B, give partner A's back a little rub-down. Give the neck a little massage as well, making sure that the head is hanging loosely.

Everybody keep breathing.

Now position yourself behind A and place one index finger on either side of the spine at the base of the sacrum. Slowly walk your fingers up your partner's spine and neck.

A, try to stack each vertebra onto the one beneath as your partner's fingers come to it, neither getting ahead nor falling behind. You will need to have some 'give' in your ankles, knees, and hips to do this.

Repeat with A walking fingers up B's spine.

⊙ Opera Cape Shrug (less than 1 minute per partner)

Working in pairs, start with partner A in a roll-down.

Partner B, walk your fingers up A's spine to a point just between the shoulder blades and stop. A's head and shoulders should still be hanging forwards.

Partner A, in this mostly rolled-up position, imagine that you are wearing a long, heavy, satin opera cape.

Easily shrug the cape off your left shoulder and leave the shoulder back.

Easily shrug the cape off your right shoulder and leave the shoulder back.

Imagine a surge of energy rising up between your shoulder blades and causing your neck to unfurl and roll up until your face is forwards.

Repeat with partner B in a roll-down.

> **Teaching tip**
>
> This exercise, which we learned from the movement teacher Debbie Green, is useful in counteracting the tendency to thrust the chest forwards in the last part of the roll-up. Many people associate that kind of military posture with 'standing up straight', but it pulls the spine out of alignment, causing an exaggeration in the lumbar and cervical curves. At the end of the roll-up, the chest should be in line with the hips; neither collapsed, nor pulled up and pressed forwards.

Sacrum Press (about 2 minutes per partner)

Find a partner who is somewhere in the neighbourhood of your height.

Partner A, roll down.

Partner B, stand to A's side. Place one hand flat on A's sacrum (the bony plate just above the tailbone). Place the fingertips of the other hand lightly on A's shoulder. You will not be pulling on the shoulder at all; the fingers are there to gently guide and help your partner feel balanced.

Partner A, bounce your knees a couple of times to make sure that they are soft and loose with plenty of 'give' in them; the exercise will not work if they are at all rigid. Think of your whole body as being easy and free, like a floppy doll's.

Partner B, on a count of three, apply a good amount of pressure down onto A's sacrum – not enough to make A stumble or feel pushed off balance, but enough to initiate a counter-lever force that will bring him or her into a roll-up. The fingers of the other hand rest lightly on the shoulder the whole time.

The roll-up will be a bit quicker than many others, but should not be so fast as to feel jarring or violent in any way.

Partner B, leave your one hand on A's sacrum and move the other so that the fingertips rest lightly on their forehead – to remind A that the head stays in line with the rest of the body.

Leaving your hands where they are, take A for a walk by applying steady and firm (but not forceful) pressure to the sacrum. You can turn A by applying a bit more pressure with either the heel of the hand or the fingers.

A, imagine that your partner's hand on your sacrum is a little motor that is moving you around the room. Start to hum as you move, imagining that the hum is coming from that motor located low on your back.

After a minute or so, B release A to walk about on his or her own.

A, imagine that that motor is still propelling you around the room from your sacrum, humming all the while.

After a minute or so of free movement, return to your partner and repeat the exercise for partner B.

As you walk around during the day, thinking of the sacrum as being the motor for your movement and of keeping the neck long can help to align your body and allow it to move more efficiently.

Teaching tip

This exercise has its origins in one described by Barbara Houseman in *Finding Your Voice* (2002). As the students are being walked around the room, if you see any who are thrusting their chests out, jutting their heads forwards, or tilting their chins up and collapsing the neck, individually stop them and help them to adjust their alignment.

Keeping It Loose

A word about 'keeping it loose' – a principle that applies at all stages of voice work. When we concentrate, we all have a tendency to get a bit fixed or frozen, sometimes through the torso, sometimes in the joints, sometimes even in the little muscles around the eyes. It's good to get into the habit of frequently doing a quick scan of your body to notice if there are any pockets of tension that can be released. This is useful not only when doing exercises, but also when sitting at the computer, rehearsing a scene, talking on the phone, or even making dinner.

Massage, physically shaking out, stretching, and wiggling can be great ways to break that pattern, and we would encourage you to do so frequently. As with all of the relaxation, release, and alignment work, however, it's possible to go through the motions and achieve very little if you are not also paying close attention to what is happening in your body and consciously engaging with images of softening and loosening.

Massage

Teaching tip

In the hands of students, massage is usually most effective as a way of helping the body to reconnect to a feeling of looseness and ease that has been deeply explored in floorwork exercises, rather than as a primary means of achieving release and relaxation.

Partners who are being massaged should be encouraged to speak out if the pressure being applied is too strong or not strong enough.

Some students may feel uncomfortable receiving massages and can stretch on their own instead. Encourage students to stay focused and avoid being overly intimate when giving massages. Assign same-sex partners, if it feels appropriate.

I. Group Massage (5–6 minutes)

All students line up one behind another. In this formation, the person at the front of the line simply receives the massage and the person at the end waits until the line turns around to receive theirs. Alternatively, if the group is big enough, the exercise can be done in a circle.

Reach up and give the shoulders and upper back of the person in front of you a quick, firm, but not too forceful rub-down. Then use your whole hand, but particularly the thumb, to massage the area where the neck joins the shoulder.

Move out along the shoulders to the upper arms, and then down either side of the spine.

Turn around and repeat with the person who was behind you.

II. Partner Massage (6–7 minutes per partner)

Get a partner who is somewhere in the neighbourhood of your height.

Partner A, begin by rubbing down B's shoulders and upper back.

Then, use your whole hand, but particularly the thumb, to massage the area where the neck joins the shoulder.

Move out along the shoulders to the upper arms, and then down either side of the spine.

Place your left forearm across your partner's upper chest, at shoulder-level, so that you have something to push against. Use the side and heel of your right hand to massage the area between your partner's right shoulder blade and the spine.

Repeat on the left side.

Return to massaging the area where the neck joins the shoulder on the right side. Work your way along the right shoulder, and then massage down the right arm to the hand. Massage back up the right arm, across the shoulders, and down the left arm to the hand. Massage back up to the area where the neck joins the shoulder.

Partner B, let your head hang forwards.

Partner A, gently massage the neck for a minute or so.

Partner B, let the heaviness of your head pull you into a roll-down.

Partner A, massage the mid and lower back.

Finally, do a 'Let Your Fingers Do the Walking' roll-up.

Repeat with partner A receiving the massage.

Joint Articulations (2–3 minutes)

We often hold tension in our joints, particularly in the arms and legs. This is a good exercise for beginning a warm-up or for re-energising the body after floor work. As with many exercises which seem repetitive or become familiar over time, it's important not to disengage the mind and rely on autopilot. Stay in the moment, and keep breathing. It's also okay to have fun and smile.

Begin standing with feet parallel, about hip-width apart, knees soft, and arms out-stretched to the side.

Loosen your wrists by circling your hands eight times in one direction and then eight times in the other direction.

Now focus on your elbows and circle your forearms eight times in one direction and eight times in the other.

Do the same with your shoulder joints by circling your arms eight times in each direction.

Now stand on the right leg. To keep your balance, it helps to focus on a point in the room about 3 metres in front of you. In this position, begin by circling your left foot eight times in each direction to release your ankle joint.

Now focus on your left knee, circling your lower leg eight times in each direction.

And now your hip joint – circle the whole leg four times in each direction.

Shake out the leg you've been standing on, and repeat these articulations with the right leg. Once you're finished, give yourself a good shake-out all over.

Loose Shoulders (about 1 minute)

Begin standing with feet parallel, about hip-width apart, knees soft, and arms to the side.

Start swinging your right arm forwards in a big circle. Allow your knees to bounce a little with the momentum of the arm movement. Let your breath come into synch with the rhythm of the movement. Send images of looseness and ease to the shoulder.

Repeat on the left side.

Repeat, swinging the right arm backwards and then the left arm backwards.

See if you can swing one arm backwards and the other arm forwards at the same time. If you find this difficult, get two partners, one on each arm, to help you.

Loose Neck

I. (about 1 minute)

Let your head drop forwards, lace your fingers together, and drape your hands over the 'fat' part of the back of your head (your occipital bone) with your elbows falling down towards the floor, as in the first neck stretch from earlier in the chapter.

After 30–40 seconds, let your arms drop and allow your head to float up.

Imagine that you are one of those bobble-headed dolls that people sometimes put on the dashboards of their cars: your neck stays long, but your head can make a small, gentle bouncing motion up and down on top of it.

Get a good, gentle, little bounce going, and then rotate your head around to the left, bouncing all the way. Then rotate around to the right and back to centre, maintaining the bobble-headed doll bounce.

II. (about 3–4 minutes per partner)

Get into pairs.

Partner A, sit in a chair with partner B standing behind you.

A, let your head drop forwards.

B, give A a neck massage for about a minute.

B, place your hands on either side of A's face. With your thumbs, feel for a little bump under each of A's ears. Rest your thumbs under these bumps.

Keeping your thumbs there, pivot your hands forwards. Leave your index finger to the side of A's eyes, and rest your middle fingers under their cheekbones. None of your other fingers will be touching A's face.

In this position, B should be able to lift up A's head and move it in any direction. Start with small, gentle movements.

A, your job is to keep breathing and completely relinquish control of your head to B. It can help to imagine that your neck is made of jelly, or that your head is getting very heavy – the way it does when you are about to fall asleep.

B, move A's head through its range of motion – 'no' and 'yes' movements, figure 8s, back and forth, side to side. Start small and gentle, becoming bolder as A really releases and gives you the full weight of their head. Avoid getting stuck in predictable patterns, but be VERY CAREFUL not to make sudden, jerky motions. The point of the exercise is not to catch your partner out, but to help them release. This requires trust.

A, as you begin to feel comfortable with the exercise, begin to breathe out on a 'fffff' sound. Then turn it into a 'vvvv' sound. Finally, try humming a bit. Notice if creating sound makes it harder or easier for you to really let go of your neck. If it becomes harder, focus even more intently on the images of the jelly-neck and the heavy head.

Continue for a couple of minutes, and then switch to partner B.

Teaching tip

This exercise is best done at some point after the 'Partnered Manipulations' exercise in the *Floor work* section. It is a good exercise to return to again and again as students become more advanced, moving from pure vocalisation to chanting nursery rhymes to speaking simple text to engaging with highly emotional text.

Loose Hips

I. (about 1 minute)

With the ankles soft and the knees slightly bent, imagine that your pelvic bowl is a cradle. Rock the cradle from front to back ever so slightly – just barely half an inch.

Let the rocking motion gradually grow until your pelvis is moving through an arc of about 7–9 inches. Keep the bottom loose throughout – if you are having to push it forwards, make the motion smaller.

II (about 1 minute)

Imagine you have a very tiny hula hoop around your waist. Begin making a tiny hula-hoop motion with your hips to get it moving.

Gradually let the imaginary hula hoop and the hula-hoop motion grow until they are enormous – as big as they could possibly be.

Move the enormous hula hoop around in the opposite direction. Imagine it gradually shrinking until you are again making a very tiny hula-hoop motion.

III. (5–7 minutes per partner)

Kevin Crawford taught us this excellent exercise.

Get a partner who is somewhere in the neighbourhood of your height.

Partner A, lie on your back; partner B sit by A's side.

Partner B, do a fairly quick version of the leg work in the 'Partnered Manipulations' exercise on both of A's legs.

Then, crouching in front of A, get a good grip on A's ankles and stand, lifting A's legs perpendicular to the floor.

B, lift A's pelvis slightly off the ground and swing it gently.

Then bounce on your toes, which will cause A's legs to shake slightly.

A, start breathing out on a 'huuuuuuh' sound. Think of the sound as being shaken out of your body from your pelvis.

After about a minute, B lower A's legs to the ground.

B, then get into a crouch and take A's legs by the ankles again. Hold the legs a couple of inches from the floor and swing them gently in an arhythmical and asymmetrical way.

A, start vocalising. Keep thinking of the sounds as being shaken out of your body.

B, continue for 30–40 seconds and then lower A's legs back to the ground.

Repeat with partner B lying on their back.

🎧 'I'm So Excited' (6–8 minutes)

1. Begin with the group in a loose circle, all standing with feet parallel and about hip-width apart, knees soft, and arms to the side.

   Lean forwards slightly from your hips, and begin to shake your bottom. Your thighs and knees will move along with it.

   Let the movement grow until your heels are coming off the floor a bit. If you're feeling very energised, you can even turn it into a little jog in place.

   Let your upper body hang very loose as you do this – arms and chest bouncing along with the bottom movement.

   Keep your neck long. Because you are leaning slightly forwards, your head will also be tilted forwards a bit; avoid compressing the back of your neck to peer up.

   Think of your whole body as a big bowlful of loose, shaking jelly. It will feel a little silly, and that's just fine.

   Once the group has established the movement, released into it, and is beginning to really enjoy it, let the movement start to shake some sound out of your body. Just a 'hah', 'huh', 'hee' or 'ho' to begin with.

   Feel how the movement of your body encourages a very free and easy release of sound.

   Take a little break to catch your breath, and stretch.

2. Come back to the bottom-wiggling movement and let it get established again.

   This time you're going to release not just sound but also a voiced thought; the thought you're going to release is, 'I'm soooooo loose!'

   As a group, practise letting that thought bubble up out of your bouncing body a few times, and then go around the circle and do it individually. Again, it will feel a little silly, and that's half the point of the exercise – to get in touch with your inner little kid and enjoy the freedom of silliness.

Take a short break again.

3. Now as a group, shaking your bottoms again, try the thought, 'I'm soooooo excited!' Pretend it's your third birthday – you are THAT excited.

Alternate between, 'I'm soooooo loose!' and 'I'm soooooo excited!' Try to find a way to keep the loose energy excited and the excited energy loose.

When an overall energy that is both excited and free is established, go around the circle and take 'I'm soooooo excited!' individually.

Teaching tip

This exercise is somewhat advanced, in that it brings the students onto voice. Much work on finding open, easy and free phonation will follow, but doing this exercise fairly early can give them a fun sense of how physical and vocal release connect.

Lead the group in coming onto vibration and then onto text. Don't let the students get away with breathy, half-hearted sound; model an engaged, fully released sound for them and encourage them to match it. If, however, you can hear that people are starting to push or even scream, take it back down to a light and easy (but not breathy) 'hah'.

This exercise and the one following grew from work done with Alexander Technique teacher, Glynn Macdonald.

We Will All Be Stars (5–8 minutes)

Begin with the group in a circle, all facing away from one another.

Start with a minute or so of bottom shaking.

While still shaking, release a loose but energised 'Oh!' a few times.

Let the shaking become smaller and release another few 'Oh's' without letting the energy drop.

Let the body become still (but not rigid) and release another few 'Oh's'.

Imagine that all of the energy that went into shaking your bottom is now circling around inside of you, just below your solar plexus (above your tummy button).

With an easy, flowing movement, raise your right hand up on a diagonal and imagine all that energy inside you pouring out your fingertips in the form of an 'Oh'. (The 'Oh', of course, will in reality come out of your mouth, but play with the image of its energy flowing through your open, loose but energised fingers).

Do the same with your left arm.

Pick up your right foot and picture all the energy in your centre pouring through it on an 'Oh' as you place it back on the ground at a bit of a diagonal from your body.

Do the same with your left foot.

Now, stretch out all four limbs in a star shape and imagine energy pouring from your centre through all of them as you say, 'Oh, for a muse of fire!'

Turn around so that everyone in the circle is facing in and try it again a couple of times.

If it's going well, try it one at a time around the circle. You may find that, when you are put on the spot in that way, you tighten up a bit and lose some of the sense of freedom and flowing energy. At this point that's not a big worry: it's good to just notice the difference.

Teaching tip

Again, this exercise is somewhat advanced; it can, however, be very useful for giving the students a sense of where they are going with the work. It is important that you model an easy (loose) but full (energised) release of sound. Students may need to come back to simply shaking their bottoms and saying 'Oh' a few times between the stages of the exercise to stay in touch with this, which is fine.

Follow-up

Reflective practice questions:

* Is there an area in your body where you have a particularly hard time 'letting go'? Does it respond more readily to stretching, image-based work, or direct manipulation?
* What relationship, if any, did you notice between breath and physical release?
* Which exercises left you feeling the most energised? Which left you the most drained?
* What aspects of relaxation, release, and alignment work do you most enjoy; which do you shrink away from; which do you find challenging?

* Are there correspondences between tension in any areas of your body? For example, does releasing tension in your arms have any effect on your neck? If you didn't notice any correspondences in class, try some out-of-class exploration.
* After doing the roll-up work, did you feel any differences in the way you move? Did any parts of your body feel wider or longer or looser than usual?

Exercises

After a few sessions of relaxation, release and alignment work, repeat the Exploration exercise. You will probably find that your old tension habits have not disappeared overnight, but you may find that your awareness of them is heightened and that you are able to relinquish them more easily.

As mentioned at the beginning of this section, relaxation, release, and alignment work is ongoing. Once the groundwork has been laid through in-depth exploration at the beginning of the course, it's a good idea to revisit at least a few exercises at the beginning of every voice class to prepare the body to work.

Further reading

Houseman, Barbara, *Finding Your Voice*, Nick Hern Books, London, 2002. Chapter 2: Body Work, pp. 15–57.

Linklater, Kristin, *Freeing the Natural Voice* (Revised edition), Drama Book Publishers, New York, 2006. Chapter 1: Workday One, pp. 31–41.

McCallion, Michael, *The Voice Book* (Revised edition), Faber and Faber Ltd, London, 1998. Part One: Body use, pp. 1–35.

McEvenue, Kelly, *The Alexander Technique for Actors*, Methuen, London, 2001. Part 1: The Alexander Technique in the Theatre, pp. 37–53.

Melton, Joan (with Kenneth Tom), *One Voice*, Heinemann, Portsmouth, NH, 2003. Chapter 1: The Foundation, pp. 3–19; and Chapter 4: The Voice/Movement Relationship, pp. 77–93.

2 Breath and Voice – Connect

Framework

Breathing is intimately linked to everything that makes us human: we breathe to live. But breath is not only for survival; it is also emotional and expressive. It connects our creative, intelligent, conscious life with our instinctive, primal, unconscious life.

The in-breath is part of our body's emotional response to an event or an object. We become conscious of this response as a feeling, which in turn can provoke thoughts – mental activities that require oxygen, the fuel of the brain. But breath is also the medium of our vocal expression – we communicate our thoughts and feelings on the out-breath. So, we conceive with the in-breath, and we express with the out-breath. This is the fundamental relationship between breath and our creative selves.

Because this fundamental, and instinctive, relationship is connected to our emotional lives, it varies as our emotions fluctuate. There is the frozen breath of fear, the rapid upper-thoracic breath of panic, and the diminished breath of depression; but there is also the inflated breath of joy, the deep breath of passion, or the relaxed breath of contentment. Emotion (after life regulation) is the primary governor of breath, and the actor, in particular, needs to be open and responsive to this emotional breath as it can be deeper, more energised and more dynamic than the passive, inexpressive breath of the person who is shut down emotionally, or cut off, or holding emotions in check. But the actor needs to manage this emotional response and not be governed by it. At its most fundamental, your voice is your breath. It is breath transformed into sound waves by your vocal folds, but it is your breath nonetheless. And if your breath is not full, free, and responsive moment by moment, your voice will not be either. Nor, for that matter, will your acting. If the actor's breath is frozen with fear, then how can she express the full breath of Juliet's passion; if it is overcome with panic, how can he communicate Romeo's joy?

So work on breath must make us aware of our habits of breathing, the inhibitions that we experience, and the potential for inspiration and expressive exhalation that is fresh and novel. This work must take us beyond the breath of our daily needs and mundane communication to a breath that moves with the character's own impulses and so moves the audience to a deeper experience of the character's drama.

This requires several stages of training: release work in order to enable the experience of a fuller breath and the development of new habits; technical/muscular work to build up the strength and responsiveness of the muscles responsible for respiration; and connecting work to link breath and voice with the thought/feeling impulse.

To understand what is involved in achieving this stronger, more responsive breath, you need to understand a bit about why and how your body breathes. As we began this chapter by saying, human beings breathe to live – our bodies constantly need oxygen, which they use to create the energy required simply to stay alive. But we also breathe to express ourselves in speech and song – and this requires more oxygen than just sitting still.

Your breath is not created by your lungs, but by the muscles surrounding them. The lungs themselves have no power to move on their own; they are little more than a collection of tubes and tiny air sacs. When you breathe in, oxygen (as well as other gases in the atmosphere) travels down your windpipe, which divides in two as it enters the two lungs. Those two pipes divide and subdivide more than 20 times into smaller and smaller tubes which eventually end in groups of little air sacs called alveoli. Each alveolus (there are approximately 300 million of them in your lungs) is surrounded by tiny blood vessels. The oxygen that has travelled down into these little pouches passes through the walls of the alveoli and the walls of the adjacent blood vessels to enter the bloodstream, which will then carry it to individual cells where it will help to create the energy we use to live. At the same time, carbon dioxide (the waste product of this energy consumption), which your blood has been picking up on its travels through your body, passes from the bloodstream into the tiny pouches. From there, when you breathe out, it travels up the tubes, into your windpipe and is then expelled through your nose or mouth. (See Fig. 3.)

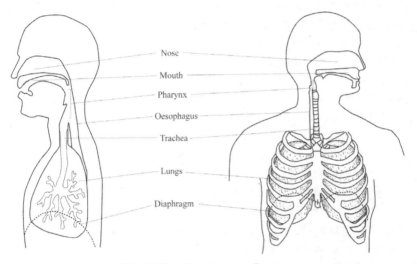

Nose
Mouth
Pharynx
Oesophagus
Trachea
Lungs
Diaphragm

Fig. 3 The Respiratory System

So, you might ask, if the lungs don't have any muscle tissue in them and can't move on their own, what is it that causes them to expand – drawing oxygen in – and deflate – pushing carbon dioxide out? The lungs are attached to a structure of muscle and bone that surrounds them in such a way that, when any part of this structure moves, the lungs move along with it. When it moves away from the lungs, the lungs are pulled with it. When it moves towards the lungs, the lungs are pushed inwards. When the lungs are pulled on, they expand; when they are pushed on, they compress. As the lungs expand, the air pressure within them drops and more air rushes in (via your nose and mouth) to bring the pressure back to normal. When the lungs are compressed, the air pressure within them rises and air rushes out (again, via your nose and mouth) to bring the pressure back to normal. Think of an old-fashioned button accordion or 'squeeze box'. When you first squeeze it (like you squeeze your lungs on an out-breath), you decrease the room inside it, increasing the pressure, and so air rushes out, making a musical note. When you expand it again (as your lungs expand on an in-breath), you increase the space inside it, decreasing the pressure, and so air rushes back in, ready to produce the next note. Try Exploration I for a human version of this 'squeeze box' image.

As mentioned, the lungs are encased in a surrounding structure of muscle and bone. The most important parts of this structure are the diaphragm and the ribs (see Fig. 4). The diaphragm is a large sheet of muscle that lies between the organs in your chest (the lungs and heart) and all the organs in your abdomen (the stomach, liver, intestines, etc.). It consists of two flexible domes connected by a central tendon. The rim of the diaphragm attaches to the bottom of your sternum (breastbone) at the front, all the way around the lower ribs at the sides, and to the lumbar vertebrae of your spine at the back. When you need to inhale, the diaphragm contracts, and the domes are pulled down and partially flattened. This pulls down on your lungs, expanding them vertically. As the diaphragm does this, it pushes down on the contents of the abdomen, causing the slight swelling of the belly we associate with breathing in. In exhalation, the diaphragm relaxes back into its dual-dome shape, passively pushing against the lungs and compressing them as it does so. When you are speaking, the muscles of the abdomen can also engage to push on the organs underneath the diaphragm, thus supporting it and giving extra pressure as it relaxes and pushes against the lungs. The diaphragm itself, however, does no active work at all on the out-breath. Try Exploration I again, and notice particularly how your diaphragm and abdominal muscles respond.

Fig. 4 The Thorax

When you are simply breathing to stay alive, your diaphragm does most of the work, but in breath for speech your diaphragm does about 75% of the work, and the muscles connected to your ribs do the other 25%. You have 12 pairs of ribs in your chest. The topmost pair lies immediately under your clavicle (collarbone), while the bottom pair can be felt most easily in the small of your back just above your pelvis. To the rear, each rib is attached to one of your thoracic vertebrae via a gliding joint that allows the rib flexible movement. At the front, the top seven ribs attach directly to your sternum; they are known as the 'true' ribs. Ribs eight to ten are indirectly connected to the sternum by means of an attachment to rib seven, and this earns them the name of 'false' ribs; but the 11th and 12th ribs don't attach to anything in the front at all, and so are called the 'floating' ribs. For most of its length, each rib is composed of bone, but shortly before the rib attaches to the sternum at the front, the bony portion of the rib ends and a portion made of cartilage begins[1].

Cartilage is a softer material than bone and has much more elasticity, so the ribs can move and twist a good deal at the front as well as the back. In the first five ribs, however, the cartilage portion of these ribs is shorter, and the joint with the sternum allows only for a slight rotating movement. This means that these top ribs have a fairly limited range of motion that has been described as being like a pump handle: lifting forwards and up, and lowering back and down (Bunch 1997:34). Ribs six through ten, on the other hand, have increasingly longer cartilage portions and the ability to rise and fall in a sideways direction, like a bucket handle. This gives them much greater flexibility than the top five pairs of ribs. Since the 'floating' ribs have no forwards attachment at all, they have considerable freedom of movement. The significance of this is that in the areas where there is greater flexibility in the rib cage, there is more room for expansion of the lungs. Equally significant is that this area of greater expansion is in the lower half of the rib cage – precisely the same area to which the diaphragm is attached. The relationship between the movement of the ribs and the movement of the diaphragm is, therefore, an intimate one which can be developed and strengthened with regular exercise. Try Exploration I again, and notice this time how your rib cage responds.

---

[1]It is this cartilage, then, that attaches to the sternum in ribs 1–7, and that attaches ribs 8–10 to rib 7. The floating ribs are simply bone.

The principal muscles that make your rib cage expand outwards are called the external intercostal muscles. They are sheets of muscles that run between the ribs. When these muscles contract during inhalation, they cause the rib cage to swing outwards and upwards, pulling the lungs along with them. The relaxation of the external intercostals, together with the effects of gravity and the elastic recoil of the cartilage in the ribs, returns the rib cage to its rest position, pressing on the lungs and causing us to breathe out. When we are breathing for speech, the external intercostals become active on the in-breath to help us take in the additional air that is needed to speak. On the out-breath, they release in a slow, steady way in order to sustain the voice.

There is another set of intercostal muscles known as the internal intercostals. Like the external intercostals, they are sheets of muscles that run between the ribs, but they lie beneath the externals. These muscles become active during exhalation, particularly to produce the small variations in air pressure that are required for stressing particular words. Contracting them will also press the ribs down further beyond their rest position, thus creating extended pressure on the lungs, and so enabling a continuation of speech where necessary.

As we have said, because the top ribs can't move very much, they can't expand the lungs very much either. Many people, when they think of taking a deep breath, think of lifting up their shoulders (which doesn't help the lungs even a little bit) and thrusting out their chests. This looks impressive, but simply lifting the chest doesn't increase the size of the lungs. In fact, when you lift your chest this way, you have to draw your shoulder blades together and probably stick out your bottom a bit. Try it. Both of these things give the lower ribs less room to open up and out, and, as we have seen, it's the lower ribs that are capable of really bringing considerable air into the lungs. The lungs themselves are quite small at the top and much larger at the bottom, and, although they stop at the point of your lowest ribs, really opening those lower ribs and allowing the diaphragm to fully descend can cause a sensation of the breath filling much lower in your body. This, not puffing the chest out, is the sign of a full, deep breath.

Much of the work on relaxation, release, and alignment we have already done is important because it allows your ribs and your diaphragm to move more fully and freely. While the lungs themselves fill only the thorax, or upper torso, your whole body is potentially involved in breathing. For example, tension in the hips can lock the abdominal muscles, which then will block the diaphragm from descending fully; misalignment in the back will limit the range of motion in the ribs. The work in this chapter on building a connection to your body's free and full breath, and between that breath and your voice will, therefore, include some stretching and visualisation exercises to help you grow further in your ability to release even very deeply held tensions throughout your body.

Beyond these habitual tensions, however, we also need to work through a very human tendency to hold our breath. We think of holding the breath as something involving a plugged nose and puffed-out cheeks that we do underwater, but, in fact, we do it all the time. When we push, pull or lift something heavy, we hold our breath, and with good reason: this breath-holding stabilises the torso, which gives the arm and shoulder muscles a fixed point to work from. When we are afraid, we also hold our breath, which makes sense too. Without the noise of breathing in our ears, we can better hear predators approaching, and with a stable torso we can better throw a punch or sprint away. However, many of the things that frighten us in modern society – for example, the threat of embarrassment, of failure, of being rejected or misunderstood – are not predators that we're going to have to fight or flee. Nevertheless, we respond to them in the same way that our distant ancestors would have responded to an approaching bear: we freeze our torsos and clamp shut our throats. Furthermore, most of us – whether we are born performers or not – will find at one time or another that standing on a stage in front of other people provokes the same response. It may very well be subtle – just a tiny tightness across the chest or rigidity in the abdominal muscles – but it is a form of holding the breath nonetheless.

In fact, simply standing still and breathing fully may be one of the most challenging things you are called upon to do if you are an actor. It requires technical skill, courage, patience and faith to release and allow your body to open wholly to the breath. It may also be one of the most *important* things actors are called upon to do. The breathing impulse is the primary impulse: if you are blocking it, what chance do other impulses have? How can you move gracefully, respond subtly, act spontaneously if you're not breathing? How can you connect to an idea or an emotion, much less communicate it powerfully to someone else, if you are disconnected from your own breath? It is not at all uncommon to find that actors who are plagued with nervous tics – under-developed gestures, unnecessary shifting of weight, shuffling feet, fidgety hands – are not allowing their bodies to breathe fully. The energy of the breathing impulse is then stymied. It has to go somewhere, though, so it darts out of the hands and feet. Once the actor has learned to open to his or her breath, to connect to that primal impulse, the energy is grounded. The energy of the voice, the text and the performance can then also flow freely and appropriately.

Our work on breath will begin with observation of how that impulse moves the body to breathe when we allow it to. Breathing is a peculiar bodily function in that we can do it both voluntarily and automatically. Every time we move our limbs, we are on some level choosing to do so (the exception being when reflex action is stimulated, like when the doctor knocks your kneecap with a little hammer). We may not be giving it a great deal of thought, but we do have control over the movement. This is called voluntary motion. Muscles like the heart, or those that line the intestines, we have no control over; we can't start or stop their motion at will. They are automatic functions. But, as we've said, breath is both automatic and voluntary. We can choose to breathe, and we do so every time we interrupt our natural breathing pattern and take in the extra air necessary to speak. We can also choose not to breathe, but only up to a point. When the physiological need for oxygen becomes strong enough, the automatic nervous system will override the voluntary and force us to breathe, even if it has to make us pass out to do it. Furthermore, if the muscles and the neural pathways are intact, our bodies will continue to breathe long after the part of the brain that controls voluntary motion has shut down. Both nervous systems are very smart and have a very finely tuned sense of how much air is necessary to do any given job, whether it be running down the street to catch a bus (controlled by the autonomic system) or speaking a line of Shakespearean verse (controlled by the voluntary).

Sometimes, however, we don't trust these systems. We stuff our bodies full of air they don't need, or we push and squeeze out the last little bit of air, when really it would make sense to just take another breath. So it's important to learn to listen to your body. To quietly observe how it works when you leave it alone. *To get out of your own way.* Once you have done this, you can begin to think about using your breath to support your voice, which is covered in the next chapter. Until you have learned to let your breathing muscles function responsively and without restraint, though, it's not very realistic to expect them to learn to work in a way that could carry you through a Shakespearean soliloquy in a 1200-seat outdoor theatre, or bring steadiness and authority to your voice in an important presentation.

As you work on opening your body to the breathing impulse through the exercises in this chapter, you will also be working on connecting your voice to your breath. It's entirely possible to make lots of noise on a shallow, tight breath. The voice that results, however, will also be shallow and tight – limited in its range and expressivity. It will often feel trapped in the throat, or squeezed, or simply disconnected from what you are thinking and feeling. The voice that is the product of a full, released breath, on the other hand, will often feel like it is originating deep in the body. It will be easy, flexible, and capable of communicating great nuance. This voice is explored simply at first – through small touches of sound connected to the natural rhythm of your breath. It is not, frankly, the most exciting thing you will ever do with your voice. It is, however, the foundation for everything that will follow. Notice what this simple connection feels like; learn to love the feeling, to nurture it, and to come back to it again and again to ground your work.

Exploration

I. **If you have asthma or other respiratory difficulties, skip this one.**
Blow out all your breath. Blow and blow and blow until you can't blow anymore; then hold your breath for a second or two until your body insists on breathing in again. As the air rushes in, notice where you feel a strong muscular response. Do it two or three times, focusing your awareness on the abdomen, the ribs to the side, the ribs to the back, and the upper chest. Put your hands on those areas to see if you can feel a response from the outside as well as the inside. Note your observations in your journal and discuss them in class.

II. When you first wake up in the morning, just lie in bed for a few minutes and notice your breathing – how often it comes, how long the little pauses between breaths are, where you feel it filling in your body. Roll over from your front to your back, from side to side; stretch out, curl up, and make the same observations in each position. Note your observations in your journal and discuss them in class.

III. Pick an activity that you do regularly and which requires you to concentrate and is a bit stressful – such as driving, doing homework, balancing your cheque book. As you engage in that activity during the day, use a little bit of your conscious awareness to notice what your breath is doing. Try to simply observe without interfering, which is not necessarily as easy as it sounds. Do your breaths come more or less frequently than when you were lying in bed? Are they more noticeable higher or lower in your body? Do they ever just stop for a while? Note your observations in your journal and discuss them in class.

Exercises

Teaching tip

The exercises in this chapter are organised under four headings: *Opening the Breath*; *Coming on to Voice*; *Breath and Voice in Action*; and *Connecting to Text*. The work on opening the breath bears very regular repeating through the initial stages of voice training and periodic revisiting thereafter, as do many of the exercises in *Coming on to Voice*. The exercises in *Breath and Voice in Action* and *Connecting to Text* begin to engage the expressivity of the voice and are designed to help root it in breathing that is open and easy. The freedom of breath and voice should facilitate freedom of impulse and thought, and vice versa.

Opening the Breath

The work on opening the breath begins with more stretching, but it is stretching that targets areas where the muscles that contribute to the breathing process tend to get locked or held. It is, therefore, particularly important not only to keep breathing in these stretches but also to focus on allowing the breath to travel deeper and more fully into the body as you hold the stretch.

The work also includes more floor work and visualisation. As always, the physical relaxation needs to be coupled with mental focus. Many of the muscles involved in breathing and speaking are not easily released through conscious command. They do, however, respond to images. A strong engagement with the images in this section can be a powerful tool to help you open up your breathing.

Side Stretches (1–2 minutes)

Begin standing with feet parallel, about hip-width apart, knees soft, and arms to the side.

Lift your arms up, and imagine your shoulder blades sliding down your back.

Imagine that there is a large barrel to your left. Keeping your waist long, lean over the barrel.

Now swing your left arm around and place your left hand on your right ribs, which should be getting quite a nice stretch (see Fig 5).

Imagine each in-breath filling your hand.

Continue breathing in this position for 30-40 seconds, and then release the stretch by relaxing your arms and torso forwards into a roll-down position. Roll up and repeat the whole sequence to the right.

Bear Hug (about 1 minute)

Begin standing with feet parallel, about hip-width apart. Bend your knees a bit – as if you were about to sit down and were interrupted half way. Imagine your tailbone curling down underneath your pelvis.

Fig. 5 Side Stretches

Let your head and shoulders gently drop forwards.

Cross your arms in front of you and reach around to your back. Try to hold the edges of your shoulder blades with your fingertips (see Fig. 6).

Your back should be getting a stretch. With each breath, feel the ribs in your back rise and fall.

Continue breathing in this position for a minute or so.

🎧 The Plough (1–3 minutes)

If you have any history of back or neck problems, you should not do this exercise.

Start in semi-supine.

If you have anything under your head – a book or a scarf – put it to the side.

Fig. 6 Bear Hug

Take a minute or so to release unnecessary tension from your body by imagining your head, your shoulders, your chest, your abdomen, and your hips all becoming very heavy on the floor.

Continue to think of your body as being heavy, soft, and floppy as you slide your hands under your bottom with the palms facing the floor.

Now draw your knees up to your chest. You may have tightened your abdominal muscles to do this; see to what extent you can release them again.

Next, push slightly against the floor with your hands and swing your knees up, bringing your pelvis up over your shoulders. It is as if you were doing a backward roll but stopped half way.

Balance about 75% of the weight of your torso and legs on your shoulders, and take the remaining 25% in your hands, with the elbows resting on the floor. There should be no weight on your neck. Roll it back and forth a few times to make sure that it is entirely free.

Let your knees hang away from each other and towards the floor.

In this position, your chest and abdomen will be somewhat compressed, which may make it feel hard to breathe – that's okay. Try to relax through the discomfort, and imagine that your back, particularly the area underneath your hands, is opening to receive the breath. Your body is resourceful at getting the oxygen it needs and will respond to this image if you don't fight it. Stay heavy, soft, and floppy.

Stay in the position for a minute or so and then use your hands to help your pelvis back down to the floor. Take a moment to observe how your breathing may have shifted; then take a stretch and a wiggle.

Teaching tip

This is based on a Yoga pose which was adapted by Catherine Fitzmaurice for voice work and passed on to us via Dudley Knight. Joan Melton also describes it in her book, *One Voice*. It is a wonderful exercise for unlocking deep tensions in the back, and opening that area to the breath. As the students become accustomed to it, it can be useful occasionally to spend up to three minutes in the pose and see what effect it has on their breathing.

Some students may feel a sensation of tightness in the lower back when they come out of the pose. If they don't have any history with back problems, this is probably not a cause for concern, and rolling over into prayer pose will usually relieve the discomfort; if it does not, the student should not repeat the exercise. Often students who have trouble staying in the pose are not getting enough of their weight up onto their shoulders or are not letting their knees drop down far enough.

🎧 The Bow (1–2 minutes)

If you have any history of back problems, you should not do this exercise.

Start lying on your stomach. Let your heels fall away from each other and your shoulders fall towards the floor.

Take a minute or so to release unnecessary tension from your body by imagining your head, your shoulders, your chest, your abdomen, and your hips all becoming very heavy on the floor.

Continue to think of your body as being heavy, soft, and floppy as you lift up your left foot and reach back with your left hand to grab the front of it. Relax the left shoulder. Then lift up your right foot and reach back with your right hand and grab the front of it. Relax your right shoulder.

Next, try to straighten your legs, keeping hold of your feet, which will stretch your arms back and lift your upper torso up off the floor. It is also helpful to think of lifting through the breastbone. You may start to rock back and forth a bit, which is fine.

Keep the neck floppy and the head hanging down towards the ground.

Imagine the upper chest unlocking and stretching.

This is a strenuous position, and your breathing may become quite fast and hard quite quickly. DON'T FIGHT THE BREATH. This is the whole point of the exercise. If you can allow the breath to move freely when you are under this kind of strain, you will be better able to allow the breath to come freely when you are under the strain of performance.

After 40–50 seconds, ease out of the pose and pull yourself back into prayer pose. It is very important to go into prayer pose immediately after doing The Bow; this exercise compresses the lower back, which then needs to be stretched back out again.

Take a moment to observe how your breathing may have shifted.

Teaching tip

This is another Yoga pose adapted by Catherine Fitzmaurice. Many students will need to be reminded to keep their heads hanging to the floor, and they will almost all need to be reminded not to fight their breathing, but rather let it be strong and deep.

Students with any history of lower back problems should sit this one out.

The Empty Torso (4–5 minutes)

Start in semi-supine. If you have back trouble which makes this uncomfortable, you can lie on your side instead. If you do so, you should change sides from time to time.

Take a minute or so to release unnecessary tension from your body by imagining your head, your shoulders, your chest, your abdomen, and your hips all becoming very heavy on the floor.

Imagine that your jaw is becoming heavy, and that the heaviness causes your mouth to drop open slightly. If you have been breathing through your nose, switch to breathing through your mouth for a while, as this is how we often breathe when we are speaking.

Focus your attention on your breath and notice it entering and leaving your body at its own tempo.

Imagine that your torso – the area between your shoulders and your pelvis – is a completely empty chamber. No muscles, no bones, no internal organs, no blood vessels or nerves – just a still, dark, quiet, maybe slightly cool space. This is not, of course, true, but the image can help you connect to a sense of openness and freedom in your breath.

Now imagine that coming up out of the top of this empty chamber of a torso is a big empty pipe. This pipe is your neck and throat. Think of it as one hollow round. The pipe comes up out of the empty torso and then turns a corner and opens into the empty chamber of your mouth. While this is also not true, you may notice that the image encourages a slight softening of the jaw, the tongue root, and the muscles of the throat.

Turn your attention back to your empty torso. Imagine that at the base, nestled in your pelvic bowl, there is a source of light, heat and energy. This may be an open flame, a red hot furnace, a ball of electricity or a bright sun – whatever image you respond to most strongly. We will call it your 'centre'.

Imagine that your centre is constantly gauging how much oxygen you need, and is responsible for calling air down to itself and then releasing air back out again. Imagine the air travelling from your lips to your centre and back again through a completely empty channel.

Focus on this image for a few minutes. Notice how your breath and your body respond to it. You, of course, are not *doing* anything; you are simply getting out of the way and letting your centre breathe through your body.

Teaching tip

We learned this exercise from Dudley Knight. It is almost entirely an exercise of the mind, but one that can have wonderful physical benefits. Talking your students through it step by step, constantly bringing them back to the sense of cool space through the torso, throat, and mouth, will help them to make a strong connection with the image.

Your students may be working with the term 'centre' in other areas of their training (e.g. movement and acting), which could cause some confusion about what it is supposed to mean to them. For the purposes of voice work, the centre is imagined to be a source of energy and impulse situated at the base of the torso. The idea of 'giving over' to the centre – letting it take responsibility for the breath – is useful in establishing a sense of the breath (and later the voice) as originating deep in the body without pushing it down. While it may be a different image and function from the centre that is discussed in other classes, ultimately all the work the students do should be bringing them to a sense of being grounded, free and present.

Once you have introduced the images of the empty torso and letting centre control the breath, it can be useful to try to implement them while doing The Plough and The Bow.

The Hanging Breath I (2–3 minutes)

Start in prayer pose, and take a moment to establish a sense of softness and looseness in your body. Notice your breath.

Come up onto all fours, with your hands directly under your shoulders and your knees directly under your hips.

Focus on your abdomen for four or five breath-cycles. On the in-breath, imagine that your abdomen is completely free to fall towards the floor as it receives the air. You don't need to push it at all – just allow it to open. On the out-breath, notice how gently and easily it floats back towards your spine.

Focus on your lower back for four or five breath-cycles. On the in-breath, imagine it swelling slightly, like bread rising in the oven. Again, you don't need to push it at all – just allow it to open. On the out-breath, notice how gravity gently pulls it back down.

Focus on your ribs for four or five breath-cycles. On the in-breath, notice where you can feel the ribs swell – probably in the lower ribs to the sides and the back. On the out-breath, feel how naturally they fall back to their original position.

Teaching tip

This exercise also works well with partners – partner A placing his or her hands on the areas where partner B is focusing as s/he does the exercise.

Coming onto Voice

The goal in this section is not to make a lot of noise, or even a beautiful noise. It is to get used to engaging your voice while maintaining a full, open breath. As you do so, you may find that your sense of your voice shifts from your throat and your mouth to your torso. This is a good thing. As we will discuss in more detail in the next chapter, your voice is indeed produced by your larynx, but it is powered by muscles as low in your body as your pelvis. Foster the sense of connection between the movement of your voice and the movement of your breath and body.

A further goal of this section is not only to connect, but also to coordinate your voice with your breath. There are two kinds of miscoordination that can happen, particularly when we say words that start with vowel sounds. One is to let a little bit of breath escape before closing the vocal folds. This results in a breathy sound and is called 'breathy onset'. Try saying, 'I'm excited about airplanes' in your very best Marilyn Monroe voice to get a sense of what this might sound like. The other is to tightly clamp shut the vocal folds before any breath gets to them. When this happens, the air pressure underneath the folds builds up until it finally bursts through with a little popping sound. This is called 'glottal onset'. Try saying 'Uh oh!' as if you were playing with a baby. If you felt a little pop or a bounce at the start of each word, you were using glottal onset. Ideally, the vocal folds should be coming together just as the breath reaches them. This is called 'simultaneous onset' and is something the exercises in this section will help you achieve.

In-breath to Out-breath (3–5 minutes)

This exercise is the essence of truth and simplicity. We learnt it from Meribeth Bunch Dayme.

Start in semi-supine. Take a minute or so to release unnecessary tension from your body by imagining your head, your shoulders, your chest, your abdomen, and your hips all becoming very heavy on the floor.

Focus your attention on your breath and notice it entering and leaving your body at its own tempo. Now begin to notice the point in your breathing cycle where the in-breath changes to the out-breath. Notice also the deepest place in your body where this change starts to take place.

As you become familiar with this point in your breathing cycle, begin to mark the change from in-breath to out-breath with a gentle *huh* sound. Think of touching this sound off from the place in your body where the change starts to take place. Just experience this process for a few breath-cycles.

As you become more confident with the sensations of breath and voice, begin to make a more committed and extended sound and let it out on an easy pitch glide so that it sounds like a sigh.

Experience this process for a few breath-cycles, and then let the *huh* sound settle on to a sustained pitch – a long *huh* on one note. Remember to stay connected to the idea of the in-breath changing to the out-breath.

With each new breath, choose a different sustained pitch to come on to voice.

After several more breathing cycles, return simply to quiet breathing. Notice any changes between how you are now breathing and how you were breathing at the beginning of the exercise.

Teaching tip

This is a useful preparatory exercise for much of the work that is to follow, as it establishes a relaxed connection between breath and voice. For this reason, it is helpful to give it plenty of time for beginners.

Look out for any habits of glottal attack as students begin to make the *huh* sound. This will be noticeable as a sharp or abrupt onset to the sound, rather like a cough, and is a potentially damaging habit. It means that the sound is being initiated in the throat and not at the place in the body where the in-breath changes to the out-breath. To counteract this tendency, just remind students to stay connected to the idea of the in-breath changing seamlessly to the out-breath – there is no stopping of the breath in the throat before making the sound.

Vibrating Breath (4–6 minutes)

Start in semi-supine. Take a minute or so to release unnecessary tension from your body by imagining your head, your shoulders, your chest, your abdomen, and your hips all becoming very heavy on the floor.

Imagine that your jaw is becoming heavy; the heaviness causes your mouth to drop open slightly. If you have been breathing through your nose, switch to breathing through your mouth for a while.

Establish in your mind's eye the image of the empty torso and the empty pipe. Imagine your centre at the base of the empty torso, glowing away. Imagine that there is nothing between your lips and your centre as it calls the air down to itself and releases the air back out again.

Now imagine that when that air descends down to your centre, it can pick up some of the centre's energy: that energy will cause the air to start to vibrate. The vibrating air will then travel through the empty torso and empty pipe and be released out of your lips. It will probably take the form of a small, quiet, 'huh'. It's small and quiet because there's not much air coming out of your body at the moment – your centre knows you don't need much oxygen to stay alive when you're lying on the floor. Do make sure, however, that all the air is vibrating, so you get a solid tone, not a breathy, Marilyn Monroe-y 'huh'.

These vibrations travel under their own energy; they don't need any help from you. They are simply catching a ride on the air you would be breathing out anyway, so creating them is no more effortful than breathing.

Try going onto and off of vibration a few times to see if you can do so without altering what's happening with your breath – it should be the same duration and come with the same frequency and intensity both ways.

Once you have established a sense of those vibrations easily floating up from centre, you can start to feed centre another stimulus and ask it to give the vibrations different forms – maybe they will come out on a different vowel sound, travel through different pitches, or vary in intensity and length. This will cause centre to alter your breathing pattern a bit, which is fine; just stay out of its way and trust it.

Teaching tip

This also comes from work done with Dudley Knight and shares some characteristics with Kristin Linklater's work. When you come to the last step of altering the nature of the vibrations, it can be useful for you to create a sound pattern for the students to follow. Keep it simple – moving, for example, from a 'huh' to a 'huh huh', maybe adding an upward inflection or moving on to a 'huh huh hum' or other vowel sounds, working your way up to easy calls, such as 'hey'.

As you are leading the exercise, listen carefully for any sign that students are 'putting on' a voice or pushing. If it starts to feel at all 'projected' or performed, a simple reminder: 'It's easier than that' will usually help them find their way to a vocal expression that is more simple and grounded. There will be plenty of opportunity to explore strong, aggressive sounds later. For right now, the focus is on connecting an easy, open voice to easy, open breath.

Once the students have made that connection, it can be very useful to revisit exercises from both this and the preceding chapter and add vibration to them; for example, Swinging, Partner Manipulation, the Hanging Breath, the Plough and the Bow. In the last two, the breath becomes much more strongly engaged, so the vibrations will become stronger as well. The challenge is to keep the channel open, and to continue to sense the vibrations coming from the same place as the breath: centre.

The Lazy Day Warm-up (10–12 minutes)

If you have any history of back injury, do this exercise with caution or skip it.

1. Lie on the floor on your side. Draw your knees up so that your thighs are at a 90-degree angle to your torso. Stretch your arms out straight in front of you, one on top of the other.

   Slowly raise your top knee. As it rises higher, it will start to pull on your pelvis, which will eventually pull your bottom knee up off the ground as well. Let your pelvis and bottom knee follow the top knee all the way up in the air and over to the other side.

   As your pelvis moves, it will also pull on your spine and your shoulder girdle. As it does so, allow your top hand to be pulled across your chest. Keep the fingers of your bottom hand on the floor and draw a large circle over your head with them as you roll from one side to the other. Your head will naturally follow your shoulders and roll over to the other side.

   Do this three or four times to get used to the motion.

2. Next, bring the breathing into synchronisation with the motion by breathing in as you are lying on your side and then breathing out on a 'fffff' as you roll from one side to the other.

   Think of the motion of the rocking pelvis moving the breath through your body; the motion of the pelvis is the motor for the breath.

   If you run out of easy breath before you've finished the motion, don't push or squeeze; just allow the breath to fill again. Over time, your body will learn to sustain the breath over the period of time that it takes to roll from one side to the other. It can't learn to do this naturally, however, if you rush in and force it to squeeze out every last drop of air.

Do four or five movement cycles on the 'fffff', and then add a touch of vibration, changing it to a 'vvvv'.

Do four or five movement cycles on the 'vvvv', and then close your lips around the vibration, changing it to a 'mmmm'.

Do four or five movement cycles on the 'mmmm', and then open it into a 'maaaa'.

Do four or five movement cycles on the 'maaaa', and then take a little break to stretch and wiggle.

3. The next step is to imagine releasing a flow of sound from your rocking pelvis, just as you have been doing, but the flow of sound will be taking a particular shape: the shape of chanting the first line of a nursery rhyme.

Do another cycle on the 'maaaa' just to get back into the rhythm, and then allow your breath to fill as you lie on your side, and chant the first line of a nursery rhyme ('Jack and Jill' and 'Humpty Dumpty' are good ones) as you move.

Repeat for at least four lines.

4. Finally, you will speak each line of the nursery rhyme as you roll from side to side, one line per cycle of movement. Do not worry about 'acting' the nursery rhyme or even about making much sense of it at this point. Focus instead on letting your voice move through your body as easily as it did when you were releasing a 'vvvv'.

Teaching tip

This exercise is a great warm-up on days when no one can face the thought of warming up! Many students may need a bit of help to grasp the arm motion. Demonstrate it once or twice, and then help students individually. Over the course of the exercise, some students may start to straighten their legs; remind them to keep them bent as if they were sitting in chairs.

💿 Vibration Pools (6–10 minutes)

1. Start in prayer pose.

Take a moment to establish for yourself the sense of the empty torso with centre at the base calling air down to itself and releasing air back out. Your front is fairly closed in this position, and your back is very open; centre, furthermore, is in a different relationship to your mouth, so the process will feel different from how it does when you are lying down.

Begin releasing a touch of vibration on each out-breath, letting it ride the air that you would be breathing out anyway. Imagine the sound rolling like a marble from centre to fall out of your open mouth.

Extend the vibration to a longer 'huh' for a few breath-cycles, and then close your lips around it so that it pools in your mouth as a 'hummm' for a few breath-cycles.

Alternate between capturing the vibrations with your lips and letting them fall on the floor, in a 'hummuhmuhmaaa'. Imagine that when you open your lips, the vibrations run like water from your centre, form a small pool on the floor in front of you and then gradually roll away.

Try some 'bubububububah's', keeping the lips very loose and floppy as you do so. Play around with lengthening and shortening the sound and moving it through your pitch range as well. Imagine it flowing from centre at all times.

2. Roll your toes under and push yourself into a squat, letting your head continue to hang forwards. Go through the process of finding just a touch of vibration at centre, then extending it, trapping it on your lips, and releasing it in a pool on the floor.

3. Float your bottom up into a roll-down and repeat the same process. This is a particularly good position for getting a sense that the sound is just falling out of your body.

4. Roll up your spine, wiggle and shake. Take a moment with you eyes closed to re-establish the image of the empty torso; of the empty stove-pipe of a throat turning a corner into the empty cavern of the mouth; and of centre. Begin releasing a touch of vibration from centre, and give yourself a few breath-cycles to establish it. Then you can start to play with giving the vibrations different forms – extending them, changing the vowel and pitch, etc.

Teaching tip

As in the floor work, it is of great help to students if you model the sounds in the last step and then have them echo you.

Three Suns (6–8 minutes)

This is an adaptation of a Qi Gong exercise. Qi Gong exercises take many forms, but all are useful for synchronising breathing and movement in ways which increase internal energy. We have added the element of voicing to this exercise.

Begin by standing with feet parallel, about hip-width apart, knees soft, and arms to the side.

Cup your hands together in front of you, palms upwards, and hold them just below your navel.

As you begin to breathe in, raise your hands vertically to chest height in time with your breathing. Then, when you feel the in-breath change to the out-breath, turn your hands over and, as you breathe out, lower your hands again to just below your navel.

On the next breath, repeat the same motion on the in-breath; when you feel it change to the out-breath, turn your hands outwards and, as you breathe out, send your hands forwards and out to the side in a breast-stroke movement before lowering your arms to your side.

As you begin to breathe in for a third time, raise your hands vertically to chest height again. But this time, keep breathing in; as you do so, turn your hands over so that you can raise them vertically above your head. Then, when you feel the in-breath change to the out-breath, turn your hands outwards and, as you breathe out, lower your arms to your side.

Repeat the exercise until you feel that the breathing and the movements are synchronising naturally. All movements should be performed continuously so that there is nothing abrupt or staccato about the process.

Once you have established the cycle of synchronised breath and movement, you can begin to add sound to the out-breath. Start by simply breathing out on a 'fffff' sound for one complete cycle, and then add a touch of vibration, changing it to a 'vvvv' for the next cycle. Use 'mmmmm' for the next cycle, and then change to vowel sounds – students can choose their own, or the instructor can use the following vowel sequence: OO, OH, AH, AY, EE.

> **Teaching tip**
>
> It will help the students if you model the whole process for them before they begin the exercise.
>
> As students get more experienced in this exercise and develop greater physical awareness, you can require them to rise up on tiptoes as they breathe in and lower their soles to the floor again as they breathe out. This has the added benefit of increasing the engagement of the breathing muscles.

The Archer (6–8 minutes)

This is another adaptation of a Qi Gong exercise, to which we have added the element of voicing.

Begin by standing with feet parallel, about hip-width apart, knees slightly bent, and arms to the side.

Now raise your left arm out to the side, with your palm facing outwards and fingers raised to the ceiling as if signalling 'Stop'.

At the same time, cup your right hand at your waist just above your right hip. The stance will look rather like an archer holding a bow.

Breathe in and turn your head to look at the fingers of your left hand as you do so.

As you breathe out, let your outstretched arm travel round in front of you until it is parallel with your right shoulder. Keep watching the fingers of your hand as it moves, and send the breath to your fingertips.

As you breathe in again, change the position of the arms so that now your right arm is raised to the right, with your palm facing outwards and fingers raised to the ceiling; the left hand is cupped at your waist just above your left hip.

Now, as you breathe out, let your outstretched arm travel round in front of you until it is parallel with your left shoulder. Keep watching the fingers of your hand as it moves, and send the breath to your fingertips.

Change the position of the arms again on the in-breath.

Remember that part of the exercise is to synchronise your breathing with the movements, so repeat the exercise until you feel that the breathing and the movements are coordinating naturally. As in Three Suns, all movements should be performed continuously so that there is nothing abrupt or staccato about the process.

Once you have established the cycle of synchronised breath and movement, you can begin to add sound to the out-breath. Start by simply breathing out on a 'fffff' sound for one complete cycle, and then add a touch of vibration by changing it to a 'vvvv' for the next cycle. Use 'mmmmm' for the next cycle, and then change to vowel sounds – students can choose their own or the instructor can lead using the following vowel sequence: OO, OH, AH, AY, EE.

Teaching tip

As in Three Suns, it is of great help to students if you model the whole process for them. You should monitor the students to ensure that they stay aligned and maintain their balance. Students often want to lean towards or away from the direction of their arm, or they will poke their heads forwards, raise their shoulders or collapse the chest. Some verbal reminders to stay long, relax their shoulders and keep their weight balanced in both feet should address these issues.

Vacuuming (3–4 minutes)

Find a place in the room where you are about six feet in front of a wall.

Take a moment to check your posture and get in touch with your breath. Imagine that your jaw is getting heavy and let your mouth drop open. Switch to breathing through your mouth.

Imagine that your torso, throat and mouth are completely empty, but your pelvic bowl, where centre is, is filled with vibrations.

Imagine next that on the wall directly in front of you, there is a giant vibration vacuum.

On your next out-breath, imagine the vibration vacuum switching on and drawing the vibration out of your pelvic bowl, through the empty torso and throat and to itself. The vibrations will probably come out in a long, mid-pitch 'Aaaaaaaaah'.

As soon as you feel that the suction of the vacuum is starting to weaken and you are having to help push or squeeze to help the vibrations out, stop and let your breath drop all the way back in again.

After three or four breath-cycles, when you have established a strong imaginative sense of the vibrations being pulled from your pelvis to a specific place on the wall, imagine that the vibrations have a colour. Your sense of their colour will probably change their vowel shape, their pitch and even their intensity. For example, a very soft pink might be a light, high 'ahhhh'; a vibrant orange might be a bright, energised 'aayyyy'. There are no right answers; just engage your imagination and focus on staying out of the way and letting the vibrations travel to the wall without being blocked or squeezed.

Try a new colour with each breath.

Try moving closer to the wall/vacuum.

Try moving further away from the wall/vacuum.

Try placing the vacuum on a wall across the room from you.

Try imagining that another person across the room from you is holding the vacuum

Try imagining that someone quite close to you is holding the vacuum.

Teaching tip

In the next chapter, the focus will shift to engaging the respiratory muscles in an efficient way so that they can support the flow of sound. To a certain extent, this will probably be kicking in already during the Vacuuming exercise. For the time being, however, the goal is to make sure that the students' sense of their voices is linked to that area of the body which will support the sound flow (the lower abdomen and pelvis) – and that there are no blocks on the way. If they are only able to release short and not particularly powerful sounds in response to the vacuum image, that's fine as long as those sounds are easy and open.

Breathing the Space (5–7 minutes)

Begin by standing in an aligned position with feet parallel, about hip-width apart, knees soft, and arms to the side.

Connect your visual awareness to your breathing in the following way: let your eyes focus on seeing in detail, each part of the room you are working in, and let the in-breath be a response to that room as you 'breathe in' the space.

Now let the out-breath out on a 'fffff' sound, and send the sound out into the room.

Think of having an effect on everything you can see in the space. Look at the specific details of objects, people, surfaces, colours. Receive these on the in-breath and communicate with them on the out-breath. Don't lose focus and generalise – stay aware and be specific.

Add vibration to the breath by changing to a 'vvvv' sound and then 'mmmmm'. Vowel sounds can then be explored – students can choose their own or the instructor can lead using the following vowel sequence: OO, OH, AH, AY, EE.

Once you have added vibrations, start to move through the space – let the sound take you to a specific part of the room on the out-breath. Let the in-breath help you find another part of the space to move towards.

Explore different levels in the room and in your voice – allow the pitch of the sound to move.

Explore different rhythms and dynamics of movement, and let the voice respond to these.

Teaching tip

This is a useful exercise for connecting students to the need for a bigger and more sustained breath in relation to the physical space. At a later stage it can be applied to theatre spaces as part of a warm-up before a performance.

I Am Here (4–6 minutes)

This exercise is designed to apply your developing awareness of release, alignment and breathing to a simple act of communication with intention.

1. Begin by standing in an aligned position with feet parallel, about hip-width apart, knees soft, and arms to the side. Be aware of your presence in the room while you focus on your breathing.

   Imagine your weight being distributed evenly across the three tripod points in each foot. Now make sure that your ankles, knees and hips are not stiff or braced. Pay attention to your pelvis also. Tell yourself that your back is long and wide; that your shoulders are loose and low; that your neck is long and free; that your head is facing forwards and the crown of your head is going up; and that you are breathing fully.

   You are now going to focus on a specific thought: *I am (whatever your first name is), and I am here.* Connect this thought to your breathing cycle by allowing the thought to form as you breathe in and imagining yourself communicating the thought as you breathe out.

   Once you have established this connection, allow your jaw to open on the out-breath and let the breath flow out freely through an open channel. Close your jaw to breathe in again and repeat the process, paying particular attention to keeping the connection between the thought and the breathing cycle.

2. Now, as you feel more confident with this, begin to add the articulatory movements of your statement to the out-breath. The aim is not to make any audible sound at this point, but simply to make the appropriate movements of the tongue and lips as you breathe out.

3. Once you have established the connection between thought, breath and articulation in this way, you can start to introduce voice to the process. Begin quietly, so that you are only speaking to yourself. Make sure that you stay aligned, released, and connected to your breath. Notice any habitual tensions that may creep in as you start to speak, and work to release these.

   Gradually increase your commitment to your statement so that your voice becomes more and more present in the space. There is no need to compete with other students in the room – this would increase vocal tension. Instead, increase your intention to state who you are and where you are, and the vocal commitment will follow.

   Explore how fully you can commit to your statement while staying aligned, released, and connected to your breath.

Teaching tip

This exercise is best used once students have gained some facility with alignment and breath work, and after they have already warmed up the body and breath. It can then be used at any point in their training as a means of connecting them to a sense of their presence. It can also be adapted to character and text work; for example, instead of using their own name, students can speak in character and/or use a short piece of text in addition to their statement.

While this is a simple exercise on the surface, it can be quite profound for students who find it difficult to assert themselves. It is therefore important for everyone to be respectful of the process and avoid competitive or negative judgements of others' abilities.

Onset Exercises (10–15 minutes)

1. Make the sound 'huhhh' just on breath – don't actually engage your voice. This is the feeling that comes with breathy onset. Make a very aggressive 'uh oh' sound just on breath – don't actually engage your voice. It should take quite a bit of bouncy breath, and you should feel a little pop in your throat. This is the feeling that comes with glottal onset. Be attentive to either of these feelings creeping in as you do the following exercises. If they do, back up and try the exercise again.

   Release an extra-breathy, voiced 'heee'. Then release a strongly popped, voiced glottal 'ee'. Now think 'heee', letting your mouth and larynx get ready to make the 'h' sound, but then simply say 'eeee' without the 'h'. This is the feeling that comes with our target: simultaneous onset.

2. As in the Vacuuming exercise, stand in front of a wall and imagine that there is a reserve of vibrations down at your centre and that your torso, throat and mouth are completely empty.

   Chant the following, imagining that as you do so, the vibrations are flowing from your centre and carrying on to touch the wall in front of you. As you chant, be sure that the sound is continuous; there should be no breaks between words:

   > Each eagle eats evil eels.

3. Now speak the sentence, still imagining the vibrations flowing out of you and touching the wall, and still connecting the words to each other in a continuous stream of sound.

4. Finally, speak each word of the sentence one at a time, still sending the vibrations to the wall but leaving a slight break between words. Ideally, there will be neither a little release of breath before each word, nor a little 'pop'. If you're having trouble getting past the aggressive, glottal attack, try thinking of a soft smile at the very back of your mouth as you start each word. If you're having trouble getting past the breathy onset, think of the vibrations being released from the middle of your nose rather than your mouth (a silly image, but a useful one).

Repeat the process with the sound 'i' (as in 'him'), using the sentence:

In India insects itch incessantly.

Repeat the process with the sound 'e' (as in 'hem'), using the sentence:

Emily ended excellent entertainment enterprises.

Repeat the process with the sound 'a' (as in 'hat'), using the sentence:

At Alice's attic ants atrophy.

Repeat the process with the sound 'uh' (as in 'hut'), using the sentence:

'Aggressively upwards', announced another understudy.

Repeat the process with the sound 'ah' (as in 'harmony'), using the sentence:

Are aardvarks on armoured articles?

Repeat the process with the sound 'awe' (as in 'hawk'), using the sentence:

It's all awfully awkward.

Repeat the process with the sound 'ay' (as in 'hay'), using the sentence:

Eighty-eight aimless aches.

Repeat the process with the sound 'eye' (as in 'high'), using the sentence:

I isolated ice isotopes.

Teaching tip

It's worth taking the time to listen to each student do at least one of these sentences to identify who might be having trouble with onset. The students themselves may not be able to hear or feel the difference until you coach them through it individually. You may choose to work with three or four of the above sentences and then have students make up some of their own.

Breath and Voice in Action

A word about breath and voice in action. The preceding exercises will have provided you with a strong technical foundation for connecting the voice and the breath. The exercises in this section allow you to start to play with that connection and explore its expressive potential. Don't feel, however, that you need to have mastered open breath and grounded voicing before working in this section. It may be that you first experience a really powerful sense of the connection between your body, your breath and your voice through these more playful exercises. Returning to the more technical exercises will then help you to achieve that sense of connection more consistently.

Breath Play (2–3 minutes each)

I.

1. Get a partner and stand about five feet away from them.

    Partner A, wave to partner B while exhaling. You can make the exhalation a bit bigger than usual just to make sure that you're connecting to it.

    A, now wave to B while inhaling – again, perhaps a slightly bigger inhalation than usual.

    A, now wave to B while holding your breath.

    Discuss the different feeling of the three waves.

2. Move in so you are just a couple of feet away from your partner.

    B, put your hand behind your back. Pretending that you have something in it, take your hand out from behind your back and offer it to your partner on a nice, full out-breath.

    Repeat on a nice, full in-breath.

    Repeat holding your breath.

    Discuss the difference in the three.

3. Now walk around the room and find a partner to hug while breathing out.

    Walk around the room again and find a partner to hug while breathing in.

    Walk around the room and find a partner to hug while holding your breath.

    Discuss the difference in the three.

II.

If you have asthma or other respiratory difficulties, you may want to sit this one out.
Stand comfortably and take a moment to become aware of your breathing; make sure

that you are allowing the belly, back and ribs to open to the in-breath but are not pumping up your shoulders and chest. Likewise, there should be no caving-in of the chest and shoulders on the out-breath.

Observe your body's natural resting breathing pattern for four or five cycles.

Start to shorten your out-breath and extend your in-breath until they are as short and long, respectively, as they can be.

Reverse that pattern, shortening your in-breath and extending your out-breath.

Try three short, sharp in-breaths in a row followed by one long out-breath. Extend it to six or seven staccato in-breaths for each long out-breath.

Reverse that pattern, using staccato out-breaths and long in-breaths.

Try three or four short in- and out-breaths followed by one long in and one long out.

Do one full minute of playing with different breathing rhythms, trying anything that comes to mind and investigating it until you are inspired (pun intended) to move on to something else.

Discuss what kinds of feeling, thoughts and images were evoked by the different rhythms.

Teaching tip

Students may have very different responses to the various breaths. Some may find action on the in-breath to be warm and inviting, while others may find it off-putting. Some may find that breathing in rapidly makes them feel panicked, while others may find it relaxes them. There's no single correct interpretation. The point to be made is that breath is connected to our thoughts, our feelings, and our interactions with other people. It influences and is influenced by everything we do.

Group Sound

All the exercises under this heading are useful for warming-up a group at the beginning of a session. By engaging you in cooperative vocal and physical activities, they can help to foster group connection, focus and energy.

I. (4–7 minutes)

Start standing, with the group in a circle. Take a moment to check your posture, and get in touch with your breath and how you are feeling at this moment.

Now, one at a time, take it in turns to go into the middle of the circle and perform a combined voice and movement expression of how you are feeling. For example, if you are feeling sleepy, you might flop on to the floor making a yawning sound; or if you are feeling happy, you might jump into the air, laughing.

After each person has performed their action, everybody else has to repeat it as precisely as possible.

Teaching tip

In introducing this exercise, it will be helpful if you can start the whole sequence off with a demonstration. Some students may start by expressing tired, half-hearted, shy or negative feelings. If this is the case, it may be helpful to require a second (and even a third) round of the exercise in which everybody has to do the opposite of what they did in the first round. With more boisterous groups it may be necessary to point out that this isn't an opportunity for a competition!

This exercise can also be used as an ice-breaker for groups who don't know each other. Ask students to say their names in combination with the movement.

II. (4–7 minutes)

Start standing, with the group spread out around the room. Take a moment to check your posture and get in touch with your breath.

Begin to walk easily around the room. Once you've established a sense of yourself in the room, you can begin to gently make physical contact with other people as you pass them; perhaps just a touch of the hands, or a soft brushing of shoulders. Let each contact move a bit of breath through you: maybe a little sigh as back moves against back, or a 'sippy' sequence of in-breaths as fingertips play off of one another.

Let the contacts become a bit more prolonged – to maybe 15–20 seconds of playing with the possibilities of shoulder against back or elbow against rib – being, of course, ever respectful, and keeping the breath engaged. This is much like the playful exploration in the Breath Play II exercise, only it is generated in response to movement with a partner.

Once everyone has had the chance to play with three or four partners, let some vibrations come with the breath.

You can expand your contact, not only to people but also to objects in the room. What kind of breath and sound move through you as you roll against a wall or tap your fingers on a window? Any variation of pitch, intensity, rhythm is possible. Play for several minutes; the more you can allow each sound to be a specific response to the stimulus of the movement, the more variety you will find.

Now begin to jog your way between contacts with people and things, and let each jog move a bit of breath/sound through you. Play with the rhythm of the jog. Add some jumps, turns, switchbacks. Play for several minutes.

Come back to walking around the room and simply breathing.

> **Teaching tip**
>
> This works best with a group of students who are already comfortable touching each other and playing in front of each other. It is important to monitor that students are contacting each other with respect and sensitivity – the exercise is not an opportunity to indulge in aggressive or flirtatious behaviour.

 III. (5–15 minutes)

Thanks to Frankie Armstrong for the general structure of this one.

Start standing in a circle. Everyone turn so that your left shoulder is in the circle and you are facing the back of the person who was to your right.

Take an imaginary shovel in your hands. Mime shovelling a pile of dirt from the centre of the circle to the outside. Find a rhythm for the movement so that you are rocking onto the front foot and then the back as you make easy, stylised shovelling motions – it should not be too strenuous. **If you experience any pain in your knees or hips, step out.**

When the beat is established, the instructor releases a call that fits with the rhythm of the movement: 'Hey-yo', which everyone echoes on the next movement.

The instructor then releases a different call in rhythm with the motion, which everyone echoes – something like 'Hee hee ho' or 'Mamamamamameeee' – any combination of sounds that fits in the space of a cycle of movement.

After the instructor has set the pattern, go around the circle with each person leading a call and the group echoing.

Don't try to decide in advance what your call will sound like – just follow the rhythm and trust that the sound will be there. Some calls may be very scat-like; others may be the release of a single vowel on a single note. The important thing is that you are staying open to the sound.

Do a couple of rounds, switching sides when your hips get tired.

Try each person giving three calls and responses in a row before moving on.

Try repeating each call three times, adding harmonies or embellishments.

Try every other person in the circle sticking with a drone ('Hi-yi' on one medium low note, or something similar) and the others playing with calls and responses on top of it.

Try not going around the circle but letting anyone who has an impulse offer a call at any time while some of the others drone and some respond.

> **Teaching tip**
>
> This exercise can be anything from a five-minute part of your warm-up – used to get the body, breath and voice working together in an easy released way – to a much longer deep exploration of sound, rhythm and impulse, depending on where your students are and what your goals are in any given session.

Connecting to Text

In the exercises that follow, your job is to maintain the connection that you've been developing between your voice and an easy, full breath as you speak a simple text – no more, no less. Remember always that you are doing exercises, not giving performances. Focus on keeping your body open to the breath and the channel for your voice free from constriction. As you strengthen your ability to stay physically open and centred from moment to moment, you will also strengthen your ability to be responsive to the text – to be mentally and emotionally 'present'. This will ultimately be invaluable to your acting, but don't think too much about that product; enjoy the process.

> **Teaching tip**
>
> Assign a piece of text to each of the students. You may have them all work with the same one or two pieces, or assign different texts to different students. The advantages of the first are that it can be easier to work as a group if everyone is on the same text, and students can learn from each other's discoveries about the language. The advantages of the second are that it can weaken the tendency students have to compare their work with others, and you can assign texts in response to students' specific needs

and temperaments. If you wish to look beyond the suggestions we make at the end of the chapter, try to find poems and/or prose passages that are relatively short and clear. They should be lively and vivid, but not intensely emotional.

The texts should be memorised – the time spent working on the language in the process is invaluable. At this point, however, the ability to rattle them off perfectly is not the point. We would advise allowing students to hold their texts in case they need to glance at them, as it helps to alleviate the anxiety that can come when one is asked to recite. If you have any dyslexic students, they may find it helpful to receive the text well in advance of the day when they will need to use it in class.

Ideally, sessions on connecting to text would start with a thorough warm-up using exercises from earlier in the chapter, and then move on to individual work. Students can benefit greatly from watching each other and hearing how effective connected breathing and voicing are. Have each student simply speak the text once, and then choose from the following exercises according to what s/he seems to need. The general goal is to help students keep the breathing free through the ribs and abdomen and away from the shoulders and upper chest. The voice should also be easy and open. You may feel inspired to introduce a new image or an element of another releasing, aligning, opening or connecting exercise. Your own thoughtful, creative responsiveness will only encourage that of the students.

Each of these exercises will take 2–5 minutes depending on the length of the text. As you perform the exercise, notice the effect it has on your experience of speaking the text: it may be easier to speak; it may feel more full of sound; it may feel more true to your intent in speaking; it may feel more *connected*. If you don't feel any change, ask your teacher or fellow students if they perceived any difference – it is likely that they did.

I. Speak the text with a partner resting their hands on your shoulders to remind you that they are not part of the channel that breath, voice and thought flow through most effectively.

II. Roll down and begin speaking the text while a partner gives your lower back a massage. Continue speaking as your partner walks their fingers up your spine, bringing you to standing.

III. Grab three partners (four, if you want someone to hold your text for you), at least one of whom is taller than you are. Have the tall partner sit on the floor, legs outstretched, hands on the ground behind them supporting their torso. Sit between that partner's legs and let your head lean back on their shoulder. The other two partners should each take an arm and gently move it, as in partnered manipulation. You must continue to relinquish control of your arms while speaking the text.

> **Teaching tip**
> You may want to use same-sex partners for this exercise. Alternatively, pick another exercise for students who might not be comfortable with this amount of touching.

IV. Stand in a comfortable, aligned position. Hold the text in your hand. Breathe in as you silently read the first line. Breathe out imagining yourself speaking it. Breathe in again, and then speak the line as you breathe out. Repeat all the way through the text.

V. Stand in a comfortable, aligned position. Chant a line of text, imagining it flowing in an unbroken column from centre; then speak it. Continue alternating chanting and speaking all the way through the text.

VI. Sit facing a partner. That partner should look you in the eye as you speak the text and focus simply on opening to their own breath while sending the thought, 'Breathe, connect, breathe, connect' to you.

Follow-up

Reflective practice questions:

* Can you identify exercises or situations in which you tend to fight your breath – to trap it high in your body or hold it altogether?
* Can you identify exercises or situations in which are you able to let your breath flow freely and easily?

* How do those two kinds of breathing feel different physically?
* Did you feel any anxiety in the stretches that constricted one area of your body (like the chest in the Plough)? How did you get past that anxiety? Did the breath move to another area of your body? If so, where?
* Have you made any discoveries about your breathing that might relate to other things you have to do when you're acting? If so, what are some of the ways in which you might implement those discoveries?
* How does thinking of your voice as originating with your breath, at the base of your torso, change how your voice feels to you? Or how you feel about your voice?
* What does 'get out of the way of your voice' mean to you?
* In which exercises did you feel that you were producing your voice with the least amount of resistance, strain and effort? Is it easier to do lying down or standing up?
* When playing vocally, what kinds of sounds do you gravitate to – low, high, loud, soft, creaky, staccato, smooth? Why do you think you favour them?
* Does introducing language make it harder or easier for you to feel that your body is open to the breath, and that the breath and voice are connected? Why do you think that is? How do you think you can bring the connection you feel in one kind of exercise to the other kind of exercise?

Once you have begun to experience what it feels like to open fully to the breathing impulse, you can practise it any time, anywhere, without anyone noticing. In your acting classes in particular, try taking just a moment before you begin a scene or an exercise to send your awareness to your breath.

Try to make bringing yourself gently and easily onto voice part of your everyday routine. Release a few 'huh's' from centre in the shower in the morning, or send some nice, open 'hi's' to yourself in the bathroom mirror. The muscles that produce your voice are like any others, and they need to be warmed up gently. You would never jump out of bed and run a marathon, so don't jump out of bed and start rehearsing Jacobean revenge tragedies without warming up a bit. Take the time to connect.

Suggested texts

Elizabeth Bishop	'Close, Close All Night'
Anne Bradstreet	'To My Dear and Loving Husband'
Robert Burns	'A Red, Red Rose'
Lucille Clifton	'Good Times'
Wendy Cope	'The Orange'
e e cummings	'o purple finch'
Elizabeth Daryush	'Still Life'
Emily Dickinson	'The Soul Selects Her Own Society'
Rita Dove	'Exit'
Robert Frost	'The Road Not Taken'
Langston Hughes	'Dream Deferred'
Vikram Seth	'All You Who Sleep Tonight'
Derek Walcott	'Love After Love'
William Carlos Williams	'This is Just to Say'
W B Yeats	'The Lake Isle of Inisfree'

Further reading

Armstrong, Frankie, 'Gossip Hoeing' in *The Complete Voice & Speech Workout Book & CD*, Janet Rogers, ed., Applause Theatre and Cinema Books, New York, NY, 2002, pp. 140–141.

Houseman, Barbara, *Finding Your Voice*, Nick Hern Books, London, 2002. Chapter 3: Breath and Support, pp. 59–73.

Linklater, Kristin, *Freeing the Natural Voice* (Revised edition), Drama Book Publishers, New York, 2006. Chapters 2–3, pp. 43–86.

Melton, Joan (with Kenneth Tom), *One Voice*, Heinemann, Portsmouth, NH, 2003. Chapter 2: Range, Resonance, and Articulation, pp. 58–62 and 64–65.

3

Breath and Voice – Supply and Support

Framework

In the previous chapter we looked at the experience of connecting breath and voice. Being connected implies that the breathing system is fundamentally responsive to expression of the thought/feeling impulse. But simply being connected doesn't necessarily help develop and manage breath capacity or vocal power – two factors which are essential in allowing a speaker to fulfil his or her potential and an actor to make artistic choices. Vocal artistry requires the ability to choose the length and strength of vocal vibration so that speakers can respond to the demands of their text and shape their expressivity for the listener's ear. We can think of this as an extension of the connection we've already established: not only must a speaker be connected internally to his or her own thought/feeling impulse; he or she must also be connected externally to the listener's thought/feeling impulses. It is through the development and management of an effective breath supply and support system that we will lay the foundations for this act of creative communication.

Breath *supply* is concerned with how, once we have sufficient air in our lungs, we maintain the flow of air from the lungs to the vocal folds. This will largely determine how long we can sustain vocal vibration. Breath *support* is concerned with how we adjust the intensity of that air flow to increase (or decrease) vocal power. This will largely determine the strength of those vibrations. But why should supply and support be so important?

To answer this, we need to take a closer look at the vocal folds. As we discussed in the last chapter, your voice is the result of your vocal folds moulding your breath into sound waves. Your vocal folds are two folds of fibrous tissue and muscle situated inside your larynx, just behind your Adam's apple – which, despite its name, both men and women possess (it's just not so prominent in women). (See Fig. 7) The folds are between 17 and 23 millimetres long and are attached to several of the cartilages which make up the larynx. If you lightly place your fingers in the middle of your throat, you can feel the larynx move up and down when you swallow.

Epiglottis

Vocal Fold

Vocalis Muscle

Trachea (Wind Pipe)

Fig. 7 The Vocal Folds

The primary function of the vocal folds is not to create our voices: it's to protect our lungs. The vocal folds act like a valve which opens and closes the space between them (the glottis), controlling what enters or leaves the lungs. Both air and food enter our bodies through our mouths (of course, air can also come in through the nose, but then it just drops from there to the back of the mouth). Usually, our tongues push food past our windpipes and it slides down the oesophagus into the stomach. Sometimes, however, it doesn't make it, and little bits drop down the windpipe instead. If this happens, the vocal folds are designed to snap shut, closing the glottis and forming a block in the middle of the windpipe, ready to catch anything that might have gone down the wrong way. If we then sharply expel some breath (by coughing), those bits of foreign matter will get blown up off the vocal folds and pushed by the tongue back down the oesophagus where they belong. That's what happens when you 'swallow the wrong way' and have a coughing fit. When you breathe, on the other hand, the muscles of the larynx draw the vocal folds away from each other, opening the glottis so that the air can get through.

As a kind of bonus feature, however, when the vocal folds are brought together with just the right amount of pressure and air passes through them, they can create sound. Try bringing your lips together loosely and then blowing through them. Because of the elasticity of your lips, if enough air pressure builds up behind them when they are shut, they will eventually blow apart. Also because of their elasticity and the laws of physics, once they've been blown apart and the air pressure is released, they will then fall back together until the air pressure builds up behind them again. This blowing-apart and falling-back-together cycle breaks the air flow up into little puffs, which creates a trilling noise. The same principle applies to the vocal folds. When they are brought together lightly as we breathe out, the air pressure builds up underneath them until they are blown away from each other. They then fall back towards each other until the air pressure builds up and forces them apart again. On a pitch of middle C, this cycle happens 261 times a second!

You need a certain amount of air pressure to make this whole system work, and this is where supply and support become important. The longer the sound you want to make, the longer you need to maintain the air pressure (supply); and the stronger the sound you want to make, the more air pressure you need (support). There are two ways to create that pressure. One is to use your muscles of respiration to create a longer and stronger flow of air. The other is to constrict your larynx, clamping the vocal folds together tightly so that more air pressure has to build up underneath them before they're blown apart. We naturally do something like this when we blow on hot food: pursing the lips creates less room for the air to move through, so more air pressure builds up behind them. Try to blow on something with your mouth wide open; then purse your lips. You may be sending the same amount of air up from your lungs, but you can feel that the air pressure increases when you resist it with your lips. When using your voice, increasing the flow of air at the source is an infinitely healthier and more efficient way to create greater air pressure than resisting it with the folds. If the folds are clamped shut tightly, they will blow apart from each other and fall back together violently.

Your vocal folds are like any other tissue in your body and will eventually become irritated if they're banged and slammed around too much. Imagine clapping or rubbing your hands together as hard as you can for ten minutes; the surface of your vocal folds will suffer every bit as much as the skin on the palms of your hands if they are subjected to the stress of rubbing up against each other violently for extended periods of time. They can even develop a kind of callus (called a nodule) which can seriously affect your vocal quality and, if left untreated, may permanently damage your voice.

While we're on the subject, being brought together too tightly in order to increase air pressure is not the only thing that can have an adverse effect on the vocal folds. Illness can irritate them and make them swell. Dehydration can make them more vulnerable. Drinking plenty of water keeps your folds lubricated from the inside and is essential for good vocal health. Alcohol and caffeinated drinks, on the other hand, are actually dehydrating. And, of course, the most popular destroyer of the folds is cigarette smoke, although cannabis is actually more irritating. Some people will be able to smoke longer than others before the damage becomes audible, but damage will happen, and there's no way of telling whose voice will go when.

Beyond helping to ensure vocal health, the development of good breath supply and support will give your voice greater strength and flexibility. It will also bring energy and authenticity to your voice and your acting. Initially, some of the work may seem quite mechanical; at first it is necessary to explore systematically how the muscles work and then introduce them to more efficient, energetic patterns of usage. The goal, however, is for a strongly engaged breath to become second nature – not just a physical habit, but a way of connecting deeply with thoughts, intentions and emotions as you prepare to communicate them.

This connection as a precondition for communication is intimately associated with the in-breath. Much of the work in the last chapter was about creating room for the muscles of inhalation to move freely, which is vital for getting a good supply of breath. In order to get in an effective supply, however, the muscles must be able to move not only freely, but also quickly and vigorously. In particular, we will work on actively engaging the muscles that run between and move the ribs – the intercostals – in order to develop the supply of air.

The most important muscles for turning that supply of air into support are the abdominals. The phrase 'abdominal muscles' is a bit misleading. The 'abs' that we work on when we go to the gym to get a 'six pack' are just one of four layers of abdominal muscles, and are not the ones that help the most in breathing. The other three layers are beneath the six-pack abs: they run from your lower ribs all the way down to your pelvis, and two of them also wrap around your sides and continue across your back to your spine (see Fig. 8). So, support from the abdominal muscles isn't just something that happens in your belly; your sides, your back, even the muscles of your pelvic floor can get involved. The contraction of the abdominal muscles as you breathe out pushes the organs beneath them in and up against the diaphragm as it relaxes back into its dome shape. This provides a firm, constant pressure against the lungs, which in turn creates strong, steady air pressure against the vocal folds (what's known as 'sub-glottic pressure'). Some of the work in this chapter will focus on learning to use these abdominal muscles to create the kind of airflow that powers a full, open voice. While this is something that needs to be practised methodically, it is not a question of teaching your body to do something that it is not intrinsically designed to do, like learning to ride a bicycle; it's a matter of building on something the body already knows how to do and practising to do it better, like training to run a marathon.

Although abdominal support provides the foundation for vocal sound, it is not sufficient in itself to provide all the sustaining power. Therefore, it is likely that a speaker who relies predominantly on abdominal support (without developing the supply system in the rib cage) will need to breathe fairly frequently and so break up the flow of thought. One possible result of this is that the speaker is

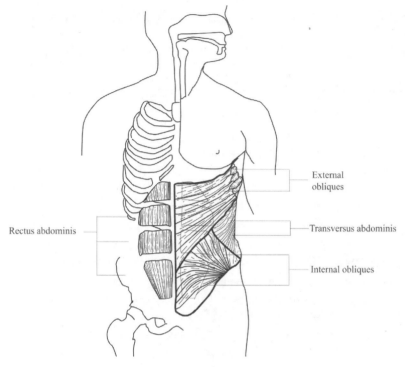

Fig. 8 Abdominal Muscles

emotionally connected and clear but lacks flow and forward energy. The dynamic choice might be strong but lack flexibility. There might be a tendency for the actor to communicate the emotion of the text at the expense of the through-line of the thought.

Intercostal supply provides the sustaining energy for the voice but is often less connected to emotional impulse. Speakers who rely predominantly on intercostal supply (without developing the support system in the abdomen) are likely to lack emotional depth in their voices. They may manage the flow of thought effectively, but can lack an emotional core in their sound. They are also unlikely to manage major dynamic shifts easily, and the resulting sound will tend to be of a fairly even intensity and possibly within a narrow pitch range.

It is vital that both parts of the supply/support system work together; when they do, the speaker has more resources for making a wider range of expressive choices. Thought and emotion can be communicated in a more balanced relationship in connection with character and situation, rather than being dictated by the speaker's habitual preferences.

So, technically, what happens when both supply and support are engaged and in balance? As we have seen, the diaphragm and intercostal muscles are the active instigators of the in-breath: their activity expands the capacity of the lungs, creating the potential supply of air for phonation. It is the relaxation of these muscles which instigates the out-breath, and so how these muscles relax will determine how efficiently that supply of air is used. For example: if, once we have breathed in, we simply stopped engaging the diaphragm and intercostal muscles, the pressure exerted on the lungs as a result of their sudden relaxation (and other physical forces such as gravity) would cause the air to rush out quickly, as in a sigh. Try it now: sigh out on a deep breath without voice. Notice how you took a deep breath in, and then just let it all go again as your breathing system collapsed. We can certainly produce vocal vibration with this air. Try it for yourself now: sigh out in the same way, but add some voice. You probably noticed several things about this sound: it didn't last very long, it lost power/intensity, and it dropped in pitch. Try it again and listen. However, if we change our intention from sighing to sustaining an AH sound – try it now – we can produce a much longer sound with relatively little change in intensity or pitch. Did you notice how your muscles of respiration behaved differently? Try it again. Our change in intention causes us to change the physical usage of the respiratory muscles. Ideally, this change will have involved a controlled relaxation of the intercostal muscles and an active engagement of the abdominal (and perhaps pelvic floor) muscles. The controlled relaxation of the intercostals (as opposed to their collapse) enables us to maintain an even flow of air over time. The engagement of the abdominals provides the muscular support underneath the relaxing diaphragm to create sufficient sub-glottic pressure for a sustained intensity of vocal vibration.

As we start to increase the power of the airflow, the work that we've done on staying relaxed and connecting the voice to the breath will become particularly important. It's no good generating lots of energy with the respiratory muscles only to block or strangle that energy with tension in the upper back, upper chest, shoulders, throat, neck or jaw. Continue to work with release exercises and images, cultivating a sense of ease and freedom in your work. Continue too to think of your body opening to the breath and your voice coming from your body. And, above all, continue to trust that you don't have to feel energy in your throat to have an expressive voice.

For actors, the creation of a good, strong, steady flow of air together with easy, appropriate engagement of the muscles in and around the larynx is not only desirable for creating strong, steady sound; it's also good for your acting. A solid muscular support for your voice also creates a solid muscular support for the ideas and emotions your voice is communicating to the listener. When the big muscles of your respiratory system don't engage, not only your larynx, but all manner of other smaller muscles in your neck, jaw, even forehead try to pick up the slack. Trying to channel all the energy of your intentions through those smaller muscles, however, will lead to a forced, pushed quality in both your voice and your acting. Grounding the energy of the breath deeper in your body will help you to ground your actions, giving them a sense of purpose and truth. It's no coincidence that 'inspiration' is another word for breathing in. And if inhalation – supply – is the moment of inspiration, then exhalation – support – is the moment of expression. Ultimately, these two principles of breath take us to the most fundamental principles of the acting process itself.

Exploration

I. Find something that makes you laugh – maybe watch a favourite sitcom, pop in a DVD of a funny movie, or call a friend with a great sense of humour. When the giggles have started, notice what's happening in your torso. Where is the centre of the action? Where else do you feel movement? If you're lucky enough to be reduced to gasping for breath, where does that gasp originate? Where does the air go?

II. **If you have back problems, you may want to skip this one**. Find something heavy you can push around your living room or a studio – a large armchair, a heavy table, a chair with a stack of books on it, etc. Think of putting all your power in your arms and push it around a bit. Think of putting all your power in your chest and push it around a bit. Think of putting all your power in your lower abdomen and hips and push it around a bit. Which focus gave you the most power? Note your observations in your journal and discuss them in class.

Exercises

Teaching tip

The exercises in this chapter are organised under four headings: *Engaging the In-breath*; *Engaging the Out-breath*; *Supporting the Voice*; and *Supporting Text*. Of course, work on the in-breath enhances the out-breath, and vice versa, so it's beneficial to move between these two sections quite freely. The work on supporting the voice and the text is best broached once the students have a good working sense of how to engage the muscles of respiration. It will help them connect that engagement with the act of expression and explore the possibilities of a strongly supported voice.

Engaging the In-breath

When we are breathing just to stay alive, the inhalation lasts for about 40% of the breathing cycle. When we start talking, the inhalation happens more quickly, taking up only 10% of the cycle (Borden and Harris 1980:66). We also use a greater volume of air when speaking, both taking in and expelling up to 125% more (Mathieson 2001:58). This means that the muscles we use to breathe in have to do more work more quickly when we're talking. As we discussed in the last chapter, the primary muscle of inhalation is the diaphragm. We'll do some work on identifying and engaging the diaphragm here, but it is, fortunately, a muscle that engages very well on its own; in fact, you couldn't stop it from contracting for long if you tried. The main thing that gets in the way of the diaphragm is tension in the muscles of the abdomen, lower back, and pelvis. If these muscles are rigid, they will hold the internal organs up against the diaphragm and it won't be able to descend very far. Try pulling in your stomach and clenching your bottom as tightly as you can and then inhaling. You can feel the diaphragm fighting to descend and not getting very far. We've done a good amount of work on stretching, softening and releasing those muscles, and it will be important that you continue to foster a sense of openness and freedom in your pelvis, stomach and lower back.

The other muscles that can help your body get more air more quickly are the intercostal muscles that move the ribs. As with any other muscles, these can be strengthened and trained to work more efficiently with practice. And, as with any muscles, working *efficiently* is not the same thing as pushing, straining or locking; on the contrary, the goal is to find ease and freedom of movement. While we will be isolating the ribs initially in order to explore their range of motion and contribution to breath, ultimately the ribs and diaphragm coordinate not only with each other, but also with the impulse to communicate to create a full, effective in-breath.

> **Teaching tip**
>
> The side stretches and bear hug from the *Opening the Breath* section of the previous chapter are particularly good warm-ups for rib work. The Sun Salutation, Granny Dance, and hip sequence from the *Stretching* section of the first chapter are also good preparation for work on the in-breath.

Find Your Ribs (3–4 minutes per partner)

1. Find a partner who's somewhere in the neighbourhood of your height.

   Partner A, position yourself in front of partner B.

   B, place your hands on A's sides with your thumbs pointing back towards you. The bottom edge of your pinkie should line up with the bottom edge of A's ribs on either side.

   A, blow out all the air you can while B presses gently on your ribs. When you've come to the end of your breath, pause for a moment, and then think of your ribs widening into your partner's hands as you breathe in. You might imagine that they are expanding like balloons.

   Focus too on keeping the shoulders and upper chest soft and quiet.

   B, maintain steady pressure, but don't try to push against A's rib expansion. If you notice the shoulders rising, you may place one hand gently on one shoulder as a reminder that they can be still while the ribs move.

   Repeat twice, A trying to engage the ribs even more strongly in widening each time.

2. Now B, move your hands forwards, so that just your thumbs are hooked around A's sides and most of your hands are stretched across the front of A's lower rib cage – your pinkies lining up with the bottom edge again.

   A, blow out all your breath and then think of your ribs expanding into B's hands as you breathe in. You might imagine them as being like flowers that are opening in fast motion.

   Repeat twice, remembering to keep the shoulders and upper chest disengaged.

3. Finally, B move your hands around to A's back, so that just your fingertips are wrapped around A's sides and most of your hand is cupping their ribs to the back, the bottom edge of your hand lining up with the lower border of the rib cage.

A, blow out all your breath and think of your ribs expanding into B's hands as you breathe in. You might imagine that they are like bread dough rising in fast motion.

Repeat twice, keeping the shoulders and upper chest mostly still.

Discuss what, A, you felt happening from the inside and, B, you felt happening from the outside.

Trade places and repeat the entire exercise.

Teaching tip

This exercise raises students' awareness of the activity of the rib cage. It can be done in a number of positions: sitting on a chair, kneeling on all fours, folded over in prayer position, and standing. It is worth exploring each of these positions in sequence, as students will often find that they are more aware of some rib activity in one position than in another. You may wish to assign same-sex partners.

Cow Belly (2–3 minutes per partner)

1. Find a partner who's somewhere in the neighbourhood of your height.

Partner A, take up a position on your hands and knees so that your spine is straight and long – neither arched nor collapsed.

Partner B, place your hands on A's back, so that just your fingertips are wrapped around A's sides and most of your hand is cupped around their ribs to the back – the bottom edge of your hand lining up with the lower border of the rib cage.

A, blow out all your breath and then expand your ribs into B's hands as you breathe in.

Repeat two or three times until you can feel that the ribs are strongly engaged.

2. A, now bring your focus into your belly. While keeping your spine straight and long, relax your abdominal muscles so that your belly just hangs from your spine, like a cow. Don't be vain – let it all hang out!

B, kneel beside A, so that you can place one hand on A's spine to remind them to keep it stable. Place your other hand under A's relaxed belly.

A, while using your abdominal muscles to lift your belly up towards your spine, blow out all the air you can on a long 'SH' sound. B, keep your hand in the same position relative to the floor – that is, don't move it with A's belly.

Now, A, relax your stomach muscles and let your belly drop back down into B's hand as quickly as possible. As you do so, you should be able to feel your lungs fill with air again.

Repeat this exercise several times until you feel confident in the connection you are building between your breath and the activity of the abdominal muscles. Remember, your abdominal muscles are active as you breathe out, and they relax as you breathe in.

A, discuss what you felt happening from the inside and, B, what you felt happening from the outside.

Trade places and repeat the entire exercise.

Teaching tip

Some students find this exercise counter-intuitive, and so may relax the abdominal muscles as they breathe out and contract them as they breathe in. It will be helpful for you to go round and check individually so that you can correct any mistaken perceptions. Students may also be more comfortable in same sex-pairs for this exercise.

Find Your Diaphragm (4–5 minutes)

This exercise was inspired by Barbara Houseman's work.

Begin standing with your feet parallel, about hip-width apart, knees soft, back and neck long.

Place your hands flat on the front of your pelvis; your thumbs should be at the base of your stomach and your pinkies at the very top of your thighs.

Take three or four breaths, and imagine that with each inhalation the area under your hands is softening, like ice cream slowly melting.

Move your hands around to where your back starts to become your bottom on either side (don't hunch your shoulders in the process), and take another three or four breaths imagining a softening under your hands with each in-breath.

Place the backs of your hands against your waist on either side, below the ribs, and repeat the pattern of breathing and softening.

Move your hands so that they are flat against your lower belly and repeat.

Lightly place the fingers of one hand about half way between the end of your breastbone (you may need to feel around for it a bit) and your navel.

Keeping your pelvis, back and lower belly as soft as possible, let out a few panting breaths. The movement that you feel under your fingers is the result of your diaphragm engaging and releasing as you pant.

Speed up the panting a bit, monitoring to make sure that your shoulders and upper chest don't start bouncing along with the breath. It can help to use Kristin Linklater's image that your diaphragm is a trampoline and a tiny person is jumping on it with each breath.

Play with increasing the tempo of the panting and then slowing it back down.

Be sure to take a break every 20–30 seconds and return to your regular breathing pattern.

Try a few sighs, imagining that your diaphragm is like a wave swelling up in you with each in-breath and running out again with each out-breath.

Finally, return again to your regular breathing and just register the sensation of your breath moving through your body.

Breath and Thought (6–8 minutes)

Form a circle with the group.

Begin standing with your feet parallel, about hip-width apart, knees soft, back and neck long.

Think of something nice to say to the person to your right.

When the instructor counts to three, turn your head and say your nice thing.

Did you breathe in as you turned to speak? Where did your body open to receive the breath? How much air did you actually get in? How deep in your body did you feel the impulse go?

Return to neutral and to the thought of the nice thing that you want to say to the person on your right. Check to make sure that your hips, bottom, lower back and lower abdomen are soft and ready to open to the breath.

On a three-count again, breathe in, opening your ribs as you turn your head to the person on your right. Open your mouth to speak your nice thing, but don't actually say anything. Your diaphragm will probably engage on its own.

Practise joining the *intent* to speak to the movement of the head and the in-breath without actually speaking once more.

Finally, on three, breathe in, opening your ribs as you turn your head, and then say your nice thing.

Discuss the difference.

Walk around the room. When the instructor says, 'Now', stop walking, look at someone across the room, consciously engage your in-breath through the ribs as you think of something nice to say to that person, and then say that nice thing.

Repeat three or four times.

Next, as you walk, think of a line from a scene or speech that you are working or have worked on.

When the instructor says, 'Now', stop walking, engage your in-breath as you connect to the impulse behind the line, and then speak it.

Repeat three or four times.

Discuss any discoveries, particularly about the relationships between breath, voice and thought.

Engaging the Out-breath

Engagement of the muscles of respiration on the out-breath is the basic mechanism of 'support'. The word 'support', however, can unfortunately conjure images of rigidity and force – great iron girders, or weightlifters straining under barbells – which are not helpful ways of thinking about breath. Respiratory support needs to be dynamic, responsive, and in harmony with how the body breathes naturally.

In this section there are some exercises on extending the out-breath. The goal of these exercises is not to count to a certain number or to be able to speak a certain amount of text on one breath *at any cost*. In the first instance, being able to speak for a long time on one breath is not in itself a particularly interesting skill. It's good to be able to keep your air flow and vocal energy up through a long thought, but sustaining sound is not the same thing as communicating effectively; it's only a tool. Furthermore, if you are straining and squeezing to get that last little bit of text out without taking another breath, you are probably diminishing rather than enhancing your ability to communicate – your voice will have less flexibility and your thought will lose its grounding. So, as you work on extending your breath, have patience with yourself and work with your body's impulses. If you are only able to count to six before you feel the need to squeeze your chest and push the sound out with the back of your neck, then stop at six. Work your way up to seven and beyond by learning to work with the impulse to engage your abdominal muscles rather than by forcing the last drop of air out of your body using any means necessary.

Birthday Candles (3–4 minutes)

This exercise was inspired by Michael McCallion's 'Blowing out Candles' exercise.

Begin standing with your feet parallel, about hip-width apart, knees soft, back and neck long.

Hold up your left index finger about six inches in front of your mouth and place your right hand flat against your lower belly.

Pretend that your finger is a birthday candle and blow it out. Notice where and how your muscles engage under your right hand to support this short, forceful explosion of air.

Hold up two fingers and blow them out one after the other.

Repeat with three, four and five fingers.

Put both hands around the sides of your lower waist and repeat (imagining the birthday candle, since there's no finger for you to focus on). Notice how the muscles engage in this area.

Move your hands around to your back, still at the level of your lower waist, and repeat.

Go back to holding up one finger, and this time blow it out with a 'hey', engaging your abdominal muscles in the same way that you did when you were blowing it out with breath.

Focus in turn on the stomach (all the way down to the pubic bone), the lower waist and the back.

If you feel any tightness or sense of effort creeping into your throat, stop, yawn, and imagine that it is an empty passage.

You may feel a burst of energy coming up from your pelvis – this can be very useful.

Blow out two then three then four then five candles on a 'hey'.

Blow out a couple of candles on a 'hah'. Go back and forth between 'hey' and 'hah'. Throw in a 'hee' or a 'hoo'; play around a bit, maintaining the strong connection between the energy of these muscles of support and the energy of the sound.

The Column of Air (7–10 minutes)

Start in supine or semi-supine.

Take a minute or so to release unnecessary tension from your body by imagining your head, your shoulders, your chest, your abdomen, and your hips all becoming very heavy on the floor.

Imagine that your jaw is becoming heavy, and that the heaviness causes your mouth to drop open slightly. If you have been breathing through your nose, switch to breathing through your mouth for a while, as this is often how we breathe when we are speaking.

Visualise your throat as an empty pipe and your torso as an empty chamber with a source of light, heat and energy at the base: that is, centre.

For a minute or so, just observe how centre moves your empty torso as it calls air down to itself and releases air back up: the gentle rise and fall of the stomach, the slight feeling of expansion and release in the hips, around the back and in the ribs.

Slip your lower lip under your top teeth as if you were going to make the sound 'F'. Simply continue to breathe, and focus on the feeling of the air sliding between your teeth and your lip.

Start to extend your out-breath so that it becomes a little bit stronger and a little bit longer. As you do, picture the air running between your centre and your lips. Think of it as being like a column of water springing up from a drinking fountain. When you feel the impulse to breathe in, breathe in – air is free, and there's little to be gained from fighting your impulses.

Notice how your body supports the flow of this fluid column of air up from centre to your lips on the exhalation and then responds to the impulse to let more air in on the inhalation. Now, imagine that this column of air continues beyond your lips, running from centre up to the ceiling. Avoid lifting your chin as you do this.

You will probably notice that your body is doing what it does when you just lie there and breathe, but it is doing it more energetically – your abdominal muscles are drawing the belly in on the out-breath and then are quickly releasing it on the in-breath. You may also feel your ribs springing open on the in-breath and gently pulling in on the out-breath.

After a couple of minutes of observing your body support the column of air on a 'fffff', imagine the air starting to vibrate, which will change it to a 'vvv'.

It may help you connect to the image of an unbroken column of vibration if you lightly place your fingers low on your breastbone, then higher on your breastbone, then on your throat, and finally under your chin to feel the slight 'buzz' moving under your fingers. Remember that the origin of this vibration is at centre.

After a couple of minutes of working with the 'vvv', take a stretch and a wriggle.

Return to the 'vvv' for two or three breath-cycles, then close your lips around the vibrations, creating a 'mmmm'. Continue to work with the image of the sound flowing from centre and the sense of your breathing muscles easily engaging to support it.

After a minute or so of working with the 'mmmm', open your lips and allow the vibrations to flow out of your mouth as a 'maaah'. Work with the 'maaah' for a minute or two. If at any point you find yourself disconnecting from the sense that there is a steady column of vibration flowing up from centre, go back to the 'vvv' or the 'mmmm' to re-establish it.

Stretch and wiggle as you finish the exercise.

Counting

If you have asthma or any other respiratory difficulty and feel a tightness in your chest or discomfort at any point, stop the exercise and return to your normal breathing pattern.

I. (5–6 minutes)

Start in supine or semi-supine.

Take a minute or so to release unnecessary tension from your body by imagining your head, your shoulders, your chest, your abdomen, and your hips all becoming very heavy on the floor.

In this and the following exercises, you will be working with your body's natural breathing pattern but shaping it in a specific way, so take a minute or two to simply observe how your body breathes when it is left entirely to its own devices before you start manipulating it. You want to work with your body's impulses, not against them.

When you feel comfortable and connected to your breath, begin to engage your breathing system more actively by focusing on your rib cage. Place the backs of your hands firmly against your lower ribs to either side. Breathe out fully, and then actively engage your intercostal muscles to widen your rib cage as you breathe in – remember that the focus of activity is in the lower ribs, and not the upper chest or shoulders.

As you develop this connection with the rib cage, begin to extend your in-breath over a two-count and breathe out on 'ffff' over a four-count. Your ribs, sides and back will be gently opening and releasing as always; they will simply be doing so over a designated period of time.

When you feel comfortable with the two/four-count, extend the in-breath to a three-count and the out-breath to a six-count. If you feel that you are stuffing your rib cage with air on the in-breath or having to squeeze the air on the out-breath, send your body images of softness, lightness and ease. If you still feel uncomfortable, switch back to two and four and simply pause while your instructor counts three and six.

When you feel comfortable with the three/six-count, extend the in-breath to a four-count and the out-breath to an eight-count. As always, if this is uncomfortable, drop back to the lower count and then gradually try to work your way back up.

After a couple of minutes of working with the four/eight-count, take a stretch and a wriggle.

Return to the four/eight-count for a few breath-cycles, and then leave the in-breath at four, but extend the out-breath to ten. Work with this for a couple of minutes until it feels comfortable.

Next, cut the in-breath to a three-count. Your body will have to bring the air in more quickly, so you will have to engage the ribs just as the impulse to inhale kicks in. Work with this for a minute or so.

Take a stretch and a wiggle as you finish.

II. (8–9 minutes)

Start in supine or semi-supine.

Begin as before by taking a minute or so to release unnecessary tension from your body. Simply observe how your body breathes in this relaxed position.

When you feel comfortable and connected to your breath, begin to engage your breathing system more actively, this time by focusing on your abdominal muscles. Place your hands on your stomach; notice how it rises and falls with your breath. Now, as you breathe in, think of filling down to centre over a two-count and breathe out on 'ffff' over a four-count – imagine the breath as a column of air running from centre, between your teeth and lip, and on up to the ceiling.

When you feel comfortable with the two/four-count, extend the in-breath to a three-count and the out-breath to a six-count. If you feel that you are stuffing your belly with air on the in-breath or having to squeeze the air on the out-breath, send your body images of softness, lightness and ease. If you still feel uncomfortable, switch back to two and four and simply pause while your instructor counts three and six.

After a couple of minutes working with the three/six-count on 'ffff', switch to working with 'vvvv' for a few breath-cycles. Then close your lips over the vibration and create a 'mmmm' for several breath-cycles.

Now fill down on a three-count and speak the word 'one' on the out-breath, feeling the abdominal muscles engage in a little pulse of support at the same time. Repeat until this feels comfortable and easy.

Now fill down on a three-count and say 'one, two', feeling a separate abdominal pulse on each word. Repeat until this feels comfortable and easy.

Gradually build up to a sequence of counting from one to ten, making sure that you take time to fill down on a three-count and that you feel a separate abdominal pulse on each word.

Take a stretch and a wiggle as you finish.

III. (9–10 minutes)

Start in supine or semi-supine and release into the floor.

When you feel comfortable and connected to your breath, begin to engage your breathing system more actively, but this time focus on both your rib cage and your abdominal muscles. Place one hand on your lower ribs at the side and place the other on your stomach.

. Now, stretch your in-breath over a two-count and your out-breath over a four-count. Your abdomen will be rising and falling as before, and your ribs, sides and back will be gently opening and releasing as before; they will simply be doing so over a designated period of time.

When you feel comfortable with the two/four-count, extend the in-breath to a three-count and the out-breath to a six-count, backing off if you feel yourself forcing the breath in or out.

When you feel comfortable with the three/six-count, extend the in-breath to a four-count and the out-breath to an eight-count. As always, if this is uncomfortable, drop back to the lower count and then gradually try to work your way back up.

After a couple of minutes of working with the four/eight-count, take a stretch and a wriggle.

Return to the four/eight-count for a few breath-cycles, and then leave the in-breath at four, but extend the out-breath to ten. Work with this for a couple of minutes until it feels comfortable.

Next, cut the in-breath to a three-count. Your body will have to bring the air in more quickly, so you will have to let the abdominal muscles release completely and engage the ribs just as the impulse to inhale kicks in. Work with this for a minute or so.

Keep the in-breath at a three-count and extend the out-breath to a twelve-count, switching from speaking the numbers to chanting (i.e. intoning) them.

As you work with this long extension of the out-breath, imagine that your throat and neck are one big empty pipe and that the vibrations are flowing up in a steady column from centre. Work with this for a couple of minutes.

Finally, take the in-breath down to a two-count and switch between chanting and speaking as you count to twelve: e.g. count once chanting and then once speaking; count to six chanting and then switch to speaking – you can play around with moving between the two. As always, if you can't get to twelve comfortably, go as far as you can. Your ability to extend and support your voice with ease will grow as you practise this exercise.

Take a stretch and a wiggle as you finish.

Teaching tip

These three counting exercises work best as a continuous sequence, but it may be necessary to do them separately to begin with, especially for students who find it hard to stay on the floor for long periods of time.

It will help the students to work consistently if you count out loud for them: e.g. 'In two, three; out two, three, four, five, six', etc. Each count should take about a second. Do remind the students that if they can't comfortably reach a given number, there's no shame in dropping out and waiting for the next cycle. They can't expect to master this skill right off the bat.

If the students are starting to drone or sitting back on their vocal folds, creating a creaky sound, ask them to picture some nice things that they can count – candy bars or puppies – or anything that will make them smile and help them stay present in the act of counting.

Beach-ball Breathing (4–5 minutes each)

I. Begin standing with your feet parallel, about hip-width apart, knees soft, back and neck long.

Place your hands on your chest – at the level of your heart.

Move your hands out away from your chest about two feet and imagine that you are holding a beach ball against your body. Take time to imagine what the beach ball looks like. What colour is it; what is it made of; what does it feel like?

As you breathe out, make a continuous 'ssss' sound. Imagine that this is the sound of the air escaping from the beach ball. As you make the sound, move your hands gradually in towards your chest and lower your elbows towards your sides, imagining that you are putting pressure on the beach ball.

When you have come to the end of your breath (just before your chest starts to tighten), release the pressure on your beach ball with your hands, and imagine the ball springing back into shape as you breathe in again.

Repeat this cycle of breathing and moving the hands. As you become more familiar with it, start to vary the speed and intensity with which the air escapes from the beach ball. Sometimes the 'ssss' may be very slow and soft; at other times it may be swift and loud.

Continue on the 'ssss' for several cycles; then imagine that the beach ball is filled with vibrations. As you gently press against it, an easy flow of 'zzzz' will come from where the beach ball is resting against your body.

Once the 'zzzz' is established, progress to 'mmm' and then 'maaah'.

If you need to, take a little break and shake out your arms from time to time.

As you work with this exercise, notice how your rib cage responds to the inflation and deflation of the beach ball – your ribs will probably open up as you imagine the ball inflating, and return to their rest position as it deflates.

II. Begin standing with your feet parallel, about hip-width apart, knees soft, back and neck long.

This time place your hands on your lower belly – at least three inches below your navel.

Move your hands out away from your belly about a foot and pretend that you are holding the beach ball against your lower stomach.

On the out-breath, think of sending up a column of air from centre, shaping it into a 'ffff' at your lips. As you do, move your hands gradually in towards your stomach, imagining that you are putting pressure on the beach ball. This will help you to engage your abdominal muscles easily.

When you have come to the end of your breath (just before your chest starts to tighten), release the pressure on your beach ball with your hands, imagining the ball springing back into shape. This will help the abdominals release quickly, allowing the in-breath to drop right in.

Continue on the 'ffff' for several cycles; then imagine that the beach ball is filled with vibrations. As you gently press against it, an easy flow of 'vvv' will come up from your centre, where the beach ball is resting against your body.

Once the 'vvv' is established, progress to 'mmm' and then 'maaah'.

If you need to, take a little break and shake out your arms from time to time.

More Counting (6–8 minutes)

Repeat the counting exercises above whilst standing.

You may find it helpful to start chanting as early as eight, and to introduce either or both of the beach-ball images/hand movements at that point.

When you get to twelve, start actually counting things in the room – elbows or ceiling tiles or chairs – anything.

Try counting to thirteen, fourteen and fifteen, physically pointing to things as you count them.

Speak the Speech (5–6 minutes)

With thanks to Dudley Knight.

Begin standing with your feet parallel, about hip-width apart, knees soft, back and neck long.

Breathe in the following thoughts and then speak them on one breath, if possible, engaging the beach-ball or birthday-candle muscles (whichever image works best for you) and keeping the throat and mouth soft and open as you do:

Speak the speech, I pray you

Speak the speech, I pray you, as I pronounced it to you

Speak the speech, I pray you, as I pronounced it to you, trippingly on the tongue

Speak the speech, I pray you, as I pronounced it to you, trippingly on the tongue, but if you mouth it

Speak the speech, I pray you, as I pronounced it to you, trippingly on the tongue, but if you mouth it, as many of our players do

[At this point you may find that your body really wants to take a quick catch breath at one of the commas; this isn't the worst thing in the world as long as that breath is achieved by releasing the abdominal muscles, rather than by gulping or gasping for air, and provided you don't let your energy drop away from the thought as you breathe. The goal is to connect intention and breath with length of thought, not to see how long you can keep speaking on one breath or how much you can fit into one breath.]

Speak the speech, I pray you, as I pronounced it to you, trippingly on the tongue, but if you mouth it, as many of our players do, I had as lief

Speak the speech, I pray you, as I pronounced it to you, trippingly on the tongue, but if you mouth it, as many of our players do, I had as lief the town crier spoke my lines.

Teaching tip

This comes from Hamlet's advice to the players, Act III, Scene ii. He is encouraging them to speak their lines with fluidity and agility rather than forceful over-muscularity. 'I had as lief the town crier spoke my lines' means that he would just as soon have the town crier deliver the speech if the actors can't get it right.

As the thought becomes longer and longer, it can be helpful for you to repeat the new words a few times before the group tries the whole thought. As you feed it to the group, model engagement with what is being said so that it doesn't become a meaningless drone. Also, make sure that the group doesn't speed up but stays at a conversational pace.

Supporting the Voice

As we move into more energetic voice use, it is particularly important to keep the effort focused in the respiratory muscles and out of the throat. As you do these exercises, you may start to get pulled back into bad habits – tightening the jaw, thrusting the back of the neck, tensing the shoulders, etc. – so it's a good idea to do some release and relaxation exercises beforehand. In addition, monitor those areas where you know you have trouble as you do these exercises. If you find yourself pushing or straining your voice at any point, stop, shake out, take a breath, focus your energy into the respiratory muscles where it can really help you, and start again. You've been developing the ability to recognise tension and release it; this is where it will really become useful. Also useful will be the image of an empty passage-way between your centre and your lips. The more power you are generating, the more important it is to keep the channel open – i.e. to 'get out of your own way'.

It can be hard to trust in your own power. Some of us get in our own way because of fear that what we have to offer is not enough – that a simple engagement of a few layers of abdominal muscles will not create a voice powerful and passionate enough to be truly interesting, arresting, affecting. So we try to help it along by pushing or straining – by 'doing' more. Some of us, on the other hand, get in our own way because of fear that what we have to offer will be more than anyone can handle – that if we truly engage, or don't clamp down and restrain ourselves, something ugly, frightening, or undesirable will be released. So we fail to commit, or we push our energy down. Some of us do both in different circumstances and for different reasons. Learning to get out of your own way is about tapping into your body's ability to support and release a strong voice. It's also about finding and using your personal power. Don't expect it to happen overnight, but don't sell yourself short and settle for less.

Baby Talk (3–5 minutes)

Begin in semi-supine.

Take a moment to release any unnecessary physical tension.

Imagine your legs and your upper body becoming lighter and lighter until they begin to lift up off the floor, resting your weight on your 'sitting bones'.

Imagine that you are a baby, old enough to hold up your head, floating on a cloud. Allow your arms, legs, chest and head to move freely as you float along.

Although this will necessitate a strong engagement of the abdominal muscles, keep everything else as soft and free as possible.

As you are floating on your cloud, release a couple of baby sighs, imagining them bubbling up from your centre.

Follow the sighs with some very easy baby sounds – 'ma ma ma ma', 'buh buh buh buh', etc. – still floating on a cloud, moving the torso, arms, legs and head freely.

Once you have established an easy flow of sound from centre, your baby talk can become more energetic and use more of your range. You can even enter into a baby dialogue with someone across the room.

Rest in semi-supine whenever your abdominal muscles start to ache.

The Chair

I. (1–2 minutes per partner)

Find a lightweight chair – a plastic or folding chair – and a partner.

Partner A, stand behind the chair with your feet parallel, about hip-width apart; knees soft, back and neck long.

B, stand behind A.

A, take the chair by the back legs and lift it up over your head. Once it's there, let your shoulder blades slide down your back as far as they will go. Check to make sure that you are not tilting your head up towards the chair and that your neck is still long.

B, place your hands on A's ribs.

A, hold the chair up for three or four breath-cycles, engaging your ribs on each in-breath. B, as A is breathing, move your hands around from the front of the ribs to the sides and the back. In this position, you should be able to feel them opening all the way around.

A, let the chair down and shake your arms out.

A, lift the chair again, keeping your shoulders low.

B, place your hands on A's lower abdomen.

A, blow out ten imaginary birthday candles. B, move your hands around from the front to the waist to the lower back. In this position, you should be able to feel the engagement of the abdominal muscles all the way around.

A, let the chair down and shake out your arms.

Repeat with B lifting the chair.

II. (about 1 minute)

Everyone get a chair and stand behind it.

Take the chair by the legs and lift it up over your head; drop your shoulders (see Chair I on the DVD for a demonstration).

Imagine your partner's hands around your ribs and open into them as you breathe in.

Engage your birthday-candle muscles to send a strong column of 'vvv's' up from your pelvis. Imagine pressure from your partner's hands on your lower belly, around your sides and across your lower back supporting the flow of sound until you start to feel pressure in your upper chest and throat.

Release and allow the breath in.

Blow out ten birthday candles with ten bursts of 'vvv's'.

Release and allow the breath in.

Blow out ten birthday candles with ten 'vah's'. Note if any tension creeps into your throat as you open onto the 'ah' sound. If it does, stop, take a little yawn; continue to think soft and open across the back of your mouth and resume the 'vah's'.

Let the chair down and shake out your arms.

III. (about 1 minute per partner)

Partner A, stand behind the chair with your feet parallel, about hip-width apart; knees soft, back and neck long.

B, stand behind A.

A, take the chair by the legs and lift it up over your head (see Chair I on the DVD for a demonstration).

Once it's there, let your shoulder blades slide down your back as far as they will go. Check to make sure that you are not tilting your head up towards the chair and that your neck is still long.

B, place one hand on the back of A's neck. Gently squeeze and release through the exercise to help A keep their neck long and soft. If at any point you feel the neck go very rigid, or A start to pull their neck away from your hand, give it a little massage to remind them to keep the effort out of the neck and in the abdominal muscles.

A, engage a strong in-breath by opening the ribs and letting the belly drop.

Blow out three birthday candles with three bursts of 'vvv's', and then blow out a fourth, opening the 'vvv' to a long 'vooooooh'.

Release and allow the breath in.

Energetically engage the birthday-candle muscles to send out an energised, 'Vvoh! For a muse of fire that would ascend the brightest heaven of invention!'

Release and allow the breath in.

Energetically engage the birthday-candle muscles to send out an energised, 'Vvah kingdom for a stage, princes to act, and monarchs to behold the swelling scene!'

Let the chair down and shake out your arms.

Repeat with partner B holding the chair.

Teaching tip

If possible, assign the memorisation of these four lines from the first Chorus speech of *Henry V* the session before you do this exercise. Review the lines several times before the students pick up the chairs so they're not exhausting their arms while trying to sort out what they're going to say.

Battles

 I. (4–6 minutes)

Do this exercise with caution if you have a history of knee or back injuries.

1. Find a partner who is somewhere in the neighbourhood of your height.

   Stand facing your partner, about a metre apart.

   Both partners should take a step forwards on to their right foot.

   Hold your hands at chest height and clasp both hands with your partner, intertwining your fingers.

   Bend your front leg a bit and shift your weight forwards. You should not be leaning forwards with your bottom sticking out; keep your pelvis under your torso. The bend in your front knee will help you to do this.

Press forwards with your right arm and receive your partner's press on your left – so your right arm is moving towards your partner and your left arm is moving back towards you. As you do this, your right hip will shift forwards.

Then, press with your left arm and receive with your right, shifting your left hip forwards as you do so.

You should never press hard enough to push your partner over.

Begin a continuous motion of pressing with the right hand and then the left, the hips pivoting from side to side.

Continuing the motion, start a fairly easy stream of 'vvv' vibrations from centre.

Because you are engaging a strong forward energy in pressing on your partner's hands, you may feel an urge to focus that energy in your jaw, eyebrows, neck and throat. If you feel yourself pushing or straining in any of these areas, consciously release the tension. Refocus the sense of effort and energy into your pelvis, and feel the muscles of support engaging in your lower abdomen.

Do three or four breath-cycles on the 'vvv'. Let each one grow in energy and volume, but if you feel a strain creeping into your throat, back off.

Take a break and shake your arms out.

2. Switch the leg that is forwards. Begin the motion again and release another easy 'vvv' from centre. On your next breath, release an easy 'vvwaaah'.

Do three or four breath-cycles on the 'vvwaaah'. Let each one grow in energy and volume, but if you feel a strain creeping into your throat, back off.

Continuing with the back-and-forth arm motion, engage a strong in-breath and, at the same time as your partner, easily speak the two lines: 'Oh, for a muse of fire that would ascend the brightest heaven of invention!'

Engage a strong in-breath and, with your partner, easily speak the two lines: 'A kingdom for a stage, princes to act, and monarchs to behold the swelling scene!'

Take a break and shake your arms out.

3. Switch the leg that is forward. Take the two pairs of lines another three times. Let each one grow in energy and volume.

Because you and your partner are pushing on each other and speaking at the same time, there may be a tendency for you to try to out-shout one another. It's fine if you feel that the exercise awakens an aggressive energy in you – in fact, it's designed to do that, and you should not back away from it – but keep the sense of power in your hips and out of your throat. Let the physical connection with your partner reinforce the sense that you are sharing energy so that you don't get into a shouting-match mentality.

II. (2–3 minutes)

If you have problems with your knees, you may want to sit this exercise out.

1. Find a partner. Stand facing them, about a metre apart.

   Take a stance in which your own feet are about hip-width apart and your toes pointed out to the sides. Imagine that your tailbone is heavy in order to counter any tendency you may have to stick your bottom out.

   Imagine that you are loosely holding a pole in each of your hands. This should help you keep your shoulders low and your hands relaxed.

   You and your partner both bend your knees and VERY GRADUALLY lower your bodies until you are all the way down in a squat. About a third of the way down, your heels may have to come up off the floor; that's fine. Your torso should be straight all the way; you should neither lean forwards nor stick your bottom out.

   When you have reached a squat, pause for a moment and then VERY GRADUALLY come up together to standing.

   This takes a great deal of effort in the thighs. Breathe into the effort, allowing the breath to drop straight down to your pelvis. Maintain eye contact with your partner and let your innate sense of competitiveness keep you from speeding up and getting ahead of him or her.

   Repeat, engaging a strong in-breath before you begin and releasing a 'vvv' from centre for the duration of the movement down and again for the movement up.

   Take a moment to shake your legs out.

2. Repeat, engaging a strong in-breath before you begin and releasing the following lines from centre: 'Oh, for a muse of fire that would ascend the brightest heaven of invention; A kingdom for a stage, princes to act, and monarchs to behold the swelling scene!' as you go down and again as you come up.

   Speak the lines at a normal pace and make both the descent and the ascent last as long as it takes to speak them.

   Because you are exerting extreme effort in your thighs and facing off with a partner, you may, again, feel a tendency to shout your way through. It's fine to release a lot of energy, but think of it as just that: allowing energy to move through you rather than pushing and grinding your way to the end of the thought.

Teaching tip

These exercises come from the Suzuki method of physical training for actors. It is important to emphasise that they are about connecting to a powerful muscular support and opening the channel to release strong sounds, and not about out-shouting one another. It can help the students if you travel around the room and, if you see anyone losing the connection to centre, simply place your hands on the ribs, the lower abdomen, the back of the neck – anywhere that is disengaged when it should be engaged or vice versa. If the energy in the room becomes too aggressive, pause for some stretching and beach-ball breathing before taking up the exercise again.

Supporting Text

As in the previous chapter, we would recommend using non-dramatic literature so that you can focus on integrating new skills with the act of communicating language that is not your own, without the pressures of 'acting'. In this chapter, however, we would encourage you to use language that is a bit more challenging: longer thoughts, more complex images and more urgent messages. You will need to bring to this strong language a strong vocal energy (which is NOT the same thing as volume) and strong muscular supply and support. Don't feel, however, that you need to work yourself up into some kind of state to demonstrate the power of the text. This approach will most likely cause you to breathe rapidly into your upper chest and cut you off from true supply and support. Continue to focus on engaging the muscles of respiration appropriately and maintaining a sense of freedom and openness in the throat. Let the energy of the voice and the energy of the language complement each other; trust that this will be enough to communicate effectively. Again, these are not performances – just exercises.

At the same time, you will need to commit to what you are saying if you want to truly support your voice. It's well-nigh impossible to trick your body into providing muscular support for an act of communication that your mind and spirit are not engaged in, so spend a bit of time making sure that you understand your text and cultivate an attitude of eager readiness to share it.

Teaching tip

Several of the poems we recommend in this chapter are very long. With these, we suggest that each student could be assigned one or two stanzas or a shorter selection from the poem. You may also wish to introduce other texts. Look for poems and/or prose passages that are energetic in tone but not overwrought. Look also for relatively long arcs of thought that will need a good supply of breath to express. As before, the texts should be memorised, although students may be able to work more effectively if they are allowed to carry the text at first. If you have any dyslexic students, they may find it helpful to receive the text well in advance of the day when they will need to use it in class.

Ideally, sessions on Supporting Text would start with a thorough warm-up using exercises from earlier in the chapter, and then move on to individual work. Have the student simply speak their text once, and then choose from the following exercises according to what they seem to need to help them find the energy of the voice in steady muscular engagement of the ribs, the abdomen and the pelvic floor. You may also feel inspired to refer back to work from previous chapters, to introduce a new image, or to incorporate an aspect of an exercise for engaging the in-breath, engaging the out-breath or supporting the voice. If at any point the students start to drone the text, losing vocal energy and creating a flat, creaky sound, have them stop, shake out, jump up and down a couple of times, and start again with a smile and the intention to engage not only their muscles but also the attention of the people they are talking to. When appropriate, use same-sex partners.

Each of these exercises will take between two and six minutes, approximately. In all cases, stay engaged with the act of communicating your text to your listeners while consciously applying the principles of supply and support that you are working with.

I. Stand in a comfortable, aligned position. Have one partner place their hands on your ribs. Have another partner place their hands on your shoulders. Focus on breathing into the hands on your ribs without moving the hands on your shoulders. Breathe out. Repeat while silently reading the first line of your text, and then breathe out.

Repeat while thinking of speaking the line to someone across the room, and then speak the line on the out-breath.

Repeat the process, taking the next two lines of the poem together. Work up to a complete thought or image of at least three lines in length.

II Stand in a comfortable, aligned position. Do a couple of cycles of Beach-Ball Breathing I or II as a warm-up.

Continue with the beach-ball hand movement as you do the following:

* hum as you go through the first two lines of your poem in your head;
* chant (i.e. intone) the first two lines;
* pick someone across the room and speak the two lines to them.

Finally, speak the two lines to that person without the hand movement but maintaining an awareness of the easy engagement of the respiratory muscles.

III. Stand in a comfortable, aligned position. Do a couple of cycles of Beach-Ball Breathing II as a warm-up.

Pick someone across the room to speak to. Recite your poem (or stanzas), echoing your breathing impulses with your hands. When you feel the impulse to breathe in, release the pressure on the imaginary beach ball; when you want to sustain a long thought, maintain an even, steady pressure on the beach ball.

IV. Find two reasonably heavy bags or backpacks and a partner. Stand in a comfortable, aligned position, and lift the bags over your head, one in each hand.

Your partner will first place their hands on your shoulders to remind you to keep them loose and low, and then massage your neck. If your shoulders start to creep up, your partner should place their hands on them again and then go back to massaging your neck.

With the bags held high, blow out five birthday candles.

Blow out five candles with a 'Hey'.

Blow out five candles with the first sound in the first line of your poem; on the fifth candle, continue straight into speaking the line.

Repeat the process on the following lines, stopping to rest when your arms become tired.

You may work your way up to speaking several lines on one breath.

V Start as in the previous exercise, with two bags and a partner to check your shoulders and massage your neck.

Blow out three candles with the first sound of the first line of your poem; on the third candle, continue straight into chanting the first line at a constant volume.

Blow out three candles with the first sound of the second line, and on the third candle, continue straight into chanting the second line at a slightly higher volume.

Blow out three candles with the first sound of the third line of your poem, and on the third one, continue straight into chanting the third line at a lower volume.

Blow out three candles with the first sound of the next line of your poem, and on the third one, continue straight into chanting a couple of lines, starting at a low volume and steadily increasing to a volume that is high, but not shouted.

Blow out three candles with the first sound of the next line of your poem, and on the third one, continue straight into chanting another couple of lines, starting at a high volume and steadily decreasing to a volume that is low, but not whispered.

Rest your arms, and then repeat – speaking instead of chanting.

VI. Find a partner, and speak your text doing the motions from Battle I, but with just one partner speaking at a time.

VII. Find a partner, and speak your text doing the motions from Battle II, but with just one partner speaking at a time.

Follow-up

Reflective practice questions:

* In which exercises did you feel the least amount of pressure and effort in your throat? In which did you feel the most? When you felt pressure and effort in your throat, were you able to move that sense of effort into your lower torso? What images or exercises helped you to do that?
* When you feel angry or aggressive, where in your body do you feel that energy focus? What exercises, techniques and images could you use to focus that strong energy in your lower abdomen and pelvis?
* How do you know when you need to breathe in? What sensations do you feel, and where are they located in your body?

* How do you know that you've breathed in fully and allowed your lungs to fill as much as they can? What sensations do you feel, and where are they located in your body?

* What is the relationship between your breath and your thought when you are speaking in a relaxed way? Does this change when you perform? If so, why do you think this happens?

* Draw two pictures of the inside of your torso – a front and a back view, including the ribs, the diaphragm, and the abdominal muscles. Don't worry about being strictly anatomically correct; draw what you feel from the inside. With a coloured pencil, draw arrows showing where and in what direction you feel everything moving when you breathe in. With another pencil, draw arrows showing where and in what direction you feel everything moving when you breathe out.

* Add a neck and head to your front and back torsos and, using whatever colours take your fancy, draw your voice inside the drawings of your body. This will, of course, be a non-literal representation of what your voice feels like in your body. It could be anything: a red ball in your belly or a blue cloud in your chest, or both. There are no right answers; this is simply a way of heightening your awareness.

* When working on your text, when did you feel your muscles of respiration engage strongly to support the thought? What images or exercises helped you to find that engagement? When did you feel disengaged? Where did the sense of effort go when disengagement happened?

Exercises

* During a phone call when you don't have to think too hard about what you're saying, sit in a comfortably aligned position with both feet flat on the floor, and use your hand to mirror what your breath is doing – moving it away from the body on the in-breath and continuously towards the body on the out-breath. After a while, move your hand to the abdominal 'beach ball' zone and use the movement to encourage your abdominal muscles to engage and gently support the flow of thought.

* Sometime when you are alone and doing a mundane chore like washing the dishes or taking a shower, start to count objects out loud. Start with five or six and then increase one by one. Stop and go back a number as soon as you feel any strain.

※ Any time when you feel tense, try breathing in on a three-count and out on a six-count, thinking of the air filling your torso to the front, back and the sides on the in-breath and pouring from centre on the out-breath.

Suggested texts

Maya Angelou	'Phenomenal Woman'
Elizabeth Barrett Browning	'A Musical Instrument'
T S Eliot	'The Love Song of J Alfred Prufrock'
Ruth Fainlight	'Introspection of a Sibyl'
Ted Hughes	'Wodwo'
D H Lawrence	'The Mess of Love'
Michael Longley	'The Butchers'
Claude McKay	'I Know My Soul'
Edna St Vincent Millay	'Love is not all'
Edwin Muir	'The Horses'
Ezra Pound	'The River-Merchant's Wife: A Letter'
Henry Reed	'Judging Distances'
Adrienne Rich	'Rape'
William Shakespeare	'My mistress' eyes ...' (Sonnet 130)
Walt Whitman	'Song of Myself' (Sections 1–3)

Further reading

Berry, Cicely, *Voice and the Actor*, Virgin, London, 2000. Chapter 2: Relaxation and Breathing, pp. 18–42.

Houseman, Barbara, *Finding Your Voice*, Nick Hern Books, London, 2002. Chapter 3: Breath and Support, pp. 73–96.

McCallion, Michael, *The Voice Book* (Revised edition), Faber and Faber Ltd, London, 1998. Part Two: Breathing, pp. 62–63.

Rodenburg, Patsy, *The Actor Speaks*, Methuen, London, 1997. Stage One: The Actor First Speaks, pp. 38–66.

4 Resonance and Range

Framework

When we listen to an engaging speaker, it is rarely just the interesting things that he or she has to say that appeal to us; we are also likely to be drawn in by the interesting way in which their voice expresses the words and ideas. For example, the melody of the speaker's voice will probably attract us by the way it moves in response to the ideas and to the speaker's enthusiasm for them. The speaker's voice may soar with delight, or plunge into awe or despair. S/he will be using pitch range to express thoughts and feelings, and we will be moved by them.

We may also be attracted to the speaker by the sound of his/her voice – its quality, its colour, or its tone. 'Rich', 'warm', 'smooth', 'dark', 'bright' – these are all descriptions of a voice's quality; that is, its resonance. 'Plummy', 'nasal', 'tight', even 'sarcastic' or 'bored' are also qualities connected with resonance. Vocal resonance is, therefore, often associated with character, personality or attitude; and, as listeners, we often make judgements about people based on the sound of their voices – judgements which are not necessarily correct. Try Exploration I over the next few days, and record your impressions in your journal.

In this chapter, we will work on developing your range and use of pitch and resonance. It helps to first have a basic understanding of how pitch and resonance are created. The pitch that we hear is produced by the vocal folds. As we discussed in the last chapter, when the vocal folds are brought together with the right amount of pressure, the air pressure beneath them builds up until it blows them apart. They then fall back together until sufficient air pressure builds up to blow them apart again, and so forth. If the folds are thin and stretched tight, this process happens very quickly; if however the folds are thick and slack, it happens more slowly. In the first instance, we would say that the sound produced has a high frequency – the folds open and close many times per second, so the sound waves come very quickly. In the second instance, we would say that the sound has a low frequency – the folds open and close fewer times per second, so the sounds waves come more slowly (i.e. they come less *frequently*). When sound waves come very fast, we hear them as high pitches; when they come more slowly, we hear them as lower pitches. For example, to sing the note middle C, the vocal folds will vibrate at approximately 261 times a second; and to sing the note A above middle C, they will vibrate at 440 times a second. Women and children generally have vocal folds that are thinner and lighter than men's, so their folds open and close more quickly and produce sound that is usually higher in pitch. The same principles apply in music – the thinnest, lightest strings on a violin vibrate more quickly and produce the highest sounds, while the thickest, heaviest strings on a cello produce the lowest sounds.

You can, however, get more than one note out of a violin string, and you can get more than one pitch out of your voice as well. The cartilage to which your folds are attached at the front (the thyroid cartilage – see Fig. 9) can tilt. When it tilts forwards, it stretches the folds; when the folds are stretched, they become thinner and tighter and open and close more quickly, making your voice 'higher'. When the thyroid cartilage tilts back, the folds become thicker and slacker. This

Vocalis muscle

Thyroid cartilage

Fig. 9 The Larynx

makes them open and close more slowly, producing a 'lower' voice. There are also muscles in the folds themselves – known as the vocalis muscles – that can also affect how quickly the folds open and close. While the vocalis muscles are particularly useful for fine-tuning the pitch of the voice, we don't have any direct conscious control over all this muscular activity. Although the violinist will consciously tighten the strings of the violin or move his or her finger up and down the string in order to change pitch, the singer or speaker cannot directly alter the thickness and tension of the vocal folds. We change pitch with our intention rather than with our fingers. It is our thoughts and feelings, or our mental image of the note we want to make, that cause our brain to unconsciously tune the muscles of the vocal folds to produce the right sound. The action of these muscles in the larynx can be affected by a number of factors: from the relatively stable – such as an individual's vocal anatomy and gender; through those that change and develop with time and experience – for example, a speaker's accent or physical and psychological maturity; to more temporary ones – a person's general energy level and state of health; to the most immediate – one's psychological or emotional state, attitude, and intention in the moment of speaking. For an actor, it is particularly desirable to have access to as wide and as flexible a pitch range as is healthily possible, and to use a 'home' note that resonates fully (sometimes referred to as the 'centre note' or 'optimum pitch').

The vibration of the vocal folds determines the pitch we hear. But without the resonance provided by the vocal tract, that vibration would just sound like the irritating buzzing of a fly. Resonance adds colour and size to those vibrations, giving them greater dimension and carrying power. Your vocal tract – the resonating chamber for your voice – is essentially a hollow but flexible tube, which extends from the larynx through the vertical space of your throat (or pharynx) into the horizontal spaces of your nose and mouth (see Fig. 10). By changing the length and shape of this tube, we alter the vocal resonance. It might be helpful to think of the vocal tract as a kind of musical instrument – perhaps a strange relative of a clarinet and a trombone. As with the clarinet, vibration is created by blowing air through a reed (in this case, the vocal folds); and, as with the trombone, it is flexible and can change its length. Unlike either instrument, though, it has two apertures (the nose and mouth) and can change its shape as well as its length.

Different shapes and sizes resonate different pitches in different ways. Some

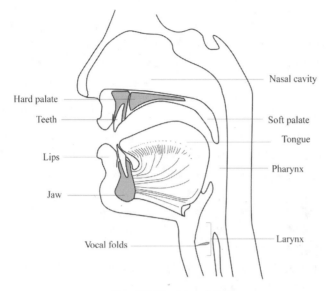

Fig. 10 The Vocal Tract

shapes, for example, will resonate high frequencies very well (as does a violin body or a flute), giving your voice richness, brightness and clarity, and carrying power at high pitches. Other shapes resonate low frequencies very well (as does a cello body or an oboe), giving your voice warmth, body, fullness and strength at lower pitches. Try Exploration II to explore how a fixed shape will resonate one pitch more effectively than others.

The shape of the vocal tract also affects the quality of your voice. Some shapes will resonate in such a way that the voice sounds full and open; others will resonate in such a way that the voice sounds pinched and narrow. Essentially, a longer tube produces a darker sound, and a shorter tube produces a brighter sound; a narrower tube produces a more constricted and restricted sound, and a wider tube produces a more open and generous sound.

The length and shape of your vocal tract are determined by a number of variables. While the structure of the bones and the overall amount of space available don't normally change except with age, you can alter all of the following: the height of the larynx; the width of the pharynx; the position of the soft palate (the back of the roof of your mouth); the shape and position of the tongue; the shape and position of the lips; and the position of the jaw. These shapes are created by the action of a number of muscles, which we generally use for eating, swallowing and facial expression, as well as for creating speech sounds. Try Exploration III to get a sense of what these muscles can do. They are affected by factors similar to those that influence the pitch-changing muscles – accent, maturity, health, energy levels, emotion, etc.

The ability of the muscles of pitch and resonance to work effectively can be limited by the habitual patterns and psychological and emotional inhibitions of our daily lives. Pitch and resonance ideally express our emotions and inner states, and are responsive to the content and context of communication. But the attitudes and repressions of our parents, our peers and ourselves will often cause us to limit that expressiveness – we restrict our pitch range so as not to sound childish or silly, or because we want to sound sweet and unthreatening; we shut down our resonance when we tighten our jaw in sullen rebellion or constrict our pharynx from social anxiety. These are patterns you need to free yourself from if you are to become as expressive as you can be. If you are an actor, the muscles of the larynx and vocal tract must be able to fully reflect the demands of character and text in respect of psychological state, accent, emotion, and intention.

If the parts of your vocal tract that can move are to be as free, agile and respon-sive as possible, the voice must be grounded in strongly supported breath. As we've discussed before, if your voice is not getting the support it needs from your respiratory muscles, other muscles will step in and try to compensate. In particular, the muscles of the throat can constrict, the root of the tongue can tighten, and the jaw can clench, all in an effort to get the sound out. This will change the shape of the vocal tract, and not in a way that gives your voice access to its full resonant possibilities. The relationship of your head and neck to the rest of your body will also change the shape of the vocal tract. If your neck is collapsed in the back or your head is jutting forwards, the space between the larynx and the back of your mouth – the pharynx – will be constricted, and your resonance will be compromised. It is, therefore, important to continue to build efficient alignment and breathing habits and to consciously employ them when working on resonance. Try Exploration IV to feel the effect of posture on resonance.

In our work on resonance in this chapter, we will do some specific excercises on the four major mobile parts of the vocal tract: the pharynx, the tongue, the soft palate, and the jaw. Much of this work will focus on releasing tension so that they can move more freely and responsively – but release is, of course, only the first step. Once the muscles are free through their range of motion, you can really explore your voice's resonant potential. As with other aspects of voice work, images and play can help you discover possibilities that you might not find through purely technical work. The physical sensation of vibration in your body can also inform your work on resonance. Strictly speaking, vocal resonance can only occur in the vocal tract: however, when you've found a shape for that channel which is particularly well suited to the frequencies being generated, the primary resonance can cause sympathetic vibration in other bones in your body. Well-resonated lower notes can cause the breastbone to vibrate, which is one of the reasons the lower voice is often called the 'chest voice'. Well-resonated higher notes can cause a sensation of vibration in the skull, which is where we get the phrase 'head voice'. We do have a certain amount of conscious control over the vocal tract, but it's not always easy to sense the exact position of every little muscle in it, or to evaluate by ear how well one's own voice is resonating. Sympathetic resonance can, therefore, be very useful to help you gauge when you've found a shape for the tract that really works. Furthermore, focusing on channelling the sense of vibration to a certain area of the body can cause the vocal tract to move in response to the image and create a shape that generates sympathetic vibrations in that area. So when you work on 'feeling' resonance in your back, you're focusing on sympathetic resonance in order to improve actual resonance; as with so many things in voice, sometimes the indirect route is the most effective.

In general, of all the resonant possibilities in your voice, the ones that will most effectively fill a large space are a mix of resonance in the pharynx, the mouth and the nose – these are often called 'balanced' or 'blended' resonances. They cause sympathetic resonance in the chest, the back, the neck, the skull and, most particularly, the face. It's the strong resonance in the front of the mouth and the nose that gives us this facial focus, which is described as 'forward placement'. To 'place' the voice simply means to focus the resonance and/or the vibrating sensation that goes along with it in a particular area. A balanced forward placement is not the only kind of resonance you will want to use, but it is an extremely effective tool. It allows you to be heard without shouting and makes it easy to speak for long periods of time without tiring the voice.

Although finding good resonance and range will give you carrying power, enabling you to be heard in large theatre spaces without straining or damaging your vocal folds, you should not feel that it limits you to making only 'good' sounds. Ideally, you should have access to a wide range of resonant possibilities. Knowing how to adjust your resonance will allow you a higher degree of control over the sound you produce. If you are an actor, this will give you a broader range of vocal options when creating a character. Try Exploration V to get a taste of this. Having a vocal tract that is free and responsive as you move through your pitch range will also enhance your ability to convey nuances of thought and feeling by developing the variety and overall richness of the voice. Resonance and range are, in so many ways, a speaker's best friends.

Exploration

I. Listen to your friends and family speaking at different times of the day or in different circumstances, e.g. over a coffee, watching television, on the phone, out shopping. Do they change the pitch or resonance of their voices? Or do their voices stay fixed in a particular quality or part of their range? Try listening to your own voice too and see if you can tell whether you change your pitch and resonance.

II. Get a can of Pringles and empty it (what you do with the crisps is up to you). Now place the open end of the empty can lightly over your mouth and hold it there with both hands making a seal with your face so that it looks as though you have grown a long beak. (Be careful not to block your nose – you still need to breathe!) You are now going to experiment with sending different sounds and pitches into the can. Start with a gentle humming, and then open into an intoned and supported AH sound: as you open into the vowel you should start to feel the can vibrate slightly. Now try moving the pitch of the AH sound around slowly – can you feel the can vibrating more or less strongly at different pitches? At what pitches does it vibrate most strongly on the AH sound? Does it make a difference if you open your jaw and relax your tongue? Now try the same exercise with different vowel sounds – EE, AY, AW, OO. Try rounding your lips actively on the AW and OO sounds. Do you notice any differences? Ask a friend to listen while you experiment with the Pringles can – can s/he hear any changes? Can you find a pitch and a sound that will make the metal end of the can vibrate like a steel drum? (Note: there isn't just one.) These exercises illustrate very clearly how pitch and resonance interact in the human voice. The Pringles can is like one shape of the vocal tract: you can hear or feel how it amplifies sounds. However, you can also hear or feel how, because of its shape, it amplifies certain sounds and pitches more than others. Thankfully, the vocal tract is flexible and can create many different shapes. This makes it potentially very responsive to the sounds we make, as long as we don't get stuck in one shape or pitch.

III. If you have a mirror over your bathroom sink, take a good look at your tongue when you brush your teeth. Notice all the movements it makes as it darts out of the way of the brush – up, down, to the sides, forwards, backwards; it can even get thinner or fatter. When you've finished brushing, run your tongue over the roof of your mouth. There's a slight ridge behind your teeth, and then a hard, smooth plate that runs about two thirds of the way back. As your tongue gets near the back molars, that hard, smooth plate will end and a softer, spongier bit will begin; that is your soft palate. Looking in the mirror, open your mouth, stick your tongue out, and see if you can make the soft palate move up and down. Most people have a little polyp of flesh, the uvula, hanging from the soft palate; as the palate raises and lowers, it too will go up and down, sometimes even seeming to disappear if the palate lifts high enough. The movements of the tongue and soft palate are two major determiners of resonance quality. Make an intoned and supported AH sound, and look at the shape your mouth makes. Now try changing that shape by altering the position of your tongue or soft palate while still intoning, or you could move the position of your jaw or lips. Notice any changes in the quality of the sound.

IV. Stand in a comfortable, aligned position. Let your jaw drop open and release a sustained, energetic AH on one note. Continuing the AH, drop your head forwards and then slowly rotate it around over one shoulder, to the back, over the other shoulder, and back down. As you do this, notice how the quality of the sound changes. Try it on an EE, an OO, and an OH. Rotating your head changes the shape of the vocal tract, which will change the resonant qualities of the vowels.

V. Try your hand at impressions. Start with a really distinctive sound like a New York Brooklyn, Liverpudlian or Australian Outback accent. Stop mid-word and notice the shape of your mouth: where is your soft palate? What is your tongue doing? How much tension is in your lips? How much space is there at the back of your mouth and in your throat? Try a very snooty, upper-class dowager and note the same things. Try a little kid voice. A clown voice, etc. In each instance, you are changing the shape of the vocal tract in order to change the resonant properties of your voice (as well as working a specific part of your pitch range and perhaps changing accent) to change your vocal quality.

Exercises

> **Teaching tip**
>
> The exercises in this chapter are organised under five headings: *Working the Channel*; *Finding the Buzz*; *Expanding the Range*; *Balancing the Sound*; and *Resonating Text*. In general, it's a good idea to begin any work on resonance and range with some work on freeing the vocal tract, and a review of engaging breath support. It's important to transfer to the major respiratory muscles the sense of effort that can get lodged in the throat and the back of the mouth. Tongue and jaw tension, in particular, can be very stubborn, so those exercises bear frequent repetition. Many of the exercises in *Expanding the Range* and *Resonating Text* have large pay-offs of fun and discovery. We find it useful to combine a series of more technical exercises with one or two of the more imaginative exercises per session to bring together the systematic acquisition of skill with the joy of expression.

Working the Channel

The 'channel' is your vocal tract – the space in which your voice will resonate. Much of the channel is shaped by bone, which tends to change only with age. There are, however, several components of the channel that can move; you will have already discovered some of the possibilities in the Explorations. The first of these moving components of the vocal tract is the larynx itself. If you place your fingers lightly on your Adam's apple and then swallow, you can feel your larynx moving upwards. Similarly, if you yawn, you can feel it drop downwards. Speaking with a habitually raised or lowered larynx will reduce the amount of resonance available to you and restrict your range. For optimum range and resonance, therefore, the larynx should rest easily and be able to move freely in your neck. We will work on maintaining this relaxed position.

Travelling further up the vocal tract, the next movable component we come to is the pharynx – the area between the larynx and the back of your mouth. As mentioned in the Framework section, the shape of the pharynx is affected by your alignment, or lack thereof, but it also has muscles of its own that can cause it to constrict or open. If they are over-engaged, your resonant possibilities will be narrowed. If, however, they are under-engaged and sluggish, they can also compromise your resonance. This is because sound waves generally resonate better against surfaces that are hard and firm than against surfaces that are soft and slack. Think about how much more clear, loud and full your voice sounds in a tiled bathroom than in a heavily curtained drawing room. We will work on finding appropriate openness and tone in this area.

The tongue we tend to think of as being part of the mouth, but in fact it descends all the way into the pharynx and attaches to the bone at the top of the larynx. Tension at the root of the tongue is very common and is one of the factors that can most affect resonance. If your tongue is bunched up at the back of your mouth, it can force some of the vibrations rising up from the larynx into your nose, which creates a very different resonance than if they are allowed to travel through the mouth. Dropping the soft palate (the back of the roof of your mouth) also prevents the vibrations from entering your mouth, sending them out of the nose instead. The balance between how much sound is resonating in the oral cavity and how much is resonating in the nasal cavity has an enormous impact on vocal quality. The front of the tongue can also be an area of tension that inhibits resonance. If your tongue tends to bunch up at the front of your mouth, it can affect the size of your oral cavity. We will work to release unnecessary tension from the tongue and to engage the soft palate appropriately so that there is a suitable balance of resonance between the oral and nasal cavities.

Finally, the position of the jaw determines how much resonating space there is in the mouth and what shape it is in. The muscles that have the primary responsibility for closing the jaw are, inch for inch, among the most powerful in the body and are a favourite place for many people to carry tension. Engaging those muscles is a common way to force back emotions that we don't want to show or act on, and it can be very hard to disengage them. Think of the clenched jaw of James Bond, Dirty Harry or a Mafia boss. Some people grind their teeth at night or have jaws that pop or click when they open. If you find that this is the case with you, or if you experience any discomfort doing the jaw exercises, you may wish to consult a specialist. In any case, even after we have found a good degree of freedom in the jaw through exercises, most of us will have to consciously bring ourselves back to that release over and over again before it becomes second nature – if it ever does.

The lips also help to shape the vocal tract, and will naturally come into play in many of the exercises in this chapter. We will work with them in more detail in the next chapter on articulation.

Teaching tip

You do not need to work through every exercise for each part of the tract in sequence. Many of them get to the same muscles through slightly different angles, and can be mixed and matched from session to session to prevent boredom and to reach as many students as possible – each one of whom will respond to each exercise differently. In particular, there are a number of exercises that involve yawning. Be careful not to overwork these exercises, as students can start to feel sleepy very easily.

Many of the exercises are designed to develop an inner kinaesthetic awareness of the different parts of the vocal tract, but it will also be useful for students to have access to a small hand mirror, particularly for work on the soft palate. You will also find it useful to combine the exercises in this section with exercises on articulation in the next chapter, where again a small hand mirror will be useful.

Larynx (1-2 minutes each)

For all these exercises, stand or sit in a comfortable, aligned position.

I. As described above, place your fingers lightly on your Adam's apple and then swallow slowly; you should feel your larynx moving upwards in the first phase of the swallow, and then relaxing downwards again.

Repeat this action, but this time try to hold your larynx in a raised position at the 'top' of the swallow, i.e. don't relax your swallow.

Now try counting from one to ten keeping your larynx raised. Notice the effect on your voice – you will probably sound like a cartoon character or a comic caricature. This is because you have drastically changed your vocal resonance.

Now relax your swallow – enjoy the sensation of an easy larynx.

II. Place your fingers lightly on your Adam's apple and then yawn slowly; you should feel your larynx moving downwards at the start of the yawn, and then relaxing upwards again.

Repeat this action, but this time try and hold your larynx in a lowered position at the 'bottom' of the yawn, i.e. don't relax your yawn.

Now try counting from one to ten keeping your larynx lowered. Notice the effect on your voice – again, you will probably sound like a cartoon character or a comic carica-ture. This is because once again you have drastically changed your vocal resonance.

Now relax your yawn – enjoy the sensation of an easy larynx.

III. Many of the muscles which raise and lower your larynx are situated at either side of your neck. Gently massage your neck on either side of your larynx, starting under-neath your jaw and working down to your collar-bone.

Now, place your fingers lightly on either side of your Adam's apple and very gently move it from side to side, encouraging the muscles to relax. It's alright – this won't damage you or your larynx. You may feel some 'clicking' movements inside your larynx – these are created by the cartilages moving around and are quite normal. But if you feel nauseous at all, stop. Moving the larynx can stimulate the 'gag' reflex, particularly if there is some degree of tension in the area. The more you work on releasing tension in other ways, the easier it will become to move your larynx from side to side.

IV. A nice way to help your larynx relax is to imagine it smiling. Think of something which genuinely makes you smile, and then think of transferring the smile down your vocal tract to your larynx. Gillyanne Kayes taught us this image, and we have found it very useful for finding a relaxed and easy larynx.

Try counting from one to ten with a smiling larynx.

Now imagine your larynx frowning and count from one to ten. Hear the difference? Go back to the smiling larynx and try speaking to a partner for a minute or two.

Pharynx (1–2 minutes each)

For all these exercises, stand or sit in a comfortable, aligned position.

I. Take a nice, big yawn. Yawning is our bodies' reflex way of opening up the vocal tract and getting a lot of oxygen into the system quickly. It produces a long and wide-open pharynx.

Notice the sensation it creates in the throat. Try to recreate that sensation in the throat without actually yawning.

Now, try to constrict that area as tightly as you can. You can do this if you imagine that you have something caught in your throat, or that you have a sore throat, or are feeling very anxious about an interview or audition.

Go back and forth between opening it wide and constricting it, and then let it come to rest in a comfortably open position – not as wide-open as for a yawn, but with an easy feeling of space.

II Yawn, sighing out loud through the yawn.

Yawn again, and hold the pharynx in the yawning position. With the pharynx wide open, release a few easy, extended 'haaah's'. These may initially come out in the middle part of your lower range; try a couple a few notes higher and a couple a few notes lower.

With the pharynx still wide open (yawn again if you feel yourself losing it), release some 'who who' calls like a dove.

Call to someone close to you and then to someone across the room.

Release the yawning posture in the pharynx and let it come to rest in a comfortably open position.

Alternate between easily calling 'hah' and 'who' to people around the room, enjoying the sense of freedom and space in the throat.

III. Smiling pharynx. Think of something that genuinely makes you smile, and then think of transferring the smile down your vocal tract to your pharynx.

Try counting from one to ten with a smiling pharynx. Now imagine your pharynx frowning and count from one to ten. Hear the difference?

Go back to the smiling pharynx and try speaking with a partner for a minute or so.

Tongue (about 1 minute each)

For all these exercises, stand or sit in a comfortable, aligned position.

I. Place one hand at the back of your neck and the other hand on the side of your jaw. This is to help ensure that you don't push with your neck and jaw but rather work the tongue itself in isolation.

Imagine a big ice-cream cone just in front of your mouth that you desperately want to lick. Reach for it with the tip of your tongue, but imagine that just as you are about to touch it, it is slowly pulled away from you, millimetre by millimetre. Continue reaching for it with the tip of your tongue as far as you can.

Hold the tongue there, reaching with the tip and monitoring your neck and jaw to make sure they don't try to help, until your tongue starts to ache – and then hold for a further 20–30 seconds.

Allow your tongue to slowly retract back into your mouth.

II. Place one hand at the back of your neck and the other hand on the side of your jaw.

Imagine the very back of your tongue slowly pushing forwards, trying to get out of your mouth. This will push your whole tongue forwards.

When your tongue is about as far forwards as it can go, continue to push from the back until your tongue starts to ache and then another 20–30 seconds longer. Keep the neck and jaw soft and loose throughout.

Allow your tongue to slowly retract back into your mouth.

III. Place your thumb underneath your chin and find the soft area in the angle made by your jaw. This soft area is the root of your tongue. Give it a bit of a massage while imagining that the part of your tongue that is in your mouth is softening and spreading.

Leaving your thumb under your chin, release a long, easy 'ahhh'.

Move from the 'ahh' directly into an 'ooo'. If you felt the base of your tongue press against or tighten under your thumb, massage the area a bit more and think of the change from one sound to the other as happening on the roof of the mouth.

Repeat this exercise regularly until you can keep the tongue-root soft as you move between vowels.

IV. Let your head hang forwards with the jaw dropped slightly open.

Allow your tongue to hang freely; it will probably come to rest on your bottom lip. Thinking of it as a floppy piece of meat or as giving into gravity can help you find release.

Continuing to let your tongue hang freely, slowly roll your head over to one shoulder and then over to the other shoulder before releasing it back down. Let your tongue roll in your mouth as you do so.

V. Let your jaw hang open and place your fingertips on either side of your chin to make sure that it stays relaxed and open.

Place the tip of your tongue behind your bottom teeth.

Roll the middle of your tongue out of your mouth, leaving the tip inside, behind the bottom teeth (see Fig. 11).

Hold this position until your tongue starts to ache and then another 20–30 seconds longer.

Let your middle tongue fall back into your mouth.

Next, roll the middle tongue back and forth in and out of your mouth fairly rapidly.

Fig. 11 Tongue

Make sure your jaw is not moving at all; it's important to be able to separate the movement of the tongue from the movement of the jaw.

Add some sound – an extended 'huh', which will probably come out as a 'huh-yuh-yuh-yuh' because of the movement of the tongue.

Try the same on a pitch-glide through your range.

VI. Finish your tongue-release work by flicking your tongue in and out of your mouth. Start slowly and then gradually build up speed.

Try the same on a pitch-glide through your range.

Teaching tip

The human tongue comes in all shapes and sizes, and so some are capable of achieving more flexibility than others. Students should be encouraged to work with goals appropriate to the shape and size of their own tongues, and not to compete with each other.

Soft Palate (about 1 minute each)

For all these exercises, stand or sit in a comfortable, aligned position.

I. Take a nice, big yawn, this time noticing what your tongue does.

Yawn again, consciously leaving your tongue resting behind your bottom teeth, and feel the lift at the back of your mouth.

If a mirror is available, take a look at what's happening. You should be able to see your soft palate lifting high up into your mouth.

Bring your mouth into position to make a 'k' sound. Before you make the sound, notice what you feel at the back of your mouth. Explode the 'k' and notice what you feel move.

Try making a 'k' sound on an in-breath and notice what you feel move.

Go back and forth between an out-breath 'k' and an in-breath 'k' four or five times, imagining that with each one you're getting a little bit more excited.

II. Make a 'ng' sound (the sound at the end of the word 'sing') and notice what you feel at the back of your mouth. Have a look in a mirror and see what is happening to make this sound.

Open the 'ng' into an 'ah' and notice the action at the back of the mouth. You should be able to see the tongue and soft palate separate if you have a mirror.

Place your fingers on either side of your chin to make sure that the jaw is still and only the soft palate and the back of the tongue move as you repeat 'ng-ah-ng-ah-ng-ah' seven or eight times. Imagine the soft palate bouncing off the back of the tongue like a trampoline as you do.

Switch to a long 'ng-ay' and then a bouncing 'ng-ay-ng-ay-ng-ay'.

Switch to a long 'ng-ee' and then a bouncing 'ng-ee-ng-ee-ng-ee'.

Jaw (I–IV: about 1 minute each; V–VI: about 2 minutes each)

If you have a jaw that 'clicks,' don't force it to open to that point when doing these exercises. If you experience a sharp pain when massaging or moving your jaw, you should see a doctor.

For all these exercises, stand or sit in a comfortable, aligned position.

I. Clench your teeth and, with your fingers, find the muscles that pop out on either side of your jaw. These are the masseter muscles. Unclench your teeth and give these muscles a thorough massage, allowing your jaw to drop open as you do so.

As you massage, make sure that you are keeping your shoulders loose and low.

II. Close your mouth.

Put a finger on your chin and use it to draw your chin down, slowly opening your mouth as wide as it will comfortably go.

Close your mouth again and, this time, place your hands on either side of your face, cradling your jawbone in your palms, with the thumbs tucked behind the ears.

Keep your shoulders loose and low.

Let the weight of your hands slowly pull your jaw down.

Keep your lips together as long as possible.

Picture the space between your back molars growing as your hands draw the jaw down.

Switch back and forth a couple of times between opening your mouth by pulling down the chin and opening it by allowing the jaw to drop open at the back. Note which one gives you the feeling of having more space in your mouth.

III. Clench your teeth and place your thumbs over your masseter muscles – the ones that are popping out as you do this.

Unclench your teeth and press against your masseter muscles with enough pressure to be uncomfortable, but not enough pressure to be painful (see Fig.12).

Fig. 12 Jaw

Hold for 20–30 seconds, keeping the shoulders loose and low and breathing deeply. Release and allow the jaw to fall open.

IV. Find the joint where your jaw hinges with your skull – it's just in front of the opening to your ear. Place your fingers here lightly, and feel how the joint moves as you open and close your jaw.

Now imagine that this joint is controlled by a wing nut (otherwise known as a butterfly nut) attached to the outside of your face. (We're indebted to Frankie Armstrong for this enjoyable image.) Tightening the nut will make you gradually clench your jaw – try it! And loosening the nut will make you gradually open your jaw – try that too!

Play with tightening and loosening the nut until you find a comfortable relaxed position for the jaw, where the lips are gently together but you can feel space between your back molars.

V. Once you have found some release in the jaw through any of the above exercises, place your thumbs under your chin and use them to gently close your jaw.

Release the thumbs and let the jaw fall open.

Imagine the masseter muscles softening, like butter melting, and see if the jaw sinks down a bit further; do not, however, pull it down.

Repeat three or four times, keeping the shoulders loose and low and the breath free.

Take hold of either side of your chin with the thumb and forefinger of each hand.

Use your hands to gently and slowly open and close your jaw. This requires the jaw muscles to release completely – think of them going wobbly, like jelly.

When you have mastered this, add a touch of sound: a continuous 'ahhhh' from centre.

VI Repeat exercise V but with a partner moving your jaw.

Revisiting the Column of Air (7–10 minutes)

You are now going to revisit the Column of Air exercise from the previous chapter, with your new awareness of the vocal tract.

Start in supine or semi-supine.

Take a minute or so to release unnecessary tension from your body by imagining your head, your shoulders, your chest, your abdomen, and your hips all becoming very heavy on the floor.

Visualise your throat as an empty pipe and your torso as an empty chamber with a source of light, heat or energy at the base: that is, centre.

For a minute or so, just observe how centre moves your empty torso as it calls air down to itself and releases air back up: the gentle rise and fall of the stomach, the slight feeling of expansion and release in the hips, around the back and in the ribs.

Now become aware of the various elements of your vocal tract. Think of your larynx at rest in your throat. Think of the open, smiling pharynx. Let your jaw relax until you can feel there is space between your back molars. Let your tongue rest in the floor of your mouth, with the tip in contact with the back of your lower front teeth. Think of your soft palate lifting away from the back of your tongue, creating space in the back of your mouth.

Slip your lower lip under your top teeth as if you were going to make the sound 'F'. Simply continue to breathe, and focus on the feeling of the air sliding between your teeth and your lip.

Start to extend your out-breath so that it becomes a little bit stronger and a little bit longer. As you do, picture the air running between your centre and your lips. Think of it as being like a column of water springing up from a drinking fountain. When you feel the impulse to breathe in, do so – air is free, and there's little to be gained from fighting your impulses.

Notice how your body supports the flow of this fluid column of air up from centre to your lips on the exhalation, and then responds to the impulse to let more air in on the inhalation.

Now, imagine that this column of air continues beyond your lips, running from centre up to the ceiling. Avoid lifting your chin as you do this.

After a couple of minutes of observing your body support the column of air on a 'fffff', imagine the air starting to vibrate, which will change it to a 'vvvv'.

Remember that the origin of this vibration is at centre.

After a couple of minutes of working with the 'vvvv', take a stretch and a wriggle.

Return to the 'vvvv' for two or three breath-cycles, then close your lips around the vibrations, creating a 'mmmm'. Continue to work with the image of the sound flowing from centre and the sense of your breathing muscles easily engaging to support it.

Remind yourself of the various elements of your vocal tract: the larynx at rest in your throat; the open, smiling pharynx; the jaw relaxed and space between your back molars; your tongue resting in the floor of your mouth, with the tip in contact with the back of your lower front teeth; and your soft palate lifting away from the back of your tongue, creating space in the back of your mouth. Imagine that behind the 'mmmm' sound there is an 'aaah' sound waiting to come out. Let your mouth form the 'aaah' sound behind your lips as you make the 'mmmm'.

After a minute or so of working with the 'mmmm', open your lips and allow the 'aaah' sound to come out freely. Work with the 'aaah' for a minute or two. Imagine the sound is just pouring out of you. If at any point you find yourself disconnecting from the sense that there is a steady column of vibration flowing up from centre, go back to the 'vvv' or the 'mmmm' to re-establish it.

Stretch and wiggle as you finish the exercise.

Finding the Buzz

Our work so far on the vocal tract has been highly technical – working on muscles directly in order to free them and prepare them to engage in a wider range of movement with greater ease. Having laid this foundation, we'll now move on to exercises that are more imaginative and experiential as we start to work on finding full, strong resonance. Some of these exercises will resonate (pun intended) more strongly with you than others. All of them, however, will work best if you have warmed up and loosened your body and are mindful of staying connected to your breath. Resonance can't be forced – you can prepare the ground, and then you just have to experiment until it comes. Be sensitive to what you feel in your body, as it will tell you a great deal about what is happening in your voice – more sometimes than what you can hear. Be aware of sensation all over your body; it's important to think of voice as a 360-degree phenomenon, not just something that is focused in the front of the body. Finally, be open to making shapes with your mouth that are unfamiliar, and to working with sounds that are outside your usual repertoire.

Teaching tip

When a roomful of students has 'found the buzz', it's easy to spot; the sound will suddenly be very full and alive. These exercises should get students well on their way, but they may need some coaching to find full resonance. If you sense that their voices are still a bit thin or are pushed, you may want to briefly revisit some of the channel work – even just yawning to open the soft palate and pharynx. Encourage them as well to shake out from time to time. Feed them images of openness, gentleness (pushing is the number one enemy of resonance), warmth and energy throughout.

Humming

I. (3–4 minutes)

1. Stand in a comfortable, aligned position.

 Take a moment to allow your breath to settle.

 Imagine a bit of vibration coming up from centre on a 'huh'.

 On the next breath, extend the 'huh' and close your lips around it so it becomes a 'hummmmm'.

 As you hum, imagine an unbroken column of vibration between your centre and your lips.

 On your next breath, think of focusing the energy of the vibration onto your lips. Over the course of the next few breath-cycles, play with the position of your pharynx, soft palate, tongue, jaw and lips to see how you can find the most buzz on your lips. Play with different pitches as well.

2. Next, think of focusing the energy of the hum in your nose. Again, play with the shape of the vocal tract as well as with various pitches to find the maximum buzz in the nose.

3. After the nose, focus the vibrations as far back in your mouth as you can.

4. Finally, try to find as much buzz as you can in the middle of your mouth.

5. On one breath, see if you can move the focus of the vibrations from your lips, up to your nose, back to the very back of your mouth and then to the middle of your mouth.

 Finally, return the vibrations to the middle of your mouth, finding as much buzz as you can. Then open your lips so the sound flows out on a full and easy 'maaahhh'.

II. (12–15 minutes)

1. Lie on the floor on your stomach with your head turned to one side.

 Take a moment to give the weight of your body to the floor and feel your body opening to the breath, particularly through the back.

 Imagine a bit of vibration coming up from centre on a 'huh'.

 On your next breath, extend the 'huh' and close your lips around it so it becomes a 'hummmm'.

 As you hum, imagine an unbroken column of vibration between your centre and your lips.

 On your next breath, imagine all those vibrations pooling in the cheek that is next to the ground. Play with the shape of your vocal tract (by changing the position of the tongue, soft palate, lips, etc.) and various pitches until you feel that your whole head is buzzing against the floor.

2. Next, imagine the vibrations pooling behind your collar-bone. Play with the image, the vocal tract, and the pitch until you feel that your upper chest is buzzing against the floor.

3. Move the pool of vibrations down to the middle of your breastbone. Spend a couple of breath-cycles exploring the feeling of resonance in this area.

4. Finally, imagine the vibrations at their source, in the pelvic bowl, and experiment with pitch and vocal-tract shape until you find the maximum buzzing sensation in that area.

5. Roll over onto your back.

   Connect again to the image of vibration flowing from centre as you recommence humming.

   Focus the vibrations into your head until you feel that it is buzzing against the floor.

6. Next, think of the vibrations as flowing to your shoulders and explore the feeling of resonance in this area.

7. Imagine the pool of vibrations moving to your mid-back – just above the lumbar curve, and adjust the quality of the hum correspondingly.

8. Finally, imagine the vibrations staying in the pelvis and buzzing against the floor there.

Touch the Buzz (10–12 minutes per partner)

Find a partner who is somewhere in the neighbourhood of your height.

Begin the exercise with partner A giving partner B a massage, such as the one described in Chapter One.

For the first half of the massage, partner B, focus simply on staying fully open to the breath.

About halfway through the massage, B, add a touch of vibration to the breath in the form of an easy hum.

Once the hum is established, think of focusing the vibration in the area that is being massaged.

When you feel you have found a good pitch and vocal-tract shape for the area that is being massaged, open the hum onto a gentle 'aaah'.

Repeat each time partner A moves to massaging a new area. B, think of the action of the massage as helping to 'shake' the vibrations out with a minimum of effort on your part.

When A has finished the massage, s/he should simply place his or her hands on different places on B's body – the neck, the top of the head, the ribs, the stomach, the hips, etc. for 30-40 seconds at a time. B, think of sending the buzzing energy of a 'hummaaah' into your partner's hands. The pitch and quality of the sound will naturally change as your partner's hands move.

Repeat, with partner B giving A the massage and A opening into sound.

Teaching tip
You may want to assign same-sex partners for the massage.

Mouths (20–30 minutes)
This is a lengthy sequence, but it really pays dividends in your connection to resonance if you work through it slowly.

1. Lying in semi-supine, take the time to allow your breath to really settle in your body. As you breathe, imagine that you have a mouth in your belly, somewhere in the region of your navel. If it helps you to imagine it, place a hand gently on your stomach.

   When you feel you have a good image of this mouth, add vibration to the breath in the form of an easy hum, but imagine that the hum is focused in your 'belly mouth'.

   Work with this image until you feel that the hum is really connected to the belly mouth. Now imagine that behind the hum there is an 'aaahhh' sound waiting to come out, and then visualise your belly mouth opening to release the 'aaahhh' sound just as your real mouth does so.

   Work with this sequence of breath, humming, and opening into 'aaahhh' from the belly mouth for about a minute until you feel fully engaged in the image and sound. Experiment with different pitches or pitch glides on your 'aaahhh' sound.

   Experiment with releasing other vowel sounds, such as 'ooooo', 'ohhhhh' or 'ehhhh', from this new mouth.

2. Now imagine that you have a mouth in the middle of your chest, somewhere in the region of your heart. Again, if it helps you to imagine it, place a hand gently on your chest.

   When you feel you have a good image of this mouth, add vibration to the breath in the form of an easy hum, but imagine that the hum is focused in your 'chest mouth'.

   Work with this image until you feel that the hum is really connected to the chest mouth. Now imagine that behind the hum there is an 'aaahhh' sound waiting to come out, and then visualise your chest mouth opening to release the 'aaahhh' sound just as your real mouth does so.

Work with this sequence of breath, humming, and opening into 'aaahhh' from the chest mouth for about a minute until you feel fully engaged in the image and sound.

Experiment with different pitches or pitch glides on your 'aaahhh' sound.

Experiment with connecting other vowel sounds to this new mouth.

3. Roll on to your stomach with your head turned to one side.

Take a moment to give the weight of your body to the floor and feel your body opening to the breath, particularly through the back.

As you breathe, imagine that you have a mouth in your lumbar region, in the small of your back. If it helps you to imagine it, place a hand there.

Now repeat the process of humming, opening into the 'aaahhh' sound, and experimenting with different pitches and vowels.

4. Now imagine that you have a mouth in your upper back, between your shoulder blades. Again, if it helps you to imagine it, place a hand there for a moment.

Repeat the process of humming, opening into the 'aaahhh' sound, and experimenting with different pitches and vowels.

5. Now roll on to one side and try combining these four mouths.

First, establish a deep connection with your breathing.

Then, as you breathe, imagine your four new mouths. If it helps, place a hand gently on each area in turn.

When you feel you have a good image of the four mouths, add vibration to the breath in the form of an easy hum, but imagine that the hum is centred in all four mouths.

Work with this image until you feel that the hum is really connected to each mouth. Now imagine that behind the hum there is an 'aaahhh' sound waiting to come out, and then visualise each mouth opening to release the 'aaahhh' sound just as your real mouth does so.

Work with this sequence of breath, humming, and opening into 'aaahhh' from the four mouths for about a minute until you feel fully engaged in the image and sound.

Roll over to your other side and experiment with connecting other vowel sounds and pitches to these new mouths.

Continue to explore your connection to these mouths as you stretch and come up to standing.

6. Standing or sitting in a comfortable, aligned position, work through the same sequence of discovery and connection, imagining a mouth first in your forehead, next in the back of your head, and finally in the top of your head.

Try combining these three mouths in the same way that you combined the mouths in your body.

Then combine all seven mouths! What does it feel like to resonate so fully?

Working with the same principle, you can explore visualising mouths in other areas. It is particularly useful to explore your side ribs, the palms of your hands, and the soles of your feet, and then to combine them with the other mouths.

Teaching tip

Some students might find the image of a mouth in different parts of the body unsettling. If students with very vivid imaginations find this too disturbing, you can suggest that they simply focus their vibrations in the particular area without visualising the mouth very strongly.

Expanding the Range

The first part of this section will concentrate on expanding and strengthening your pitch range – the number of notes you use in your voice. The second part is about extending the figurative range of your voice – the arsenal of sounds that you can possibly use. Moving through your pitch range, manipulating the vocal tract, and actively engaging your imagination can help you to find sounds you'd never imagine yourself making. The ability to be creative not just with your body and your mind, but also with your voice, is a particularly precious skill if you are an actor.

The issue of pitch is sometimes a loaded one. For one thing, it's often tied up with people's feelings about their singing voices. A belief that 'I can't sing high' can influence how one approaches using the upper register of one's speaking voice, just as a developed ability to sing bass parts can lead one to favour the lower register. There are also cultural influences. Most obviously, lower voices are often associated with manliness and higher voices with femininity. Both the outright acceptance and the outright rejection of gender stereotypes can lead one to limit one's use of the pitch range. We may also associate certain characteristics with pitch; lower tones may seem more warm or sincere or authoritative, where higher tones may feel more friendly or unthreatening or weak. A lot of choices – made almost unconsciously as we grow up, and related to how we want to be perceived – influence how we pitch our voices.

We'll start with a couple of very simple exercises to help identify what is sometimes called 'optimum pitch'. As you found with the empty Pringles tube, any fixed, hollow shape will resonate one or two particular pitches more effectively than other frequencies. To the extent that the shape of your vocal tract is fixed by your bone structure, it too will resonate a couple of pitches better than others. Identifying an 'optimum pitch' doesn't mean that you should speak in that pitch all the time, but it can help you to recognise if you have a habit of either pressing your voice down lower or lifting it up higher than where it might naturally settle. If you know where your ideal pitch is, you can also use that part of your voice when you want maximum carrying power with minimum effort.

The true ideal, however, is for the voice to be free to move through a wide range of pitches. This gives you the ability to express with precision a broad spectrum of thoughts and feelings. If you are an actor, it also gives you a variety of options when creating a character. Furthermore, even if you rarely use your very highest or lowest note, working all the way through your range will strengthen your voice and add resonant depth to the notes you do use.

Optimum Pitch

Teaching tip

Identifying optimum pitch (also known as 'centre note') is an imprecise science, partly because this pitch will change slightly as the student develops his or her voice. At this stage of training, it's not vital to identify precisely the exact note at which a student's voice is strongest and most resonant. Move through whichever of these exercises you choose (doing them all is not necessary) with a minimum of fuss to help the students get a general idea of whether or not they are habitually pitching their voices above or below a range in which they might work more effectively.

I. (about 1 minute per partner)

Get a partner. Partner A stand in front of partner B.

Partner A, wait 15–45 seconds, and then ask B a simple question that you know s/he will answer with a neutral 'mm-hmm' sound; for example, 'Do you have brown [or another colour] eyes?' or 'Do you have a mobile phone?' or 'Do you like chocolate?'

Help B to isolate the pitch that is the 'hmm' part of the 'mm-hmm'. That will usually come out at about his or her optimum pitch.

B, try counting from one to ten on this pitch – how does it feel? Familiar? Higher than usual? Lower than usual?

Now repeat with partner B asking the question. (Note that if the question is too provocative, then the pitch of the answering 'mm-hmm' will be quite extreme and will not be close to the optimum.)

II. (about 1 minute per partner)

Get a partner. Partner A stand behind partner B.

Partner A, wait 15–45 seconds – enough time for B to be unable to anticipate your movements, and then, without warning, give B just a little push between the shoulder blades – enough to make him/her lurch forwards a small step, but nowhere near enough to make him/her lose his/her balance.

B, when you are pushed, release an 'Oh!' That 'Oh!' will usually come out at about your optimum pitch.

Try counting from one to ten on this pitch – how does it feel? Familiar? Higher than usual? Lower than usual?

Now repeat with partner B behind parner A.

III. (about 1 minute)

Find the lowest comfortable note that you can make without effort (that is, don't growl!). Use that note as the bottom of a scale, and then sing up the scale for a total of eight notes (an octave). The top three or four notes of the scale are likely to be in the area of your optimum pitch.

Explore which note sounds fullest or strongest. Try humming the notes with your fingers in your ears – which one creates the loudest or richest sound in your head? Try speaking on this pitch – how does it feel? Familiar? Higher than usual? Lower than usual?

The Cat Sequence (6–7 minutes)

In general, high pitches resonate better in a small space. Think about making sound by blowing across the top of a bottle filled with water; the less space, or air in the bottle, the higher the note that is produced. Joan Melton has pointed out that this principle can be applied to the shape of the body when doing pitch work: small, scrunched-up poses seem to encourage high notes, while stretched, expansive poses seem to make it easy to find low notes. This exercise builds on her work. As with all the pitch exercises, it's important to do some warm-up work first. You will need to engage with abdominal support in the exercise and avoid straining or pushing to reach the high or low pitches.

1. Start in prayer pose, and then bring your arms in so that your forehead is resting on your fists.

   Think of a newborn kitten and, engaging the abdominal muscles of support, make a few little mewling 'hmmm's as high in your pitch range as you comfortably can.

   Next, open the little 'hmmm's into very small, very light 'meow's.

   Move from the 'meow's into 'reow's, opening your mouth wide as you do and imagining the sound travelling straight out the top of your head into the floor.

   Play with this light, newborn-kitten, whimpering sound for a minute or so.

2. Come up onto your hands and knees. Allow your back to settle into its natural curves, neither slumped nor arched. Keep your head in line with your spine – neither lifted nor hanging.

   Imagine now that the helpless newborn has grown into a playful kitten.

   Engaging the abdominal muscles of support, make a few more energetic 'hmmm's, still high in your pitch range, but focused less on the top of the head and more in the forehead and behind the nose.

   Open the 'hmmm's into 'meow's and 'reow's. Play with all the possibilities of this young kitten persona.

3. Still on your hands and knees, widen your stance a bit and imagine the kitten turning into a mischievous young cat.

   Lift your head up just enough to make eye contact with the other cats. Explore the possibilities of communication through young-cat sounds – flirtations, idle conversation, threats. Try out some 'meow's and 'reow's in the middle of your range.

4. Next, sit back on your haunches with your arms in front of you. You are now the mature, King (or Queen) of the House cat. Try out some 'meow's and 'reow's lower in your range. See how little energy you can expend and still command the most respect with your meowing.

   Rise up off your haunches so you are kneeling. Open your arms to your side, with the palms facing forwards. Tilt your nose up about 30 degrees, thinking length through the back of the neck as you do so. Let your jaw drop open. Imagine a wide, open pipe running from your lips to your pelvis. Yawn to re-enforce that sense of space.

137

Picture an old lion. He's the most powerful animal in the room, but can't be bothered to make a lot of noise about it. Engaging the abdominal support muscles, release an easy 'raaahhhr'. Try another one a bit lower in your pitch range. Play with this deep, grumbling sound for a minute or so.

Get into a roll-down position.

On a 'meow', start at the top of your pitch range and, as you roll up, glide down to the bottom of your pitch range.

Roll down, moving from the bottom of your range to the top on a 'oweem'.

Sirening (3–4 minutes)

Teaching tip

Sirening is, in general, a great warm-up tool for the whole of the pitch range.

Stand in a comfortable, aligned position.

Allow your jaw to release and your lips to hang slightly open.

Lift the back of your tongue up against your soft palate, and let the front of your tongue relax on the floor of your mouth.

Starting somewhere in the middle of your pitch range, make a gentle siren sound on a long 'Ng' for 10–15 seconds.

Now, make a siren starting a couple of notes (or so) higher for 10–15 seconds, then a couple of notes higher than that, and so on until you are sirening at the highest note you can easily make.

Put your hand on your lower abdomen and notice how those muscles give a little pulse of support with each pulse of the siren.

Next, come down, two (or so) notes at a time until you are sirening on the lowest note you comfortably can.

Make one, continuous siren on 'Ng' from the top of your range through to the bottom.

Make one, continuous siren on 'Ng' from the bottom of your range through to the top.

Keep a hand on your abdomen and keep engaging support from there.

Starting back down at the bottom of your range, siren up about three notes, and then open your mouth to create a 'Ngahhh'. Sustaining the note this way will feel a bit like singing.

Siren up another three or so notes from there, and then open onto a 'Ngahhh' again. Repeat to the top of your range.

Open Eagle (3-4 minutes per partner)

> **Teaching tip**
>
> This exercise is particularly useful for opening up the lower part of the range.

If you have ever had trouble with dislocating your shoulders, you should skip this exercise.

Grab a partner who is somewhere in the neighbourhood of your height.

Partner A, stand in front of partner B. Partner A should have a fairly narrow stance and B a fairly wide one.

Partner B, take A's wrists in your hands, and gently pull A's hands behind his/her back.

A, slowly lean forwards, giving a third to a half of your weight to B. Let your chest open up, allowing your shoulder blades to be drawn together.

B, you may want to bend your knees or put one foot forwards and lean slightly back to help balance A's weight.

A, you should feel a stretch across your upper chest. Tilt your nose up about 30 degrees, thinking length through the back of the neck as you do so. Let your jaw drop open. Imagine a wide, open pipe running from your lips to your pelvis. Yawn to re-enforce that sense of space.

A, release a 'Hiyiyiyi' from centre. Follow it with some Santa Claus-like 'Ho ho ho's'.

'Ho ho ho' your way as far down your pitch range as you can.

On a medium-low note, release from centre a 'Get out of my way' a few times – don't allow the aggressiveness of the thought to drive your sense of vocal energy back up into your throat and face; let the energy from centre do your work for you.

Staying in the lower part of your range, and thinking great openness from the pelvis to the lips, release: 'Oh for a muse of fire that would ascend the brightest heaven of invention'.

When A is finished, B gently help him/her come back to standing.

A, on your own two feet, take a moment to reconnect to a sense of openness from the pelvis to the lips, and particularly across the upper chest.

Release some 'Ho ho ho's' quite low in your pitch range and then bring them up to the lower of your middle notes.

In those lower middle notes, speak 'O for a muse of fire ...' again.

Speak the text one more time, letting it settle wherever it wants in your pitch range and noting where you feel the focus of the vibrations in your body.

B stand in front of A and repeat the exercise.

More Baby Talk (3–4 minutes)

> **Teaching tip**
>
> This exercise is particularly useful for opening up the upper part of the range.

Stand in a comfortable, aligned position.

Briskly massage your neck, your face, and your whole head, including the top.

As you are massaging, gently hum fairly high in your pitch range.

After a minute or so of humming, open the hum onto some easy, 'humamamamah's'.

Finish the massaging, and allow the 'humamamamah's' to develop into proper, nonsensical baby talk.

Turn to someone near you and have a nonsense baby conversation.

Turn the nonsense into an actual conversation about what you had for breakfast this morning and the route you take into school or work, still using baby tones and intonations.

Let go of the sing-song baby intonations, but stay in that open place of your upper register and talk about what your favourite foods were as a child.

Still in the high, open voice, release the following: 'Oh for a muse of fire that would ascend the brightest heaven of invention'.

Repeat two or three times, allowing your voice to come down closer to its centre note each time.

Speak it one final time, letting it settle wherever it wants to in your pitch range and noting where you feel the focus of the vibrations in your body.

The Sound Pool (10–15 minutes)

1. Get into a group of 10–12 people and stand in a circle, close enough together to hold hands comfortably.

   Let go of your neighbours' hands and close your eyes. It isn't essential to keep your eyes shut for this exercise; if it makes you feel uncomfortable, you can have them slightly open and unfocused. But the exercise is about listening and giving/receiving sound with awareness, so having your eyes shut (or open and unfocused) will help you find that awareness without being distracted by the others in the group.

Imagine that in the middle of the circle there is a pool – not of water, but of sound vibrations. You can receive vibration from the pool with your in-breath and give back to it with your voice. Your responsibility as a group is to fill the pool with vibrations.

Allow your breath to deepen, and then start with some easy and sustained humming so that you establish a group sound that is centred, supported and resonant. Then begin to improvise with different vowel sounds, pitches and pitch glides.

You don't have to be making the same sound as everyone else, but don't try to be deliberately awkward or discordant. The exercise is about an experience of group resonance rather than individual sound. If you can stay aware of and connected to the group sound, you can improvise quite freely within it. Listen and receive from the pool as you breathe in; give voice to the pool as you breathe out.

On the instructor's cue the sound will eventually fade away.

Discuss the experience with the rest of the group. What did you feel, hear or experience?

2. You are now going to repeat the exercise, but this time each member of the group will have the opportunity to take a turn 'bathing' in the pool.

Repeat the exercise up to the point where the group is improvising with vowels and pitches. Then, on the instructor's cue, take it in turns to step into the pool and listen to and feel the vibrations. There's no need to carry on vocalising when you are in the pool; just be silent and receptive. After a short while, step out of the pool and start sounding again. Continue until everyone in your group has had a turn. Then let the sound fade away.

Discuss the exercise with the rest of the group. What did you feel, hear or experience? Did it make a difference being in the pool? What does the exercise teach you about range and resonance?

Teaching tip

This exercise works best with a group of 10–12 students; it can work perfectly well with 8 or 14, however. If you have a larger group in a big enough space, you can break it into a number of smaller groups spread around the room.

In leading the exercise with just a single group, we have found it useful to be part of the group so that students don't become self-conscious about being listened to. This is not an issue when there is more than one group working at the same time. In this case, you need to stay outside the groups in order to monitor overall engagement.

One of the tricks in this exercise is to let the first phase of the sound pool continue long enough to fully develop without going on so long that everyone becomes bored and disengages. There will probably be a first lull, when it seems that the sound is becoming same-y. It's worth pushing past this point to find what lies beyond the students' first impulses. This may lead to a bit of a crescendo, before the sound starts to die down again. When it starts to die down is a good time to murmur, 'Let's bring it down now,' and let it come to a natural fade. You can then introduce the second phase of the exercise, which has its own in-built timing.

Sound Paintings I (6–10 minutes)

Stand in a comfortable, aligned position with enough space around you to stretch in all directions without invading other people's space.

Think of the space around you as the inside of your personal sphere. Begin to stretch into this space with your arms, exploring all the physical dimensions of this sphere around you: above and below you; in front of and behind you; and out to either side.

As you stretch and move in your sphere, breathe out on a 'shhh' sound and fill the sphere with your breath. Think of your breath having an effect on the space around you.

Now stretch into your sphere with other parts of your body – your legs, your back, your head. Keep connected to your breath as you do so, but now breathe out on a 'ffff', filling the sphere with your sound.

Add vibration to your breath so that the sound becomes a 'vvv'. Imagine that, as well as the vibration, the sound has a colour – brown perhaps, or green. Imagine painting that sound on the sphere around you with your breath and body. Use different pitches and dynamics of sound. Use different physical gestures – sweeping movements, dabbing movements, delicate movements. Think of the sound having an effect on the space around you.

Change to an 'oooo' sound and paint its colour on your sphere. Is it a blue colour, or maybe a red? What shade of that colour is it? Be specific in your intention and in your gesture.

Once you've really engaged your imagination, experiment with other vowels and consonants. What colours do you associate with them? How do they make you want to move? What visual images come to mind?

Paint your sphere as if it were a canvas – perhaps it's a landscape or an interior, or it's an abstract. Don't be general; have a specific effect on the space around you. Use different pitches and dynamics of sound. Use different physical gestures. Take some time to enjoy being an artist.

On the instructor's cue, bring your painting to a completion.

Imagine hanging it up on the wall in front of you, so that you can stand back and look at it in your mind's eye. Perhaps you'd like to sign it. Perhaps you'd like to give it a title.

Leave it hanging there while you discuss the experience with the rest of the group.

What did you feel, hear or experience in your voice? How did introducing the ideas of colours change your voice use? What does the exercise teach you about range and resonance?

Teaching tip

This is another exercise which you may need to engage in at the same time as the students. If you model the work with them, they will feel less self-conscious.

You may also need to be patient and allow time for the imaginative connection to establish itself. Some groups 'get' the idea immediately; others need a bit of encouragement. When you feel that they have had sufficient time to 'create' their pictures, tell them that they have another minute to finish their paintings, and then bring it to a close.

Sound Paintings II (10–15 minutes)

Teaching tip

We learned this exercise from Jules Craig, who remembers learning it at Rose Bruford College from Lynn Darnley. For it, you will need to get decent quality reproductions of two paintings. In general, abstract paintings work best – such as Paul Klee's works or some of JMW Turner's more impressionistic seascapes. Choose paintings that have several dominant colours and some distinctive shapes. The reproductions should be at least six by eight inches. If you can't find any big enough in an art book, enlarge using a colour copier. Very large posters, on the other hand, may be unwieldy.

Divide the class into two groups.

Group A, sit in a circle, facing each other, with just enough room for someone to sit in the middle of the circle. Be patient for a few minutes.

To one side, group B gather around one of the paintings.

Take a good look at the painting and think about one part of it – a line, a shape, a patch of colour – that appeals to you.

On the instructor's three-count, everyone place your finger on the part of the painting you've chosen. If there is more than one person on any part, redistribute so that each person has a different detail. You are going to represent that part of the painting with your voice but without language.

Group A, close your eyes. Your job is to listen with an open mind and be aware of what pictures pop into your mind's eye or what feelings are evoked during the exercise.

Group B, stand surrounding group A, with the instructor sitting in the middle of A's circle, holding the picture so you all can see it.

B's, when your instructor points to you individually, come in with some kind of non-verbal sound inspired by your part of the painting. If the first thing that comes out of your mouth doesn't feel quite right, feel free to experiment until you find something that seems to capture the essence of your colour and shape. Keep looking at it throughout to make sure that you are continually responding to it in the moment rather than just settling into a mechanical drone of sound.

As more and more B's join in, be mindful of listening to each other and working together to capture not only each individual part, but also the overall feeling of the painting.

Once all of the B's have joined in, your instructor may conduct you – making hand signs to bring out some sounds for a little while or to move others into the background.

After a minute or so, your instructor will signal you one by one to drop out until you are all silent.

Group A, open your eyes. Discuss what images and feelings were evoked over the course of the exercise. There are no wrong answers – the point of the exercise is not to guess what the picture is, but to explore the relationship between sound and images.

Finally, the instructor will show the picture to group A.

Swap groups so that B sits in a circle and A creates a new sound picture with the other painting.

Sound Stories (20–30 minutes for the entire sequence)

> **Teaching tip**
>
> The following sequence is good for exploring the creative possibilities of vocal sound. Any number of the steps could also be used together or on their own as a warm-up to an improvisation session. However, it's easy for students to get excited by their imagination and so lose touch with a centred and supported breath. The first two steps are, therefore, designed to help integrate breath and imagination. An occasional reminder thereafter to stay connected to breath and open the throat should keep them on track. Again, the exercise works best with groups of 10–12 students.

1. Get into a group, and sit or stand in a loose circle. Your task is simply to pass your breath around the circle. To do this, person A begins by breathing in and then, looking at person B on the left, breathes out easily. Person B 'receives' the breath by looking at A in a relaxed and open way. B then breathes in and passes the breath to C on his/her left, and so on round the circle.

2. Repeat the exercise in the opposite direction, but as you do so, instead of simply breathing out, use your breath to make an expressive sound: it might be a sigh, or a 'shhh' sound, a whistle, or a moan. Person B 'receives' the sound by repeating it after A as exactly as possible. B then breathes in and passes a different sound to C, and so on round the circle. Pass the sound a couple of times around the circle.

3. Now you are going to try your hand at a bit of 'sound storytelling'. Decide on the kind of story you are going to tell – a ghost story or a fairy story is a good idea to begin with. Instead of telling the story with words, you are going to create the soundtrack of this story with your voices. Whoever begins (A), start with the opening of the story – perhaps it is the sound of wind blowing in the trees – and pass this to the person on your left (B). As in the previous step, B repeats this sound as exactly as possible before adding his/her sound to the story – maybe a bird whistling in the trees – and passes it on. C copies B's sound and creates his/her own – say, a creaking door – and passes it on. And so on round the circle until you reach a conclusion to your story.

   If you have time in the session, you could repeat this step with another type of story.

4. We'll come back to storytelling in a moment, but this time person A, start by creating some kind of repeatable motion pattern with your hands. Avoid things that make

sounds, such as clapping or snapping fingers. Once you've established a pattern, find a vocal sound to go along with it.

When you have the movement and the sound, pass them to the person on your right – letting him/her copy you until you feel that s/he really has them down exactly, and then stopping and letting him/her take over.

The person who has 'received' the movement and the sound will then transform them by extending them, shrinking them, letting them grow into something new. When you are satisfied with your new movement and sound, pass them to the person on your right.

Let the movement/sound go around the circle at least twice.

5. We are now ready to combine steps three and four to tell a story in both sound and movement.

Let it be the story of a day in the life of a strange shape-changing creature. Whoever begins (A), start with the opening of the story – perhaps the sound and movement of the creature asleep – and pass it to the person on your left (B).

B repeats both the sound and the movement as exactly as possible before transforming them into the next event in the story – maybe it's the creature waking up – and passes it on.

C copies B's sound and movement and creates his/her own – the creature brushing its teeth – and passes it on. And so on round the circle until you reach a conclusion to your story.

Discuss the experience with the rest of the group. What does the exercise teach you about range and resonance?

Balancing the Sound

Much of this work is about finding the balance between nasal and oral resonance that will give your voice the energy and brightness to fill large spaces without your having to think about 'talking louder'. The process of achieving this mix is different for everyone. In general, many Americans err on the side of too much nasal resonance, while many British people can have trouble finding enough. Exploring new balances of resonance may feel and/or sound strange to you at first, but once you've learned to join the nasal and the oral, you'll be able to feel a fullness and power in your voice that you'll want to cultivate.

🔊 Nasal into Oral (5–10 minutes)

Some elements of this exercise have their origins in the work of Kristin Linklater.

1. Stand in a comfortable, aligned position.

    Allow your jaw to release and your lips to hang slightly open.

    Place the front of your tongue against the back of your bottom teeth and let it rest gently there.

    On a note somewhere in the middle of your pitch range, make a siren sound on a 'NnnnNnnnNnnn' for 10–15 seconds.

    Massaging the sides of your nose and the sinuses alongside them, turn the 'NnnnNnnn' siren into a straight 'nnnnn' drone.

2. Finish the massage, and open the 'nnnnn' onto the nastiest 'nyah' that you can, wrinkling your nose as you do.

    As well as wrinkling your nose, wag your bottom a bit too, to keep everything loose, and try a really mean, taunting, little-kid 'nyah nyah nyah nyah nyah'. The sound should be strong, shrill and, frankly, not very pretty.

    Moving from 'nyah', try a 'neee' and then a 'meee'. Use the same, taunting tune on a 'meee meee meee meee meee'.

3. Now imagine that you have a Halloween witch's claws for hands (who knows why it helps, but it does) and screw your face up into an ugly witch's mask.

    Thinking support from centre and openness in the throat and back of the neck, try a witch's cackle on 'me hee hee hee hee'. If it's not quite clicking, you can try one of the suggestions in the *Teaching tip*.

    If at any point you feel strain in your throat, stop, shake out, yawn a couple of times and then return to the exercise, thinking of keeping the throat open and soft, placing the effort in your abdominal muscles, and focusing the vibrations squarely in your nose.

    In your strong and brassy (and probably not very pleasant) witch's voice, try on a few witch's phrases, such as 'Toil, toil, boil and bubble!'

4. Having fully explored the witch voice, return to a simple 'meeee', massaging your nose and sinuses and focusing the sound there.

    Sustaining the 'meeee', move your fingers from the sides of your nose out across the top of your cheekbones. When you get to the area just under the middle of your eyes, switch to a quick 'may', flicking your fingers away from your face as you do. Imagine that the sound is shooting like lasers from under your eyes – very focused and very powerful.

Move between the 'meeee' and the 'may' a few times.

Finally, move from a 'meee' to a 'may', and hold it. Then, slowly open you arms out until they are held fully out to the sides and change to a 'maaaah'. Imagine your entire body opening around the sound.

Repeat two or three times.

Pick a spot across the room, and use your wide, open 'maaah' voice to send the following to that spot: 'O for a muse of fire that would ascend the brightest heaven of invention. A kingdom for a stage, princes to act, and monarchs to behold the swelling scene!'

5. To check that you have moved sufficiently from nasal placement to oral placement as you've opened from the 'may' to the 'maaah', say the following sentence in your 'maaah' voice: 'Each early girl and boy eats an apple every other day.'

Pinch your nose shut and say it again; the quality of your voice should be essentially unchanged. If your voice sounds muffled with your nose closed, think a big smile across the back of your mouth to lift the soft palate.

Teaching tip

This exercise is very useful for giving students an experience of both nasal and oral resonance, and of moving between them. In the exercise, it's well worth taking the time to listen to each student individually, particularly when doing the witch's laugh. This can be quite difficult for some students to find, and they may need some help. If the sound is somewhat weak, moving back and forth between the 'nya nya' and the 'mee hee hee' can help. Putting one foot in front of the other and leaning forwards with a finger outstretched, as if to bore a hole with the voice, can also work. If the student is producing a muffled sound, wrinkling the nose and thinking of lifting the soft palate off the tongue a bit will be useful.

Another point at which it's good to listen to the students individually is when they are plugging and unplugging their noses. The quality of sound should not change substantially at all except on the 'm', 'n', and 'ng' sounds. If it does, ask the student to try to smile at the back of the mouth to lift the soft palate.

Wall Work (10–12 minutes)

This exercise grew out of the work that Rebecca did with Nigel Rideout.

1. Find a bit of open wall that you can stand in front of.

   Stand facing the wall in a comfortable, aligned position. Your toes should be just a few inches away from it.

   Keeping your shoulders loose and low, bring your hands up to form a megaphone around your mouth. The outer edge of your hands should be touching or almost touching the wall.

   Find a supported 'meeee' that is strongly focused in your nose; then, move into a 'maaay' that is strongly focused under your eyes; finally, open the sound into a 'maaah' and imagine that the vibrations are forming a ball between your hands.

   Repeat a couple of times.

2. On your next time through the 'meeee, maaay, maaah' cycle, when you get to the 'maaah', slowly back away from the wall a foot or two, your hands still at your mouth. Imagine, however, that you are leaving the buzzy ball of 'maaah' vibrations at the wall.

   Check to make sure that you are not thrusting your head forwards – focus on the image that you are moving away from the sound rather than sending the sound forwards.

   It will take a fair amount of abdominal support to do this: if you feel that you lack power or are straining in your throat at all, take a moment to get in touch with your beach-ball breathing muscles and consciously focus your sense of effort there.

   If you feel that you are losing the connection with the wall, simply go back and start again.

   Repeat until you are able to back away three or four feet and still feel that the energy of your voice is staying at the wall and that you are not having to push or strain to keep it there.

3. Return to the wall, and establish the ball of vibration between your hands with the 'meeee, maaay, maaah'. Then, as you back away from the wall, move into chanting (i.e. intoning), 'Moth man makes many mighty moons'.

   Repeat the entire process on a higher note.

   Repeat on a note higher still.

   Return to your centre note.

   Repeat on a lower note.

   Repeat on a note lower still.

Return to your centre note.

Begin to chant and back away from the wall again, but this time switch into your speaking voice half-way through.

Repeat the process entirely in your speaking voice.

Try the exercise with some nursery rhymes – chanting first, then moving from chanting to speaking and finally using just your speaking voice.

4. Now, turn so that your back is to the wall.

Bend your knees a bit so that you can press your back against the wall. Your head should not quite touch the wall behind it.

Take a moment to make sure your thighs and the wall are doing the work of holding you up so that your lower belly can release.

Open your arms against the wall at the level of your mid-chest.

Pick a point across the room from you. Go through the 'meeee, maaay, maaah' sequence once, thinking of placing the ball of vibration at that point. You will not have your hands at your face to help you focus the sound, so you will have to engage your imagination particularly strongly.

5. Move on to chanting, 'meeee, maaay, moth man makes many mighty moons', still placing the energy of the sound at that particular point across the room.

Let a breath drop in and switch to speaking 'meeee, maaay, moth man makes many mighty moons', concentrating on directing the energy of the sound to that point across the room.

6. Stop and shake out.

Check that your jaw and tongue are loose.

Consciously allow your ribs, abdomen and pelvis to open to a full in-breath, and then hum a bit while engaging your muscles of support.

Return to your position with your back against the wall.

Repeat the above step with a nursery rhyme. Pick a person to be the focus of your sound, rather than a point in the room.

Teaching tip

Wall work is wonderful for finding and developing forward resonance. Make sure that students stand up straight when they initially position themselves against the wall – i.e., make sure that their bottoms are not sticking out and they are not dropping their heads or thrusting them forwards. Make sure, as well, that they keep their shoulders loose and low as they raise their hands up to their mouths. As the students are working, if you see any shoulders starting to creep up, you can gently place your hands on them as a reminder to keep them soft. It can also be helpful to rub students' backs between the shoulder blades to remind them to keep this area open to vibration. We've divided the exercise into steps; if students are becoming physically rigid, have them step away from the wall and shake out between steps.

Slug Tongue (3–4 minutes)

Stand in a comfortable, aligned position.

Give your jaw muscles a bit of a massage, and then let the jaw hang comfortably open.

Allow your tongue to slowly creep forwards – think of it as a slug or oozing goo – until it is resting on your bottom lip, the tip just sticking out of your mouth. It should be soft and fat.

Leaving your jaw and the front of your tongue where they are, try to speak the nursery rhyme 'Jack and Jill'.

Because only the back of your tongue and soft palate can move, you will not be able to form many of the sounds in the rhyme, particularly the consonants – don't worry about this; just give voice to the tune of the rhyme and to as many of the vowel sounds as you can.

If you feel that your jaw wants to 'help' by moving up and down, gently place the thumb and forefinger of one hand to either side of your chin to encourage it to stay still and open.

If you feel that your tongue wants to pull back into your mouth, gently hold the tip with the thumb and forefinger of one hand to remind it to stay put.

Note where the energy of your voice seems to be focused. It will probably be at the front of your mouth, just behind your upper teeth.

Go through the rhyme again, noticing how the muscles of breath support engage to help power the sound.

Repeat the rhyme as you let your tongue slowly creep back into your mouth. As the tongue moves back and starts to become involved in articulating the sounds of the words, imagine the focus of the sound staying forwards, just behind the top teeth. The jaw may start to move a bit, but should stay mostly released.

Speak the rhyme again, thinking not only of the focus of the sound staying forwards, but also of the muscles of support engaging.

Teaching tip

This is a great 'quick fix' exercise. It encourages a release of tension in the tongue and jaw and brings the sound forwards in the mouth. It can also help to enliven articulation, and so is useful to apply to any piece of text a student is working on.

Soundball (5–10 minutes)

As a group, form as large a circle as the room will allow.

The first person, A, begin with a simple hum. Hold your hands cupped in front of your mouth, and imagine the hum forming a ball of vibration between them.

Keeping your hands in front of your mouth, begin to move them – in and out, up and down, wiggling the fingers, anything – and allow the movement of the hands to shape the ball of sound. Maybe it will stay a hum but get very nasal or very low in pitch. Maybe it will open up into a light, high 'ahyahyah' or become a bright, brassy 'wahwahwah'. Anything goes; just think of keeping the vibrations focused in your hands.

Once you have found a shape for your vibrations, use your arm to 'throw' the sound to someone across the circle (i.e. make the physical gesture of throwing), and allow your voice to follow across the space.

That person will 'catch' the sound by repeating it, hold it in a ball between his/her hands for a moment, and then move the hands, which will change the shape of the sound – and so forth.

Repeat until everyone in the circle has had a chance to throw at least two or three sounds.

Teaching tip

This is another exercise which is good for exploring the creative possibilities of vocal sound. However, as with the Sound Stories exercises, it's easy for students to get carried away by their imaginations and so lose touch with a centred and supported breath. An occasional reminder to stay connected to their breath and open the throat will help to keep them on track.

Resonating Text

A word on resonating text: it is not uncommon for students to do a long session on resonance in which they employ a glorious range of full, interesting sounds, and then to come on to text and return to a narrow repertoire of pinched, muffled resonances. While it is important to make oneself understood through language, the power of pure sound to communicate should not be overlooked. The group exercise in this section is designed to help you discover how sense and sound can work together, and how resonance can contribute to expression. While you may find readings of the text that might be exciting when transferred into a performance context, there is a danger in becoming too concerned about whether or not one would really 'do it this way'. An exploration of exaggerated pitch and resonance possibilities is a good way to open up the voice, which is a worthy end in itself. Increased flexibility and sensitivity to nuances of thought and sound will eventually bring life and colour to even the most naturalistic of performances.

Puck (15–20 minutes)

Teaching tip

You will need to prepare the text, preferably double-spaced and in a large, easy-to-read font, to hand out to the class. If you are aware of having any dyslexic students in your class, it may help them if you copy the text onto paper that is not white (green is often a good colour) and hand it out the session before you do the exercise. See *Suggested Texts* for the passage.

1. The group should stand in a circle.

   Read through the text, with each student taking one line.

   If there are more than 12 students, simply read through it again until each student has had the chance to speak a line. If there are fewer, continue to read through to get the sense of the full passage; in the exercise, however, each student should work with only the first line that he/she read.

   Take a seat and discuss the meaning of the text. In line 2, 'behowls' means 'to howl at'. In line 4, the ploughman (someone who pushes a plough) is worn out ('foredone') by his work. In line 5, the last embers ('wasted brands') of the evening fire are burning out. In lines 6–8, the owl makes the poor, wretched person ('the wretch that lies in woe') think of the cloth that dead people are wrapped in ('a shroud') and, by extension, death itself. In lines 10–11, the graves are opening ('gaping') wide to let out the spirits ('sprites') to haunt the graveyard.

   Take the line that you read, and read it out loud to yourself, drawing out the vowel sounds a bit. Note that we're working with the sounds here, not the letters: for example, the letter 'o' in 'now' makes an 'ow' and not an 'oh' sound. Pick three vowel sounds in the line that you think are particularly juicy or expressive: for example, in line 1, you might pick the 'ow' in 'now' over the short, non-descript 'uh' in 'the'.

Memorise those three sounds.

2. As a group, close your eyes and use the vowel sounds that you have picked to create the sounds of a haunted graveyard at midnight on Halloween.

You can work with one vowel for a while, or move back and forth between vowels frequently.

Challenge yourself to find as many possible variations in pitch, resonant placement, volume and duration in each vowel. For example, the 'ow' could be made quite quietly with a very tight, high-pitched nasal resonance in short little bursts, or it could be made quite loudly with a wide, back-of-the-mouth resonant focus low in the pitch range and sustained for a long time.

Listen to what is going on around you and try to contribute to a complete, varied sound-scape. For example if there are lots of low, moaning sounds, try a high squeak.

On the instructor's cue the sounds will eventually fade away.

3. In this step, you will create the sound-scape again, but using all the consonant and vowel sounds in your line in sequence. In effect, you will be speaking the line, but some of the sounds may be so distorted that the words are unrecognisable. Feel free to stop on any sound for a while and play with it before moving on to the next.

If you get to the end of your line before the instructor has cued the fade, start again at the beginning.

Keep your eyes open so you can read the line if necessary.

4. After the complete line sound-scape, stand up and find a comfortable, aligned stance.

In this step, you will go around the circle one at a time and each read your line, keeping in as many varied graveyard sounds as you can but stringing them together so that the words are recognisable. The focus, however, is very much on the sounds rather than the words.

Next, shift the focus from the sounds to the words, but let some of the graveyard sounds bubble to the surface from time to time – for example, a bit of a howl on an 'ow' sound or a screech on an 'ee'. Don't worry about whether or not you would actually 'do it this way'; look for how the sound can help communicate the meaning or the mood of the words.

5. Everybody shake out and run around the room.

Return to the circle, and without thinking too hard about anything but communicating with energy and specificity, go around the circle and speak your lines one at a time.

Take a seat and discuss the process and any discoveries you've made.

Teaching tip

As with the 'Sound Bath' exercise, one of the tricks in this exercise is to let the sound-scape continue long enough to fully develop without going on so long that everyone becomes bored and disengages. There will probably be a first lull, when it seems that all the sounds are becoming very same-y. It's worth pushing past this nadir to find what lies beyond the students' first impulses. This may lead to a bit of a crescendo. As with other imaginative work, students can easily lose touch with centre and support; a specific reminder to stay connected to their breathing may be necessary from time to time. It may also be useful for you to contribute some unexpected sounds along the way to prompt the students to dig a bit deeper. After the second or third natural build, whisper, 'Let's bring it down now,' and let it come to a natural fade.

When the group begins to integrate the graveyard vowels into the text, there can be a tendency for students to get stuck in one kind of sound – e.g. everyone starts using 'spooky ghost' voices or 'creaky' voices. Encourage the students to try something different with each of the vowels.

Individual Work

Teaching tip

The discoveries made in group work can next be brought to bear in individual work. We have made some suggestions for texts at the end of the chapter, and advise that each student should memorise one – or in the case of longer poems, a stanza or two. If you would like to use other texts, look for poems or passages that are rich in imagistic detail and have a lushness of sound and expression. Each session of text work should begin with a good general warm-up, emphasising freeing the channel and finding the buzz. Let each student simply speak his/her piece, and then choose from the Individual Work exercises or adapt other resonance exercises to suit the student's needs.

Each of these exercises will take between 5 and 10 minutes.

I. Stand in a comfortable, aligned position in the corner of the room, facing the wall. Have a partner stand behind you and massage your back. Begin humming and focus on filling the corner with the vibrations of your voice.

Open the hum onto a 'mmaaaa'. Your partner should now place his/her hands in the middle of your back; you should focus on filling his/her hands with your vibrations. After a couple of breath-cycles, move onto chanting the first line of your text. On the second line, move from chanting to speaking.

As you continue speaking the text, your partner should move his/her hands to a different place on your back or neck with each new line, and you should think of allowing your sense of vibration to move into that area.

When you have finished the piece, turn from the wall. Your partner should place his/her hands on your back again.

Speak the text again, still focusing on sending the vibration back into your partner's hands. This should encourage a fullness of resonance through your pitch range as you speak.

II. Lie on the floor in semi-supine and chant your text. With each line, switch to a different note and move your hand to the area of your body where you feel the strongest sense of secondary resonance.

Roll over into prayer pose. Chant the first half of your text and then move into your speaking voice for the second half, imagining the vibrations pouring out of your body and pooling onto the floor beneath you.

Bring yourself to standing and give your temples and the muscles that run along the side of your jaw a good massage. Leave the jaw hanging open.

Allow your tongue to slowly creep forward – think of it as a slug or oozing goo – until it is resting on your bottom lip, the tip just sticking out of your mouth. It should be soft and fat.

Leaving your jaw and the front of your tongue where they are, try to speak the first half of your text. It won't make much sense, which is just fine.

For the second half of the text, allow your tongue to slide back into your mouth, but leave the focus of your voice forwards – imagine a small ball of energy floating just in front of your lips.

III. Pick a particularly vivid image or sequence of images from your text.

Stand in a comfortable, aligned position five or six feet in front of a big, blank section of wall.

Warm up with a few easy hums and ha's, and then use your voice to 'paint' the image on the wall, using only sounds, no words. Feel free to move around as you look for ways to vocally express the precise colours, shapes, textures and moods of the images in detail.

Next, 'paint' the images on the wall using the sounds from the words of the text. The words themselves will probably be very distorted as you draw out, abbreviate or repeat different sounds as you see fit. Do be mindful of staying connected to a supported breath and keeping the sense of effort out of your throat as you work.

Next, use your hand to 'paint' the images as you speak through the section of the text you are working with again. Let the words take intelligible form this time, but try too to let your voice move with your hand.

Finally, turn around and simply speak the text, letting the movement and colours you've discovered inform your voice.

IV. Go through your text with a pencil and circle all the vowel sounds, with the exception of short sounds in short words (e.g. the 'uh' in 'the' or 'of').

Find a partner and stand in a comfortable, aligned position about four feet in front of them.

Try to communicate the thoughts and images of your text to this partner by speaking only the vowels. You may draw them out, repeat them, separate them from each other, run them together, and move through your pitch range as you see fit.

Finally, speak the entire text to your partner, focusing on communicating with the words but allowing the vowel sounds to be part of the expression of the thoughts and images.

V. Find a partner.

As you speak your text, your partner will move their hand up and down (not too suddenly or violently). You must follow the movements of your partner's hand with your body and your voice – moving up when the hand goes up and down when the hand goes down, or maintaining a constant pitch and physical posture when the hand is still.

Next, work on your own. Move your own hand and follow it with your voice and body as you speak the text.

Finally, simply stand and speak the text, allowing your voice to move freely up and down with the images and rhythms of the text.

VI. Stand in a comfortable, aligned position.

Have a partner stand behind you and hold your neck to remind you that you don't need to push or press from there.

Hold your hands cupped in front of your mouth and chant just the first word of your text a couple of times, feeling a ball of vibration forming between your hands.

When you feel that the energy of your voice is strong in your hands, make the motion of easily throwing the vibrations to someone across the room as you speak the word.

Repeat with each word in the first line of your text.

If you feel any tightening or jerking in your jaw or any strain in your throat, chant the word using beach-ball breathing or think of blowing out a couple of birthday candles with it to get back in touch with your breath support. Then, return to the throwing.

When you have worked your way through the line, chant the first word into your hands again a couple of times, and then throw the first phrase (3-5 words). Chant the first word of the next phrase and then throw that phrase. Continue through the piece.

Finally, stand across the room from the rest of the group. With each line, find someone new to talk to and move your hand in an arc towards that person as you speak (i.e. start with your hand at your shoulder and move it forwards and slightly up through the length of the line.)

VII.Stand in a comfortable, aligned position.

Chant the first couple of lines of your text to get warmed up.

After those first two lines, the instructor will call out a musical instrument. With your body, mime playing the instrument, and with your voice look for the particular resonance of that instrument (e.g. something low and rumbling for a cello, bright and brash for a trumpet, etc.) as you speak the next two lines.

Your instructor will call out a different instrument every couple of lines until you finish the text.

As soon as you finish, speak the text again, letting your voice move through different resonances at will.

Follow-up

Reflective practice questions:

* Which exercises and images best help you release your jaw?
* Which exercises give you the greatest sense of space in the back of your mouth?
* In what area of your body do you most easily feel a sense of secondary resonance?
* Do you find that you have a tendency to favour either higher or lower pitches?
* What words or images would you use to describe your 'normal' voice?
* Were there any exercises in which you felt you were using a voice that was not 'your own'? If so, what words or images would you use to describe this 'other' voice or voices? How did producing this 'other' voice feel physically different from producing your 'normal' voice?
* In the *Balancing the Sound* exercises, when did you feel your voice had the most energy with the least amount of effort? Where was the effort focused in your body? Where did you feel the 'buzz'?
* Did you find that introducing language expanded or narrowed the resonances you were able to find in your voice? Why do you think you had this experience?
* In doing individual text work, what discoveries did you make about your voice? Did the resonance work lead to any discoveries about the text?

Exercises:

* As part of your brief morning warm-up, spend a minute or two chanting 'mah, may, mee, moh, moo' over and over on different pitches.
* Play with finding the place in your voice where you can get the strongest feeling of buzz in a variety of spaces. For example, chant and then speak some nursery rhymes in the shower, in a closet, in the kitchen, facing curtained windows in a small room, facing a blank wall in a large room, etc. and try to find where your voice feels the most energetic with the least amount of effort. If theatre spaces are available to you, try the same in them. Look for the most effective resonant placement from the lip of the stage, the back of the stage, facing stage right, stage left, sending your voice to the front row, the back of the house, etc.

Suggested texts

Puck:

'Now the hungry lion roars
And the wolf behowls the moon,
Whilst the heavy ploughman snores,
All with weary task foredone.
Now the wasted brands do glow
Whilst the screech-owl, screeching loud,
Puts the wretch that lies in woe
In remembrance of a shroud.
Now it is the time of night
That the graves all gaping wide,
Every one lets forth his sprite
In the churchway paths to glide'.

(From *A Midsummer Night's Dream* by William Shakespeare)

W H Auden	'Some say that love's a little boy'
Aphra Behn	'Song. Love Arm'd'
Lewis Carroll	'Jabberwocky'
e e cummings	'i thank You God for most this amazing'
Carol Ann Duffy	'Warming Her Pearls'
Langston Hughes	'The Weary Blues'
Gerard Manley Hopkins	'As Kingfishers Catch Fire'
Michael Ondaatje	'The Cinnamon Peeler'
Alice Oswald	'Wedding'
Sylvia Plath	'Blackberrying'
Christina Rossetti	'Goblin Market'
William Shakespeare	'Full fathom five' (Ariel's Song from *The Tempest*)
Wole Soyinka	'In the Small Hours'
Dylan Thomas	'Fern Hill'
W B Yeats	'He Wishes for the Cloths of Heaven'

Further reading

Houseman, Barbara, *Finding Your Voice*, Nick Hern Books, London, 2002. Chapter 5: Releasing the Sound: Freeing the Voice, pp. 138–152; and Chapters 6 and 7, pp. 162–192.

Kayes, Gillyanne, *Singing and the Actor* (Second edition), A&C Black, London, 2004. Chapter 5: Developing the three octave siren, pp. 45–57; and Chapter 8: Tuning the oral resonator, pp. 90–98.

Linklater, Kristin, *Freeing the Natural Voice* (Revised edition), Drama Book Publishers, New York, 2006. Chapters 4–10, pp. 87–197.

McCallion, Michael, *The Voice Book* (Revised edition), Faber and Faber Ltd, London, 1998. Part Three: Tuning, pp. 81–86 and pp. 93–117.

Rodenburg, Patsy, *The Actor Speaks*, Methuen, London, 1997. Stage Two: Extending the Voice into Resonance, Range and Speech, pp. 91–103.

Turner, J Clifford, *Voice and Speech in the Theatre* (Sixth edition, edited by Jane Boston), A&C Black, London, 2007. Chapter 3: The Tone, pp. 26–36 and pp. 47–52; and Chapter 4: The Note, pp. 53–65.

5 Articulation and Muscularity

Framework

Ultimately, all the voice work that we undertake is done to facilitate communication. And while communication can happen in many different ways, speech is one of the most important tools we have with which to convey our thoughts and feelings to others. Good articulation gives clarity and precision to speech, making the act of verbal self-expression infinitely more affecting and effective. If a dancer's steps are vague or mistimed, or if a guitarist's fingering is fumbled or misplaced, their artistic interpretation of the choreography or music is severely limited. For actors, the lips, tongue and other articulators are the equivalent of the dancer's feet and the guitarist's fingers: if they do not move with accuracy and energy, they cannot be responsive to the artistic intention.

Articulation work is not the same thing as elocution, however. Making sounds with purpose and exactness is not necessarily the same thing as making sounds 'beautifully'. Nor is it the exclusive domain of people who may be thought of as 'well-spoken'. There are rap artists who slur their words together into an unintelligible blur, but there are also rap artists who fully form each word, even when going at an astonishing speed. There are classical actors who speak with tremendously effective ease and lucidity, but there are also classical actors who seem to chomp at each word to such an extent that their performances have neither flow nor spontaneity. The aim of good articulation is to form all the sounds needed to make each word easily understood with an economy of effort, not to attack them or push them or lavish too much attention on them. It is also to achieve a balance of sound. If vowels predominate, we get a wash of sound and feeling and can lose the sense and clarity. If consonants predominate, we can get a lot of energy and punch but without a sense of space and ease.

Achieving good articulation is, furthermore, not about changing your accent; it's possible in any accent. If you are an actor, you may have some specific habits that are common to the region where you grew up – for example, dropping 't' sounds at the ends of words, as many UK and US speakers do – which you might want to modify so that you can be better understood on stage; but, in most instances, you do not have to fundamentally change the way you speak to attain good articulation.

In some cases, there may be sounds that are more difficult for a person to pronounce clearly or 'correctly'. In general, the practising of individual sounds is done in speech rather than voice classes, so this book does not address the specific formation of each English sound, nor does it give extensive drills for each one. There are many excellent resources listed in the *Further Reading* section at the end of the chapter, and these describe in detail the most efficient way to form individual speech sounds. If a particular sound proves particularly difficult for you to make in a standard way ('s' and 'r' are commonly problematic), and you are seriously planning to make acting your career, it will be worth your while to find a personal speech tutor to help you with them.

What we do want to accomplish in this voice course is the releasing and toning of the muscles of articulation so that they can move precisely and freely. Those muscles involved in forming speech sounds are numerous. There are, for example, four different sets of muscles that make up the body of your tongue, and then another four sets of muscles that attach to your tongue and help to move it around. These muscles are also attached to the jaw, the soft palate, the wall of the pharynx and the bone at the top of your larynx (see Fig. 13 on the next page). Unnecessary tension or movement in the tongue when you are speaking, therefore, can affect the overall quality of your voice by pulling the soft palate down or raising the larynx up.

The soft palate itself functions as an articulator when we lower it to send the air out of the nasal passage in making the 'n', 'm' and 'ng' sounds. This is one of the simpler articulation movements – only four muscles are involved in lowering and raising the soft palate. There are, however, ten different sets of muscles that can be used to move your lips. Some are within the lips themselves, but some run up to your cheekbones and others go out to your

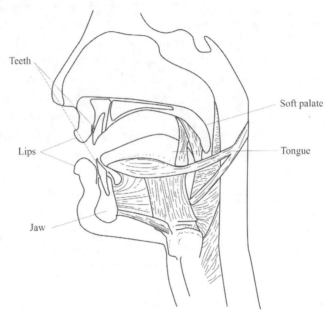

Fig. 13 The Articulators

cheeks and down to your chin (see Fig. 14). It takes great co-ordination for all these muscles of the tongue, the soft palate and the lips to come together and make sounds – the years that it takes young children to learn how to talk is a

witness to this. Even after we have left our toddler-hood well behind, we can still learn to use these muscles more efficiently, much as an athlete learns to perform common acts like running and jumping more effectively.

We've mentioned the tongue, the soft palate and the lips – there is one other active articulator of importance, and that is the jaw. The jaw, however, is tricky. While we often want the tongue and the lips to become livelier and more engaged, we usually want the jaw to become less so. The tongue and the lower lip are attached

Fig. 14 Lip Muscles

to the jaw, so when it moves, they move too. Sometimes, instead of moving the lip and the tongue on their own to make speech sounds, we just move the jaw up and let the lip and tongue go along for the ride. As an illustration, first allow your jaw to drop open about a finger's width. Leaving the jaw where it is, make a 'duh' sound by moving just the tip of your tongue. Now bring your tongue down so that the tip is behind the lower teeth. Leave the tongue where it is and make a 'duh' sound by moving your jaw up. It's rare to consistently make speech sounds exclusively with the jaw, but it is quite common to 'help' with the jaw. This 'help', however, actually serves to make the sounds less sharp and defined. It also narrows the space in your mouth, decreasing resonance – a lose/lose situation. The lips and the tongue, therefore, must learn to work independently of the jaw.

While we want to free the actions of the lips and the tongue from the jaw, we also want to connect them to a strongly supported breath. As with just about anything to do with speaking, articulation will flow most easily if the body is aligned and the channel from the lips to the pelvic bowl is released and open. Focusing the effort of speaking in the muscles of support at one end and the articulators at the other can help to keep that passage clear. Furthermore, the muscles of support and the articulators have a kind of symbiotic relationship with each other: commitment in one area can encourage commitment in the other. If you are having trouble at any point finding a good, strong engagement of your articulators, try working on your breath support for a little while. Conversely, if you feel that you are losing touch with a solid, supported breath, try working with some articulation exercises. Waking up one area can send a message to the brain that you are serious about the act of communication, which wakes up the other area. In its essence, good articulation is about this very commitment to communication. It's about focusing and specifying the strong need to make yourself understood.

Exploration

I. Bring your jaw up so that your back teeth are almost touching but there is still a bit of space between your lips. Keep your jaw held in this position and speak the alphabet, moving your lips and tongue as little as possible. Note how this affects your sense of your voice and your overall energy.

II. Speak the alphabet again, this time moving your jaw as much as you can – almost as if you were 'chewing' each sound. Note how this affects your sense of your voice and your overall energy.

III. Purse your lips tightly and then blow through the most powerful 'puh' sound you can.

Repeat, adding your voice to make a 'buh'.

Place your lips together as lightly as possible and blow through as little air as you can to make a tiny 'puh'.

Repeat, adding your voice to make a 'buh'.

Press the tip of your tongue as hard as you can up against the ridge behind your top teeth (the alveolar ridge), then blow through a strong 'tuh'.

Repeat, adding your voice to make a 'duh'.

Place the tip of the tongue so that it is just barely touching the alveolar ridge and blow through just enough air to make a small 'tuh'.

Repeat, adding your voice to make a 'duh'.

Push your soft palate down hard onto the back of the tongue and blow through a 'kuh'.

Repeat, adding your voice to make a 'guh'.

Let your soft palate rest on the back of your tongue and blow through just barely enough air to make a 'kuh'.

Repeat, adding your voice to make a 'guh'.

Note how both the very tense and the very lax articulations affect your sense of your voice and your overall energy.

Return to each of the sounds and play with the amount of effort you use to produce them. Look for an engagement that is energetic but not tense.

Exercises

Teaching tip

The exercises in this chapter are organised under three headings: *Toning the Articulators*; *Specifying the Sounds*; and *Articulating Text*. Work on *Toning the Articulators* can be introduced fairly early in a course of voice work. Frequent repetition of a repertoire of exercises over a long period of time is probably the most effective approach. It is also useful to work on these muscles in conjunction with breath work; as noted, effective breath support and effective articulation often go hand in hand. However, it is also worth noting that a focus on articulation work can distract students from breath support, release and alignment. It is vital, therefore, to keep reminding students to pay attention to their alignment, to keep released and to stay connected to a centred breath. Work on articulation in text can be introduced at any time, but is often most useful after students have become adept at connecting breath to the act of speaking, supporting long, energetic thoughts, and employing a full range of resonant sounds within language. Articulation work is a good way to segue between technical voice work and the specific communication of an idea that is the concern of text and acting work.

Toning the Articulators

The same principles apply here as in all the physical work we have done; the goal is to release tension so that the muscles can learn effective patterns of engagement. Many of the muscles involved in articulation are found in the vocal tract, and we've already done some release work on them in the previous chapter. In this chapter, we will continue that work while developing the ability of all the muscles involved in articulation to work independently and with precision. This will allow you to use the appropriate tool for the job. For example, if you can separate the action of the tip of your tongue from the action of the middle of your tongue, you will be able to make a 't' sound with less effort and more clarity – why use a shovel when a teaspoon will do?

Teaching tip

As with any muscles, it takes time and repetition of exercises for the articulators to learn a new pattern of usage. In any given voice session, you may want to do just a couple of exercises for each of them. Rotating through all the exercises will help to prevent boredom and give each muscle group a slightly different workout from day to day.

Jaw (about 1 minute each)

For all these exercises, stand or sit in a comfortable, aligned position. Any of the jaw exercises from the previous chapter are also good for finding release in this area.

🎧 I. Give the masseter muscles a gentle massage, allowing the space between your back molars to gradually increase as you do.

Hold your hands in front of you and extend your thumbs. Place your hands on the sides of your face with your thumbs hooking under your ears. Your jawbone should be nestled in the centre of your palms.

Slowly draw your hands down the length of your jaw. When you get to the chin, let your hands slide forwards off your face, and make a small gesture of throwing away all the tension through your fingertips.

Repeat three or four times, adding a small sigh the last couple of times.

🎧 II. Place the tips of your fingers along the side of your jaw at the level of your lower gums, under the back molars and wisdom teeth.

Let the weight of your arms hang from your fingers and allow that weight to gradually draw your jaw open. Imagine that the jaw muscles are clay, slowly yielding beneath your fingers. Keep the shoulders soft and low.

When the jaw is open as far as it will comfortably go, take hold of either side of your chin with the thumb and forefinger of each hand and use your hands to gently and slowly open and close your jaw.

Soft Palate

Tone up the soft palate with the exercises from Chapter Four.

Tongue (about 1 minute each)

For all these exercises, stand or sit in a comfortable, aligned position and place one hand at the back of your neck and the other hand on the side of your jaw; this is to help ensure that you don't push with your neck and jaw but work the tongue in isolation.

I. Push the whole of your tongue straight out of your mouth and hold for a few seconds.
Reach for your nose with the tip of your tongue and hold for a few seconds.
Reach for your left ear and hold for a few seconds.
Reach for your chin and hold for a few seconds.

Reach for your right ear and hold for a few seconds.

Repeat this sequence several times, gradually building up speed.

Now, make a huge circle from the nose to the left ear to the chin to the right ear and then another in the opposite direction. Repeat several times.

Allow your tongue to slowly retract back into your mouth.

II. Imagine that each of your teeth is covered with a different flavour of ice cream. Use your tongue to taste each tooth one at a time, front, bottom and back.

Be particularly mindful of keeping the jaw as still as possible without locking it while the tongue moves.

III. Get a mirror to look at your tongue.

Stick your tongue out of your mouth about an inch.

Try to make it as thin and wide as possible.

Without retracting your tongue or sticking it out more than a further half an inch, try to make it as thick and narrow as possible.

Go back and forth between thin and thick several times.

IV. Imagine that you are a cat lapping milk with your tongue. Be particularly careful that the jaw and the back of the neck don't tighten or push forwards as you do this.

V. Imagine that you've been eating ice cream in a fancy restaurant, and now there's some of it on your upper lip.

Try to lick the ice cream away as discreetly as possible. See if you can move just the tip of your tongue along your upper lip while keeping the rest of it in your mouth.

Next, imagine ice cream on your bottom lip and try to lick it away with just the tip of your tongue.

Finally, move the tip all the way around your lips, keeping the body of the tongue in your mouth.

Lips (about 1 minute each)

For all these exercises, stand or sit in a comfortable, aligned position.

I. Massage your face. Start around your lips and then move up the sides of the nose, out across the cheeks and cheekbones, around the eyes, onto the temples and then up across the forehead.

Pull your face in as if you were making a fist with it – eyes scrunched closed, lips tightly pursed. Then, open your face out as wide as it will go – eyebrows up, mouth stretched open. Go back and forth a couple of times.

II. Make sure your hands are clean for this one. Hook your pinkies into the corners of your mouth and pull them out as far as they'll go. Move the pinkies around your lips, pulling them in all directions.

Take your fingers out of your mouth and blow through your lips, making a noise like a horse.

Add some voiced vibrations, making a shivering sound.

Continuing to blow through your lips, move from the bottom of your pitch range to the top and back.

III. Place one hand at the back of your neck and the thumb and forefinger of the other hand on the sides of your chin; this is to help ensure that you don't push with your neck and jaw but work the lips in isolation.

Lift just your top lip; thinking of sneering can help. Move it up and down six or seven times.

Try to lift just the left half of your upper lip and then just the right. Move back and forth between the two. This is something that you can get better at with practice.

Now lower just your bottom lip – thinking of a ventriloquist's dummy or of a little kid who is about to cry can help. Move it down and up six or seven times.

Try to pull down just the left half of your lower lip and then just the right. Move back and forth between the two.

IV. Keep one hand at the back of the neck and the other monitoring your jaw at the chin.

Push both lips straight out as if you were going to give someone a kiss. Open and close your lips as much as you can while keeping them stretched forwards. Don't let the jaw become involved.

Next, pull your lips in over your teeth.

Keeping your jaw more or less still, move your lips back and forth from pushed out to pulled in, six or seven times – ending with your lips out.

Leaving the top lip pushed out, pull just the bottom lip in.

Pull the top lip in as well.

Push out just the bottom lip, leaving the top in.

Push out the top lip as well.

Continue pulling in and pushing out each lip in isolation until you have gone through the cycle four or five times.

End by blowing out through your lips.

V. Keep one hand at the back of the neck and the other monitoring your jaw at the chin. Push your lips out and make an OO sound.

Now spread your lips and make an EE sound.

Move between these two sounds as accurately and agilely as you can.

Now, build up the following sequence of vowels, starting slowly and increasing the speed as you repeat the sequence six or seven times: OO–EE–OO–AY–OO–AH–OO–OH–OO–AW.

Note the following:

OO = the vowel sound in 'food'

OH = the vowel sound in 'hope'

AW = the vowel sound in 'awe'

AH = the first vowel sound in 'father'

AY = the vowel in 'say'

EE = the vowel in 'speak'

Specifying the Sounds

The focus in this section is not on mastering the ideal formation of every English speech sound. As mentioned, that is more commonly the domain of the speech class. Rather, the work here is designed to develop the articulators' capacity to move economically and precisely. Before beginning these exercises, it can be useful to revisit the Exploration exercise of using too little and too much effort to form sounds. In the exercises that follow, you will be looking for a happy medium – an engagement of the articulators that is energised but not forced. One indicator that they are working well is that they can move between sounds quickly. Speed, itself, however, is not the point; it's a neat trick to be able to rattle off text in record time, but unless you're doing a Gilbert and Sullivan patter song, you're never going to get paid for it. The goal is easy clarity; speed is just a tool to help you gauge your progress.

In this section, we recommend that you frequently monitor your jaw, to make sure it is not trying to do the work of the other articulators. Do this by placing the forefinger and thumb of one hand on either side of your chin. Ideally, your jaw should rest in a comfortably open position that will allow you to work your other articulators freely. It may feel that you have to stretch your tongue and lips more than you are used to in order to make certain sounds without closing the jaw. Give yourself some time to get used to the new sensations, and to become comfortable with the new movement patterns: with time and practice they will become second nature. Do note, though, that to cleanly make the sounds 's', 'sh', 'z', 'zh' (the sound in the middle of the word 'pleasure'), 'ch' (in 'church') and 'dg' (in 'judge'), the jaw may have to close a bit. The trick then is to learn to let it release again when it is not needed.

You may have found in exercises from the previous chapter that an easily released jaw also allows you to find fuller resonances. Because the movements of the articulators change the shape of the vocal tract, it is important to keep those movements free and specific so that they don't interfere with your resonance. For example, if your tongue root tenses and your soft palate drops every time you make an 'l' sound, the vowel that follows will have only a small space to resonate in. If you can isolate the action in the tip of the tongue, the resonance will stay open and full. You may find it useful to move back and forth between the *Working the Channel* and *Finding the Buzz* exercises from Chapter Four and the exercises here to develop a good relationship between articulation and resonance.

> **Teaching tip**
>
> It is helpful to do a bit of warming up with exercises from *Toning the Articulators* before moving into *Specifying the Sounds*. This section lists a number of sound and word combinations that are useful as drills, and then some tongue-twisters to practise crisp, engaged articulation. There are many resources for other tongue-twisters, and introducing new ones frequently can help to prevent boredom while also running the articulators through a wide range of sound combinations. You may want to occasionally have elimination rounds with a tongue-twister, in which each person in a circle has to speak it more quickly than the previous person and drops out if s/he makes a mistake. Or do tag-team tongue-twisters, with partners in pairs alternating lines in a race with other pairs. A little bit of fun encourages the lightness of touch that is a hallmark of good articulation.

The Basics

I. (2–3 minutes)

Stand or sit in a comfortable, aligned position.

Allow the jaw to drop open about a knuckle-width. Place the forefinger and thumb of one hand on either side of your chin to encourage your jaw to stay easily open. You may feel a little tug on the skin beneath your fingers, but the jawbone underneath should stay more or less still.

Breathe in, and then bring your lips together energetically (but not too forcefully), and release them energetically to make a voiceless 'puh'. Repeat four or five times in rapid succession.

With the same motion of the lips, add voicing to make a 'buh'. Repeat four or five times in rapid succession.

Leaving the jaw where it is, breathe in and lift the tip of your tongue up to make firm contact with your alveolar ridge (right behind the top teeth), and then release it vigorously to make a voiceless 'tuh'. Repeat four or five times in rapid succession.

With the same motion of the tongue, add voicing to make a 'duh'. Repeat four or five times in rapid succession.

Still leaving the jaw comfortably open, breathe in and bring the soft palate and the back of the tongue together with a firm contact, and then let them spring quickly apart to make a voiceless 'kuh'. Repeat four or five times in rapid succession.

With the same motion of the soft palate and tongue, add voicing to make a 'guh'. Repeat four or five times in rapid succession.

Now put these three motions together into a sequence. Start first with a slow, distinct 'puh tuh kuh'.

Keeping the jaw released and the motions distinct, gradually increase your speed in repeating 'puh tuh kuh' until you are going quite quickly indeed. Remember to keep your breath flowing and to stay released in the back of your neck. Place a hand there, if it helps.

Next, put the motions together in a slow, distinct 'kuh tuh puh'. Repeat seven or eight times, increasing speed.

Now, put the two patterns together: 'puh tuh kuh kuh tuh puh'. Slowly build up speed, keeping your jaw released.

Next, put the motions together in a slow, distinct 'buh duh guh'.

Keeping the jaw released and the motions distinct, gradually increase your speed in repeating 'buh duh guh' until you are going quite quickly indeed. Remember to keep your breath flowing and to stay released in the back of your neck.

Next, put the motions together in a slow, distinct 'guh duh buh'. Repeat seven or eight times, increasing speed.

Finally, put the two patterns together: 'buh duh guh guh duh buh'. Slowly build up speed, moving through your pitch range as you do so and keeping your jaw released.

II. (5–6 minutes)

Stand or sit in a comfortable, aligned position.

Allow the jaw to drop open about a knuckle-width. Place the forefinger and thumb of one hand on either side of your chin to encourage your jaw to stay easily open – although note that it may need to close a little when making 'ss' and 'zz'.

Go through the following sound combinations at a conversational speed, breathing as necessary and thinking of moving your articulators in a purposeful but not overly deliberate manner.

Make sure that you fully form each sound in the combinations. For example, on 'BAYLD' you may find that you have a tendency to stop just short of making a full 'L' sound, replacing it with a 'W' sound, or to make an incomplete 'D' sound. If you find that you have dropped or not quite completed a sound, go back and repeat the entire line two or three times, focusing on finishing that sound without over-stressing it.

Note the following:

OO = the vowel sound in 'food'

OH = the vowel sound in 'hope'

AW = the vowel sound in 'awe'

AH = the first vowel sound in 'father'

AY = the vowel in 'say'

EE = the vowel in 'speak'

LOOPT	LOHPT	LAWPT	LAHPT	LAYPT	LEEPT
LOOBD	LOHBD	LAWBD	LAHBD	LAYBD	LEEBD
GOOKT	GOHKT	GAWKT	GAHKT	GAYKT	GEEKT
GOOGD	GOHGD	GAWGD	GAHGD	GAYGD	GEEGD
BOOLT	BOHLT	BAWLT	BAHLT	BAYLT	BEELT
BOOLD	BOHLD	BAWLD	BAHLD	BAYLD	BEELD
MOOMD	MOHMD	MAWMD	MAHMD	MAYMD	MEEMD
ROOFT	ROHFT	RAWFT	RAHFT	RAYFT	REEFT
ROOVD	ROHVD	RAWVD	RAHVD	RAYVD	REEVD

TOOST	TOHST	TAWST	TAHST	TAYST	TEEST
TOOZD	TOHZD	TAWZD	TAHZD	TAYZD	TEEZD

Take a little break to give your jaw a massage, blow through your lips, massage under your chin and flap your tongue in and out. Continue with the following, making sure you pronounce those L sounds:

PROOLN	PROHLN	PRAWLN	PRAHLN	PRAYLN	PREELN
PROOLM	PROHLM	PRAWLM	PRAHLM	PRAYLM	PREELM
PROOLZ	PROHLZ	PRAWLZ	PRAHLZ	PRAYLZ	PREELZ
TROOPL	TROHPL	TRAWPL	TRAHPL	TRAYPL	TREEPL
TROOBL	TROHBL	TRAWBL	TRAHBL	TRAYBL	TREEBL
BROOTL	BROHTL	BRAWTL	BRAHTL	BRAYTL	BREETL
BROODL	BROHDL	BRAWDL	BRAHDL	BRAYDL	BREEDL
DROOKL	DROHKL	DRAWKL	DRAHKL	DRAYKL	DREEKL
DROOGL	DROHGL	DRAWGL	DRAHGL	DRAYGL	DREEGL
KROOFL	KROHFL	KRAWFL	KRAHFL	KRAYFL	KREEFL
KROOVL	KROHVL	KRAWVL	KRAHVL	KRAYVL	KREEVL
GROOSL	GROHSL	GRAWSL	GRAHSL	GRAYSL	GREESL
GROONL	GROHNL	GRAWNL	GRAHNL	GRAYNL	GREENL

Take a little break to give your jaw a massage, blow through your lips, massage under your chin and flap your tongue in and out. Continue with the following:

SPOOSTS	SPOHSTS	SPAWSTS	SPAHSTS	SPAYSTS	SPEESTS
SPOOFTS	SPOHFTS	SPAWFTS	SPAHFTS	SPAYFTS	SPEEFTS
SPOOVST	SPOHVST	SPAWVST	SPAHVST	SPAYVST	SPEEVST
SNOOKST	SNOHKST	SNAWKST	SNAHKST	SNAYKST	SNEEKST

(for the following, use the voiceless 'TH' sound in 'thin')

SNOOTTH	SNOHTTH	SNAWTTH	SNAHTTH	SNAYTTH	SNEETTH
SLOOTTHS	SLOHTTHS	SLAWTTHS	SLAHTTHS	SLAYTTHS	SLEETTHS
SLOOTHT	SLOHTHT	SLAWTHT	SLAHTHT	SLAYTHT	SLEETHT

(for the following, use the voiced 'TH' sound in 'this')

SLOOTHD	SLOHTHD	SLAWTHD	SLAHTHD	SLAYTHD	SLEETHD
SKOOTHZ	SKOHTHZ	SKAWTHZ	SKAHTHZ	SKAYTHZ	SKEETHZ

SKOOLVZ	SKOHLVZ	SKAWLVZ	SKAHLVZ	SKAYLVZ	SKEELVZ
STROONDL	STROHNDL	STRAWNDL	STRAHNDL	STRAYNDL	STREENDL
STROOMBL	STROHMBL	STRAWMBL	STRAHMBL	STRAYMBL	STREEMBL

III. (2–3 minutes)

Monitoring the jaw with your fingers, repeat each of the following phrases four times at a conversational pace, slightly exaggerating the specific movements that each combination of sounds requires:

Paper poppy

Lily lolly

Mommala poppala

Unique New York

Red leather yellow leather

Will you won't you (be sure on this one that you are really saying 'won't you', not 'won chew')

Go through the sequence again at a conversational pace. This time don't exaggerate the movements, but do notice them.

Repeat three or four times, increasing your speed each time.

Combinations (10–30 seconds per tongue-twister)

Repeat the following tongue-twisters seven or eight times each, gradually increasing your speed. You may want to slightly exaggerate the movement of the lips and tongue initially, and then relax into them:

Peggy Babcock

Toy boat

Three tree twigs

Find five fine friends.

The Leith police dismisseth us.

Rubber baby buggy bumper

Let little Nelly run

A cheep chick sleeps in cheap sheets

Strange strategic statistics

The sixth sheik's sixth sheep's sick

Do daily deeds diligently. Don't dilly dally

Two toads totally tired of trying to trot to Tewksbury

A regal rural ruler

Around the rough and rugged rock, the ragged rascal ran

One smart fellow, he felt smart. Two smart fellows, they felt smart. Three smart fellows, they all felt smart

A thin little fellow picked six thick thistle sticks

Can you imagine an imaginary menagerie manager managing an imaginary menagerie?

Articulating Text

While it is vital that the articulators become skilled at forming speech sounds, often the primary cause of unclear speech is unclear thought. If you have only a general sense of what it is you are trying to say or do with a line, an active tongue is not going to be able to make that line lucid. If your mind fails to grasp the importance of words or phrases, your lips will not be able to give them definition. It is common for actors to stumble over words that they don't understand, because it's hard to trick the articulators into strongly committing to something that the brain isn't familiar with. It's important to do your homework – to look up words you don't know and find the logic behind the phrasing of difficult thoughts. It's important too to build up your stamina – the ability to hold long, complicated thoughts in your mind without letting any of the details slip away. The text work that we've included in this chapter is not only intended to drill the mechanics of articulation, but also to encourage the mental discipline required to communicate with specificity and conviction. Ultimately, the highest quality voice work is done in conjunction with the highest quality thinking and acting.

Henry V (15–20 minutes)

Teaching tip

You will need to prepare the text – preferably double-spaced and in a large, easy-to-read font – to hand out to the class. If you are aware of having any dyslexic students in your class, it may help them if you copy the text onto paper that is not white and hand it out the session before you do the exercise. See *Suggested Texts* for the passage.

If you have already done the Puck exercise from the previous chapter, the group should catch on to this pretty quickly. As in that exercise, there may be a moment when everyone seems stuck making very similar sounds, at which point it is worth staying with the exercise a bit longer to see what direction it might take. After the second or third natural build, whisper, 'Let's bring it down now,' and let it come to a natural fade.

1. The group should stand in a circle.

   Read through the text with each student taking one line.

   If there are more than 14 students, simply read through it again until each student has had the chance to speak a line. If there are fewer, continue to read through to get the sense of the full passage, but in the exercise each student should work with only the first line that s/he read.

   Take a seat and discuss the meaning of the text. It is the Chorus's introduction to Act IV of Shakespeare's *Henry V*. At this point in the play, it is late the night before a major battle, and the English and French armies are camped out making their final preparations. In lines 1–3, the listener is invited to imagine ('entertain conjecture') a specific scene. In line 5, the sounds made by both armies are said to move between the camps 'stilly', or 'quietly' so that, in lines 6–7, the guards on either side ('fixed sentinels') can almost hear each other's whispers. In lines 8–9, the campfires on either side seem to be communicating, and through the pale ('paly') flames, each army ('battle') can see the darkened ('umbered') faces of the other. In lines 12–14, the armourers are doing their job, which is to use hammers and rivets to secure the armour on the knights – 'accomplishing', or finishing their preparation. This sound could fill the listener with dread of what's to come.

   Take the line that you read, and read it out loud to yourself, leaning into the consonant sounds a bit. Note that we're working with the sounds here, not the letters: for example, the letter 'c' in 'conjecture' makes a 'k' sound, not a 'see' sound.

   Pick three consonant sounds, or combinations of consonant sounds (such as the 'kt' in 'conjecture') in the line that you think might be particularly evocative of the scene that is being described.

   Memorise those three sounds.

2. As a group, you will now close your eyes and use the consonant sounds that you have picked to create the sound-scape of armies preparing for battle and of the battle itself. Think about the whispers and clangs that Shakespeare is describing.

Think too about the sounds that will come – the clink of sword on sword, the swish of arrows, the moans of the dying, the laboured breathing.

You can work with one consonant for a while or move back and forth between consonants frequently. Challenge yourself to find as many possible variations in each consonant. For example, the 'k' could be made lightly and frequently, like crickets chirping in the night; or it could be strongly exploded, like a sword hitting another sword. The quality of the sound will change too depending on whether the lips are spread or pursed. Play around and try to find as many qualities of sound with each consonant as you can.

Listen to what is going on around you and try to contribute to a complete, varied sound-scape.

On the instructor's cue the sound-scape will eventually fade away.

3. Now, in the next step, you will create the sound-scape with all the sounds in your line in sequence. In effect, you will be speaking the line, but some of the sounds may be so distorted that the line is unrecognisable. Feel free to stop on any sound for a while and play with it before moving on to the next. If you get to the end of your line before the instructor has cued the fade, start again at the beginning. Keep your eyes open so you can read the line.

4. After the complete line sound-scape, stand up and find a comfortable, aligned stance.

In this step, you will go around the circle one at a time and each read your line, keeping in as many varied army sounds as you can but stringing them together so that the words are recognisable. The focus, however, is very much on the sounds, rather than the words.

Next, shift the focus from the sounds to the words, but let some of the army sounds bubble to the surface from time to time – for example, a bit of an explosion on a 't' or a murmur on an 'm'. Don't worry about whether or not you would actually 'do it this way'; look for how the sound can help communicate the meaning or the mood of the words.

5. Everybody shake out and run around the room.

Return to the circle, and without thinking too hard about anything but communicating with energy and specificity, go around the circle and speak your lines one at a time.

Take a seat and discuss the process and any discoveries you've made.

Nephelidia (12–15 minutes)

> **Teaching tip**
>
> You will need to prepare the text – preferably double-spaced and in a large, easy-to-read font – to hand out to the class. If you are aware of having any dyslexic students in your class, it may help them if you copy the text onto paper that is not white and hand it out the session before you do the exercise. See *Suggested Texts* for the passage. If there are not enough groups to take all the lines, don't worry about completing the poem.

Divide into groups of two or three students.

Each group should take two lines of the text.

In your group, identify the three or four consonant sounds that seem to dominate your lines of text.

Identify what exactly you do with your articulators to make each of those sounds.

For each sound, create a large, total-body movement that echoes the movement of the articulators. For example, you may pull your body into a tight circle on a 'w' sound or bring your elbows to your knees and then pull them up and away on a 'k'.

Integrate the movements into the speaking of the lines.

Practise the lines a few times.

The groups should form a circle in the order that their lines appear and, one by one, share what they've done so far.

Go around the circle again, this time making your physical movements only half as big.

Go around the circle again; let your body be still but your articulators full of life and movement.

Go around the circle one last time, and don't think of anything but sharing the text with the other groups.

Take a seat and discuss the process and any discoveries you've made.

Lord Chancellor (5–6 minutes)

> **Teaching tip**
>
> You will need to prepare the text – preferably double-spaced and in a large, easy-to-read font – to hand out to the class. If you are aware of having any dyslexic students in your class, it may help them if you copy the text onto paper that is not white and hand it out the session before you do the exercise. See *Suggested Texts* for the passage.

Stand in a circle in a comfortable, aligned position.

As a group, read the entire piece aloud at a conversational pace (resist the temptation to speed up as you go). Focus only on making sense of what you're reading.

Go back to the beginning and read Section 1 at a slower pace, focusing on keeping your jaw as released as possible.

Speak Section 2 at more of a conversational pace again, focusing now on fully forming each sound with the articulators. This doesn't mean you have to exaggerate them – just use the muscles you need to make them clear and distinct.

Speak Section 3 at the same pace, shifting your focus to your breathing – engaging the muscles of support as you speak and allowing them to spring open on the in-breath, like a beach ball springing back into shape. Place a hand on your lower abdomen and a hand alongside the ribs if it helps you.

Speak Section 4 at a slightly quicker pace, focusing on engaging both the breathing muscles and the articulators in harmony with each other.

Speak Section 5, allowing it to become faster and faster as you go. Let your breath and articulators do whatever they need to keep you going.

Individual Work

> **Teaching tip**
>
> The discoveries made in group work can next be brought to bear in individual work. We have indicated some suggested texts at the end of the chapter and advise that each student should memorise one – or, in the case of longer poems, a stanza or two. If you would like to use other texts, look for poems or passages that feature strong sounds requiring a high degree of muscular commitment. Each session of text work should begin

with a good general warm-up, emphasising toning the articulators and specifying the sounds. Let each student simply speak his or her piece, and then choose from the *Individual Work* exercises or adapt other articulation exercises to suit the student's needs.

Each of these exercises will take 3–6 minutes.

I. Stand in a comfortable, aligned position.

Have a partner hold your neck to remind you not to push from there.

Do a couple of cycles of beach-ball breathing on 'ffff'.

Keeping one hand on the lower belly to encourage connection and support, whisper your text. This should be a true, not a stage, whisper – no voice should be involved, nor should the breath be forced or strained. With no voice energy involved, the focus of your impulse to communicate will be solely on your articulators.

When you come to the end of your text, go back and repeat it with voicing. Engage your articulators, however, as if you were still whispering. Notice the effect this has on your speech – does it feel more energised, or more present, or perhaps loud and domineering?

Finally, simply stand and speak the text.

II. Stand in a comfortable, aligned position. If you don't have your text memorised, have a partner hold it in front of you.

Hold your hands in front of you, one on top of the other.

Speak the first few lines of your text extremely slowly. As you do so, use your hands to re-create the movements inside your mouth. For example, on a 't' sound, the fingers of the bottom hand may rise up and flick against the fingers of the top hand. On a 'ng' sound, the heels of the top and bottom hands may join together.

Now let your hands drop. Close your eyes and speak those lines a bit more quickly than before, but still rather slowly. Focus your attention on the movement of the articulators.

Repeat these steps until your have worked your way through the entire text.

Finally, speak the text at a conversational speed, focusing on communicating with your audience while maintaining the awareness of your muscularity.

III. Stand in a comfortable, aligned position.

Place the thumb and forefinger of one hand on either side of your chin to encourage your jaw to stay loosely open as much as possible.

Have a partner set up two chairs in front you, about ten feet apart.

When your partner stands at the chair to your left, you will speak as slowly as you can. When your partner stands at the chair to your right, you will speak at quickly as you can.

When your partner stands in the middle of the space between the chairs, you will speak at a conversational pace.

You must speed up as s/he moves to the right and slow down as s/he moves to the left. S/he can choose to stand still from time to time, to speed up or slow down him or herself, or to double back before reaching a chair. Your partner's intent should be to keep you on your toes, but not to trip you up.

When you have reached the end of your text, go back and speak it again at a conversational pace.

IV. Stand in a comfortable, aligned position as far away from the rest of the group as possible.

Have a partner hold your neck to remind you not to push from there.

Begin speaking your text at a fairly loud volume, but not shouting.

Gradually take the energy out of the volume and put it into the articulation, so that you are speaking increasingly more quietly but more distinctly.

When the group can no longer make out what you are saying, they will raise their hands.

Return to the volume/energy of articulation that you were using a couple of moments before the group could no longer understand you. Staying at this volume, let your articulation become progressively lighter – less effortful. Again, the group will raise their hands when they can no longer make out the distinct sounds in each word.

Return to a conversational tone and speak the text with just the articulatory energy necessary to reach the group across the room.

V. Imagine that you are wearing a very fine tuxedo or evening gown. Angle yourself so that you are not quite facing your audience head-on, and put on your very best dashing international man/woman of mystery persona.

Without changing your accent, speak your text, channelling the crisp sophistication of your character into the consonants.

Shake off the persona, but try to stay in touch with a sense of easy precision as you speak the text again.

VI. Sit in a comfortably aligned position. The rest of the class should sit on the floor around you.

Imagine that your text is a story you are going to tell to a group of four year olds (note: childish behaviour is not needed from the group – these are very interested, well-behaved four year olds).

Without allowing your pitch to go up more than a couple of notes above your ordinary speaking range, speak the text, using the sounds of the consonants and vowels to draw the children into the story.

The class should return to their normal position and adult personas. Stand and speak the text to them, using as much of the story-telling energy of articulation as is appropriate.

Follow-up

Reflective practice questions:

* Which sounds does your jaw most like to 'help' with?
* Which consonant combinations are hardest for you to say?
* When drilling sounds or tongue-twisters, which articulators get the most tired? The lips? The tip of the tongue? The back of the tongue? The jaw?
* What, if anything, did you notice about the relationship between breath and articulation?
* In line 9 of the *Henry V* passage, why do you think Shakespeare chose the word 'battle' when 'army' probably would have been easier to understand? In line 10, why did he pick the less common 'steed' over 'horse'? Are there other words that may have been picked for their sound?
* In the text you worked on individually, are there any words that you think were picked for their sound?
* In doing your own text work and watching others, how did the articulation work contribute to the overall energy and clarity of the final performance?
* When you watch theatre, TV or films, note which actors' articulation is particularly clean and clear. Which actors are sometimes not clear in their speech? Which actors seem to overdo their enunciation of sounds? How is

this related to the characters they play? How well would the film actors' articulation work on stage? How would the stage actors' articulation work on screen?

Exercises:

* Work a couple of minutes of tongue-twisters into your morning warm-up, always taking the time to release the jaw before you start.
* In situations where you might ordinarily use volume to reach someone, see to what extent you can get your message across by sharpening the clarity of the speech sounds.
* From time to time, try reading aloud, concentrating on bringing together the energy of the thought, the energy of the breath and the energy of the articulation.

Suggested texts

Chorus from *Henry V* by William Shakespeare.

1. Now entertain conjecture of a time
2. When creeping murmur and the poring dark
3. Fills the wide vessel of the universe.
4. From camp to camp through the foul womb of night
5. The hum of either army stilly sounds,
6. That the fixed sentinels almost receive
7. The secret whispers of each other's watch.
8. Fire answers fire, and through their paly flames
9. Each battle sees the other's umbered face.
10. Steed threatens steed in high and boastful neighs
11. Piercing the night's dull ear, and from the tents
12. The armourers, accomplishing the knights,
13. With busy hammers closing rivets up,
14. Give dreadful note of preparation.

Nephelidia by Algernon Charles Swinburne.

From the depth of the dreamy decline of the dawn through a notable nimbus of nebulous noonshine,

Pallid and pink as the palm of the flag-flower that flickers with fear of the flies as they float,

Are they looks of our lovers that lustrously lean from a marvel of mystic miraculous moonshine,

These that we feel in the blood of our blushes that thicken and threaten with throbs through the throat?

Thicken and thrill as a theatre thronged at appeal of an actor's appalled agitation,

Fainter with fear of the fires of the future than pale with the promise of pride in the past;

Flushed with the famishing fullness of fever that reddens with radiance of rathe recreation,

Gaunt as the ghastliest of glimpses that gleam through the gloom of the gloaming when ghosts go aghast?

Nay, for the nick of the tick of the time is a tremulous touch on the temples of terror,

Strained as the sinews yet strenuous with strife of the dead who is dumb as the dust-heaps of death:

Surely no soul is it, sweet as the spasm of erotic emotional exquisite error,

Bathed in the balms of beatified bliss, beatific itself by beatitude's breath.

Surely no spirit or sense of a soul that was soft to the spirit and soul of our senses

Sweetens the stress of suspiring suspicion that sobs in the semblance and sound of a sigh;

Only this oracle opens Olympian, in mystical moods and triangular tenses -

'Life is the lust of a lamp for the light that is dark till the dawn of the day when we die'.

Mild is the mirk and monotonous music of memory, melodiously mute as it may be,

While the hope in the heart of a hero is bruised by the breach of men's rapiers, resigned to the rod;

Made meek as a mother whose bosom-beats bound with the bliss-bringing bulk of a balm-breathing baby,

As they grope through the graveyard of creeds, under skies growing green at a groan for the grimness of God.

Blank is the book of his bounty beholden of old, and its binding is blacker than bluer:

Out of blue into black is the scheme of the skies, and their dews are the wine of the bloodshed of things;

Till the darkling desire of delight shall be free as a fawn that is freed from the fangs that pursue her,

Till the heart-beats of hell shall be hushed by a hymn from the hunt that has harried the kennel of kings.

Lord Chancellor's Song from *Iolanthe* by WS Gilbert.

1. When you're lying awake with a dismal headache, and repose is taboo'd by anxiety,

    I conceive you may use any language you choose to indulge in, without impropriety;

    For your brain is on fire – the bedclothes conspire of usual slumber to plunder you:

    First your counterpane goes, and uncovers your toes, and your sheet slips demurely from under you;

2. Then the blanketing tickles – you feel like mixed pickles – so terribly sharp is the pricking,

    And you're hot, and you're cross, and you tumble and toss till there's nothing 'twixt you and the ticking.

    Then the bedclothes all creep to the ground in a heap, and you pick 'em all up in a tangle;

    Next your pillow resigns and politely declines to remain at its usual angle!

3. Well, you get some repose in the form of a doze, with hot eye-balls and head ever aching.

    But your slumbering teems with such horrible dreams that you'd very much better be waking;

    For you dream you are crossing the Channel, and tossing about in a steamer from Harwich –

Which is something between a large bathing machine and a very small
second-class carriage –

And bound on that journey you find your attorney (who started that morning
from Devon);

He's a bit undersized, and you don't feel surprised when he tells you he's
only eleven.

4. Well, you're driving like mad with this singular lad (by the by, the ship's now
a four-wheeler),

And you're playing round games, and he calls you bad names when you tell
him that "ties pay the dealer";

But this you can't stand, so you throw up your hand, and you find you're as
cold as an icicle,

In your shirt and your socks (the black silk with gold clocks), crossing Salisbury
Plain on a bicycle:

5. And he and the crew are on bicycles too – which they've somehow or other
invested in –

The shares are a penny, and ever so many are taken by Rothschild and
Baring,

And just as a few are allotted to you, you awake with a shudder despairing –

You're a regular wreck, with a crick in your neck, and no wonder you snore,
for your head's on the floor,

and you've needles and pins from your soles to your shins, and your flesh is
a-creep, for your left leg's asleep,

and you've cramp in your toes, and a fly on your nose, and some fluff in your
lung, and a feverish tongue,

and a thirst that's intense, and a general sense that you haven't been
sleeping in clover;

But the darkness has passed, and it's daylight at last, and the night has been
long – ditto, ditto my song – and thank goodness they're both of them over!

Maya Angelou	'Touched by an Angel'
Hilaire Belloc	'Tarantella'
John Betjeman	'A Subaltern's Love Song'
Noel Coward	'I am No Good at Love'

T S Eliot	'Skimbleshanks: The Railway Cat'
W S Gilbert	'My Name is John Wellington Wells'
Liz Lochhead	'Bawd'
Dorothy Parker	'One Perfect Rose'
George Peele	'What Thing is Love?'
Harold Pinter	'The Ventriloquists'
Edgar Allen Poe	'The Raven'
Cole Porter	'Let's Do It, Let's Fall in Love'
Peter Porter	'A Chagall Postcard'
Vikram Seth	'Round and Round'
William Shakespeare	'When I Do Count the Clock ....' (Sonnet 12)

Further reading

Berry, Cicely, *Voice and the Actor*, Virgin, London, 2000. Chapter 3: Muscularity and Word, pp. 43–75.

Houseman, Barbara, *Finding Your Voice*, Nick Hern Books, London, 2002. Chapter 8: Shaping the Sound: Firming Up Your Articulation, pp. 193–229.

Lessac, Arthur, *The Use and Training of the Human Voice*, Mayfield Publishing Company, California, 1997. Chapter 5: The Dynamics of Consonant NRG, pp. 63–121.

Linklater, Kristin, *Freeing the Natural Voice* (Revised edition), Drama Book Publishers, New York, 2006. Chapter 19, pp. 295–311.

McCallion, Michael, *The Voice Book* (Revised edition), Faber and Faber Ltd, London, 1998. Part Four: Speech, pp. 125–190.

Rodenburg, Patsy, *The Actor Speaks*, Methuen, London, 1997. Stage Two: Extending the Voice into Resonance, Range and Speech, pp. 104–122.

Turner, J. Clifford, *Voice and Speech in the Theatre* (Sixth edition, edited by Jane Boston), A&C Black, London, 2007. Chapter 5: The Word, pp. 66–102.

Appendix 1

Vocal Workout

In this appendix we provide you with a short vocal workout that can be easily performed at home or at work, in a classroom, office space or dressing room. It assumes a level of competence appropriate to someone who has completed the work of *The Vocal Arts Workbook*. We would like to thank those students who helped to refine it: Jonathan Bonnici, Sonya Cassidy, Lauren Crace, Katie Georgiou, Mike Grady-Hall, Antonia Kinlay, Siu Hun Li, Antonio Magro, Tim Pritchett, Georgina White, and Jonathan Wright.

1. Begin on the floor, lying in semi-supine, and connect to your breathing.

   Let your breath deepen, and then focus particularly on the movement of your ribs.

   Place your hands on the sides of your ribs so that you become aware of the lateral widening of your rib cage as you breathe in. Encourage this sideways movement on each in-breath by thinking 'Ribs widen'.

   On the out-breath, begin by releasing a steady, sustained SH sound for a mental count of ten.

   Repeat, and then produce an easy, sustained SS sound for a mental count of 12.

   Repeat, and then produce a clear, sustained ZZ sound for a mental count of 12.

   Repeat, aiming to keep the sound at a steady intensity for its whole length.

   Now bring your lips gently together to create a hum (MM) on your next out-breath. Monitor how long you can sustain this sound. As you do so, imagine there is an AH vowel waiting behind the hum – let your tongue rest in the floor of your mouth, feel the tip of your tongue resting against the back of the lower front teeth, let your jaw soften, creating space between your back molars, and think of lifting the soft palate away from the back of the tongue.

On your next out-breath, establish the hum in this way and then let the jaw drop open to release the AH vowel.

Repeat, and then do the same with the vowels OO and EE. Aim to maintain all of these vowels for a mental count of 12. If you find yourself running out of breath before that, don't worry – just keep exercising regularly and the muscles will respond. If you can sustain for longer than 12, keep up the good work.

2. Still on the floor in semi-supine, focus your attention on your abdominal muscles as they respond to the movement of your diaphragm.

Place your hands on your stomach; notice how your hands rise as you breathe in, and lower as you breathe out. Encourage your abdominal muscles to release as you breathe in and to engage as you breathe out – place the impulse for breathing in this action of the abdominal muscles.

Now, on the out-breath, produce a sustained SH sound with a steady engagement of the abdominal muscles throughout.

Repeat, but this time complete the sound with a CH, and feel the added contraction of the abdominal muscles supporting this sound.

Build on this sense of abdominal support by producing a long FFF sound, feeling the engagement of the abdominal muscles sending the air to where the sound is made at the teeth and lip.

Do the same on a long VVV sound, feeling the vibrating air focused on your teeth and lip. Now use the engagement of the abdominal muscles to touch off a short, easy HUH sound – think of it as a little dart of sound going up to the ceiling.

Repeat, feeling the support of the abdominal muscles.

Do the same with a HAY sound, but give yourself an imaginative impulse – for example, calling to a friend across the street. Repeat, and then do the same with a HI sound (greeting a friend you haven't seen for a while, for example).

3. Now bring yourself up on to all fours.

In this position, think of your back lengthening and widening as you breathe. Focus on the movement of the ribs again, but think particularly of them widening in your back as you breathe in. (If you find it difficult to be aware of this movement, try lowering yourself into a prayer position for a while as this can create a greater sensation of the ribs opening across the back.)

Release your out-breath on a hum (MM), imagining an AH vowel waiting behind it. Repeat and open the jaw to release the AH vowel, thinking of sending the sound into the floor.

Repeat, and then do the same with the vowels OO and EE.

Now focus your attention on your abdominal muscles. Think of engaging the muscles to lift your stomach up towards your spine as you breathe out, and then release the muscles to allow the stomach to drop towards the floor as you breathe in. Release your out-breath on a SH sound.

Repeat, but this time complete the sound with a CH, and feel the added contraction of the abdominal muscles supporting this sound.

Continue with the exercises in (2) in this position.

4. Now sit well forwards in a chair, so that there is space between your back and the chair. (The chair should be of a height where you can sit comfortably upright, feet flat on the floor, and thighs parallel with the floor.) In this position, think of your back lengthening and widening as you breathe. Think of your neck being free not fixed, and your head facing forwards with the top of your head parallel with the ceiling. Focus again on the movement of the ribs, and feel them widening out to the sides from the spine as you breathe in. Encourage this sideways movement on each in-breath by thinking, 'Ribs widen'.

Release your out-breath on a hum (MM), imagining an AH vowel waiting behind it. Repeat and open the jaw to release the AH vowel, thinking of sending the sound across the room.

Now focus your attention on your abdominal muscles. Think of engaging the muscles to bring your stomach towards your spine as you breathe out, and then release the muscles to allow the stomach to move out as you breathe in.

Release your out-breath on a SH sound.

Repeat, but this time complete the sound with a CH, and feel the added contraction of the abdominal muscles supporting this sound.

Now combine your awareness of the ribs and the abdominal muscles. Allow the ribs to widen and the abdominal muscles to release as you breathe in. Release your out-breath on a hum (MM), imagining an AH vowel waiting behind it. Feel your abdominal muscles actively engaged to support this sound.

Repeat and open the jaw to release the AH vowel, thinking of sending the sound across the room.

Repeat several times, focusing on the AH vowel – let your tongue rest in the floor of your mouth, feel the tip of your tongue resting against the back of the lower front teeth, let your jaw soften creating space between your back molars, and think of lifting the soft palate away from the back of the tongue to create space in the back of the mouth.

Repeat with the vowel sounds AY (as in 'hay') and OH (as in 'hoe'), feeling the space in the back of your mouth.

Continuing to use a supported breath, now begin to work your pitch range by sirening on a pitch glide using first a NG sound (as in 'sing') and then on AH.

5. Stand up and continue to sound on AH while shaking out, swinging your arms and sirening through your range.

Now stand easy, think of your back lengthening and widening as you breathe. Think of your neck being free not fixed, and your head facing forwards with the top of your head parallel with the ceiling.

Now combine your awareness of the ribs and the abdominal muscles again. Allow the ribs to widen and the abdominal muscles to release as you breathe in. Release your out-breath on a hum (MM), imagining an AH vowel waiting behind it. Feel your abdominal muscles actively engaged to support this sound.

Repeat and open the jaw to release the AH vowel, thinking of sending the sound across the room.

Repeat several times, focusing on the AH vowel – let your tongue rest in the floor of your mouth, feel the tip of your tongue resting against the back of the lower front teeth, let your jaw soften creating space between your back molars, and think of lifting the soft palate away from the back of the tongue to create space in the back of the mouth.

Repeat with the vowel sounds OO, OH, AW, AH, AY, EE.

6. Complete the workout with the following work on the articulators.

Enjoy a full open-mouthed yawn, and then scrunch the face up, and release.

Repeat several times, to waken up the muscles in the face.

Massage the muscles of the jaw to encourage it to open fully.

Massage the muscles around the lips. Now blow your lips out on a BRRR sound (the 'shivering' sound we make when we are cold) – glide this sound through your pitch range.

Flick your tongue in and out of your mouth very quickly, making a rapid series of LA sounds – and glide this sound through your pitch range.

Now stick your tongue out and point it and flatten it several times.

Anchor the tip of your tongue behind your lower front teeth, then stretch the body of your tongue forwards into a hump over the lower front teeth, and then release it back into your mouth.

Do this several times, making a YA-YA-YA sound as the tongue moves forwards and back. Glide this sound through your pitch range.

These exercises have helped to release tension from the jaw, lips and tongue. Maintain this sense of release as you exercise the articulatory muscles on the following sound sequences:

BUH-BUH-BUH **BUH-BUH-BUH BAH**
PUH-PUH-PUH **PUH-PUH-PUH PAH**
MUH-MUH-MUH **MUH-MUH-MUH MAH**

DUH-DUH-DUH **DUH-DUH-DUH DAH**
TUH-TUH-TUH **TUH-TUH-TUH TAH**
NUH-NUH-NUH **NUH-NUH-NUH NAH**

GUH-GUH-GUH **GUH-GUH-GUH GAH**
KUH-KUH-KUH **KUH-KUH-KUH KAH**
NGUH-NGUH-NGUH **NGUH-NGUH-NGUH NGAH**

Play with your pitch range on these sequences, and instead of AH at the end of each sequence, try substituting other vowel sounds. Let your body be free and keep your neck and jaw relaxed.

Appendix 2

Sample Curricula

These outline programmes are provided to indicate two ways in which the work of this book may be incorporated into a formal curriculum. These are not meant to be definitive models, as it is expected that teachers will adapt them to suit the learning needs of their particular students. We have assumed a minimum of three hours a week.

15-week model (One Semester)

Block 1 **Introduction**

Week 1   Initial work from Chapter 1 on *Stretching, Floor Work, Roll-ups* and *Keeping it Loose.* Work on *Opening the Breath* from Chapter 2.

Week 2   As for Week 1, and add initial work on *Coming on to Voice* from Chapter 2.

Week 3   Continue as above, and add later work from Chapters 1 and 2, including work on *Breath and Voice in Action.*

Week 4   Continue as above as appropriate, but focus on *Engaging the In-breath* from Chapter 3.

Week 5   Continue as above as appropriate, but focus on *Engaging the Out-breath* from Chapter 3. Work on *Connecting to Text* from Chapter 2.

Block 2 **Development**

Week 6   Review the work of Weeks 1–5.

Week 7   Continue with the work of Weeks 1–5, and add work on *Working the Channel* from Chapter 4. Further work on *Connecting to Text* from Chapter 2.

Week 8   Continue as above as appropriate, but focus on *Supporting the Voice* from Chapter 3.

Week 9   As for Week 8, and add initial work on *Finding the Buzz* from Chapter 4.

Week 10   As for Week 8, and add initial work on *Expanding the Range* from Chapter 4. Work on *Supporting Text* from Chapter 3.

Block 3   Consolidation

Week 11   Review the work of Weeks 7–10, and add later work on *Finding the Buzz* and *Expanding the Range*.

Week 12   Continue as above as appropriate, but focus on *Toning the Articulators* from Chapter 5. Work on *Resonating Text* from Chapter 4.

Week 13   Continue as above as appropriate, but focus on *Balancing the Sound* from Chapter 4.

Week 14   Continue as above as appropriate, but focus on *Specifying the Sounds* from Chapter 5.

Week 15   Warm up. Work on *Resonating Text* from Chapter 4 and *Articulating Text* from Chapter 5.

30-week model (Three Terms)

Term 1   Introduction

Week 1   Initial work from Chapter 1 on *Stretching, Floor Work, Roll-ups* and *Keeping it Loose*.

Week 2   Work on *Opening the Breath* from Chapter 2.

Week 3   As for Weeks 1 and 2, and add initial work on *Coming on to Voice* from Chapter 2.

Week 4   Continue as above.

Week 5   Continue as above, and add later work from Chapters 1 and 2.

Week 6   Continue as for Week 5 and add work on *Breath and Voice in Action* from Chapter 2.

Week 7   Continue as above as appropriate. Work on *Connecting to Text* from Chapter 2.

Week 8   Continue but add work on *Engaging the In-breath* from Chapter 3.

Week 9   Continue as above as appropriate, but focus on *Engaging the Out-breath* from Chapter 3.

Week 10   Warm up. Further work on *Connecting to Text* from Chapter 2.

Term 2   Development

Week 1   Review the work of Term 1.

Week 2   Continue review of Term 1, including *Connecting to Text* work as appropriate.

Week 3   Continue with the work of Term 1, and add work on *Working the Channel* from Chapter 4.

Week 4   Continue as for Week 3 as appropriate.

Week 5   Continue as for Week 3 as appropriate, but add work on *Supporting the Voice* from Chapter 3.

Week 6   Continue work on *Supporting the Voice*. Work on *Supporting Text* from Chapter 3

Week 7   As for Weeks 5 and 6, and add initial work on *Finding the Buzz* from Chapter 4.

Week 8   Continue as for Week 7.

Week 9   Continue as for Weeks 5 and 6, and add initial work on *Expanding the Range* from Chapter 4.

Week 10   Continue as for Week 9. Further work on *Supporting Text* from Chapter 3.

Term 3   Consolidation

Week 1   Review the work of Term 2, and add later work on *Finding the Buzz* and *Expanding the Range*.

Week 2   Continue as for Week 1.

Week 3   Continue as above as appropriate, but focus on *Toning the Articulators* from Chapter 5.

Week 4   Continue as for Week 3.

Week 5   Continue as for Week 3, and add work on *Balancing the Sound* from Chapter 4.

Week 6   Continue as for Week 5. Work on *Resonating Text* from Chapter 4.

Week 7   Continue as above as appropriate, and add work on *Specifying the Sounds* from Chapter 5.

Week 8   Review the work from Chapter 4.

Week 9   Review the work from Chapter 5.

Week 10   Warm up. Work on *Resonating Text* from Chapter 4 and *Articulating Text* from Chapter 5.

Appendix 3

Bibliography and Resources

Recommended Books

Practical Voice and Speech

Berry, Cicely, *Voice and the Actor*, Virgin, London, 2000.

Berry, Cicely, *Your Voice and How To Use It*, Virgin, London, 2000.

Bunch Dayme, Meribeth, *The Performer's Voice: Realizing Your Vocal Potential*, W W Norton, New York, 2005.

Kayes, Gillyanne, *Singing and the Actor* (Second edition), A&C Black, London, 2004.

Houseman, Barbara, *Finding Your Voice*, Nick Hern Books, London, 2002.

Lessac, Arthur, *The Use and Training of the Human Voice*, Mayfield Publishing Company, California, 1997.

Linklater, Kristin, *Freeing the Natural Voice* (Revised edition), Drama Book Publishers, New York, 2006.

McCallion, Michael, *The Voice Book* (Revised edition), Faber and Faber Ltd, London, 1998.

Martin, Stephanie and Darnley, Lyn, *The Teaching Voice* (Second edition), Whurr Publishers, London and Philadelphia, 2004

Melton, Joan (with Kenneth Tom), *One Voice*, Heinemann, Portsmouth, NH, 2003.

Morrison, Malcolm, *Clear Speech* (Fourth edition), A&C Black, London, 2001.

Rodenburg, Patsy, *The Actor Speaks*, Methuen, London, 1997

Turner, J Clifford, *Voice and Speech in the Theatre* (Sixth edition, edited by Jane Boston), A&C Black Publishers, London, 2007.

Vocal Anatomy and Vocal Health

Borden, Gloria J and Harris, Katherine S, *Speech Science Primer*, Williams & Wilkins, Philadelphia, 1980.

Bunch, Meribeth, *Dynamics of the Singing Voice* (Fourth edition), Springer-Verlag, Austria, 2001.

Davies, D Garfield and Jahn, Anthony F, *Care of the Professional Voice: A Guide to Voice Management for Singers, Actors and Professional Voice Users*, A&C Black, London, 2004.

Mathieson, Lesley, Greene and Mathieson's *The Voice and Its Disorders* (Sixth edition), Whurr Publishers, London and Philadelphia, 2001.

Bodywork

Allain, Paul, *The Art of Stillness: The Theatre Practice of Tadashi Suzuki*, Methuen, London, 2002.

Lam Kam Chuen, Master, *The Way of Energy*, Simon & Schuster, New York, 1991.

Macdonald, Glynn, *The Complete Illustrated Guide to Alexander Technique*, Element, Dorset, 1998.

Macdonald, Robert and Ness, Caro, *Secrets of Alexander Technique*, Dorling Kindersley Ltd, London, 2001.

McEvenue, Kelly, *The Alexander Technique for Actors*, Methuen, London 2001.

Essay Collections

Armstrong, Frankie and Pearson, Jenny (editors), *Well-Tuned Women*, The Women's Press, 2000.

Hampton, Marion and Acker, Barbara (editors), *The Vocal Vision*, Applause, New York, 1997.

Journal

The Voice and Speech Review, the official Journal of the Voice and Speech Trainers Association, covers contemporary issues in professional voice and speech training. Published biannually, the *Review* is packed with articles, pedagogical essays, and book and theatre reviews from across the English-speaking world. It has reached five volumes at the time of writing:

1. *Standard Speech*, edited by Rocco Dal Vera, 2000.
2. *The Voice in Violence*, edited by Rocco Dal Vera, 2001.
3. *Film, Broadcast and Electronic Media Coaching*, edited by Rocco Dal Vera, 2003.
4. *Shakespeare Around the Globe*, edited by Mandy Rees, 2005.
5. *Voice and Gender*, edited by Mandy Rees, 2007.

These can be ordered online at www.amazon.com.

Recommended poetry anthologies

Staying Alive, edited by Neil Astley, Bloodaxe Books, Northumberland, 2002.
Being Alive, edited by Neil Astley, Bloodaxe Books, Northumberland, 2004.
The Rattle Bag, edited by Seamus Heaney and Ted Hughes, Faber and Faber Ltd, London, 1982.
The School Bag, edited by Seamus Heaney and Ted Hughes, Faber and Faber Ltd, 1997.
The New Faber Book of Love Poems, edited by James Fenton, Faber and Faber Ltd, 2006.

Recommended websites

Poetry

www.famouspoetsandpoems.com
www.poemhunter.com
www.poetryarchive.org
www.poets.org

Organisations

www.british-voice-association.com The website of the British Voice Association
www.cssd.ac.uk/pages/icv.html The website of the International Centre for Voice
www.vasta.org The website of the Voice and Speech Trainers Association
www.voicecare.org.uk The website of the Voice Care Network (UK)

Practitioners

www.frankiearmstrong.com (Frankie Armstrong)
www.fccake.com (Meribeth Bunch Dayme)
www.fitzmauricevoice.com (Catherine Fitzmaurice)
www.roy-hart.com (Roy Hart Theatre)
www.vocalprocess.co.uk (Gillyanne Kayes)
www.methodsworkshops/dudley (Dudley Knight)
www.kristinlinklater.com (Kristin Linklater)

Appendix 4
Professional Histories

David Carey

David Carey trained during the 1970s as a speech and drama teacher at the Royal Scottish Academy of Music and Drama in Glasgow, where his voice teachers were John Colson, Jacqui Crago, and Jim House. John was the husband of Greta Colson, Co-Director of the New College of Speech and Drama, London. Greta Colson was a graduate of the Central School of Speech and Drama and author or co-author of a number of books on voice, speech and phonetics. The New College of Speech and Drama, which was later absorbed by Middlesex Polytechnic (later Middlesex University), was one of a number of drama schools in the 1960s which were training voice teachers in the UK. Jacqui Crago and Jim House were both graduates of New College. Jacqui's classes in phonetics and poetry were a particular influence on David's decision to become a voice teacher.

However, David's initial introduction to voice and speech work was literally at his mother's knee. Elna Carey (nee Graham) trained during the 1930s as a Speech Teacher at the Central School of Speech and Drama under Elsie Fogerty. Gwynneth Thurburn and J Clifford Turner were also on the Central faculty at this time. She married actor Brian Carey, who came from a theatrical family in Dublin, and so David was brought up with a deep awareness of the importance of voice, speech and articulate communication.

Following his training in Glasgow, David completed a BA degree in English Language and Linguistics at Edinburgh University before taking up a position as Lecturer in Voice and Speech at Queen Margaret College, Edinburgh, where he taught on the College's undergraduate drama programme for five years. His work at this time was strongly influenced by both Cicely Berry and Kristin Linklater through their seminal books, *Voice and the Actor* (first published in 1973) and *Freeing the Natural Voice* (first published in 1976). Berry had trained under and worked with Gwynneth Thurburn at the Central School of Speech and Drama (CSSD), while Linklater had trained under and worked with Iris Warren at the London Academy of Music and Dramatic Art (LAMDA). David found that the rigorous and muscular work of Berry was complemented by the more kinaesthetic and image-based approach of Linklater, and that a combination of the two was well suited to the needs of developing students.

David left Edinburgh in 1982 to join the Royal Shakespeare Company as Assistant Voice Director, working under Cicely Berry and alongside Patsy Rodenburg. The four years that David spent at the RSC were a rich period in the company's history: Judi Dench, Fiona Shaw, Juliet Stevenson and Harriet Walter, Kenneth Branagh, Brian Cox, Derek Jacobi, Alan Rickman and Antony Sher were all members of the acting company. In addition to Joint Artistic Directors, Terry Hands and Trevor Nunn, other directors included Bill Alexander, John Barton, Ron Daniels, Howard Davies, Barry Kyle and Adrian Noble. Notable plays and productions of this period with which David was associated were *Richard III* with Antony Sher, *Henry V* with Kenneth Branagh, and the world premieres of *Les Liaisons Dangereuses* and Howard Barker's *The Castle*. David's understanding of voice, text and acting was deeply informed by the opportunity to observe these actors and directors, but most especially by the experience of watching Cicely Berry's unique collaboration with these theatre artists. Her passion for language and its ability to express the human experience, particularly through the work of Shakespeare, left an indelible impression on David and continues to influence his work to this day.

David left the RSC to take up the post of Senior Lecturer (later, Principal Lecturer) in Voice Studies at the Central School of Speech and Drama, where he was responsible for developing and sustaining the school's postgraduate programme in Voice Studies, a course of professional development for graduates who wished to follow a career in voice teaching. David was responsible for all aspects of teaching and learning, from course design and admissions to assessment, timetabling and pastoral care. He taught modules in vocal anatomy, vocal pedagogy, voice and text, and phonetics, as well as supervising dissertations and independent practical projects.

Under his leadership, the course became recognised as a national and international benchmark in the field. British graduates were regularly employed by all of the leading HE drama training institutions in England and Wales. As UK universities diversified their provision with respect to practice-based drama courses, graduates also found employment in this part of the sector. The course also served a world-wide demand for well-qualified teachers of voice and speech, attracting a regular number of international applicants from North America, Europe, Asia and Australia. In the USA, graduates went on to work at (amongst others) Yale University, Southern Methodist University, and the University of Utah. Other graduates were successfully employed in HE drama training institutions in Australia, Canada, Japan, Singapore, South Africa, Holland and Denmark. In his 17-year tenure, David was responsible for training over 200 voice teachers, many of whom are now at the top of their profession, including the Heads of Voice at the Royal

National Theatre in London, the Stratford Ontario Festival Theatre, and the Oregon Shakespeare Festival.

Through the course at CSSD, David introduced a generation of voice teachers to the work of a wide range of practitioners, including Frankie Armstrong, Kevin Crawford, Meribeth Bunch Dayme, Catherine Fitzmaurice, Nadine George, Barbara Houseman, Gillyanne Kayes, Christina Shewell, Andrew Wade, and Joanna Weir-Ouston.

In 2000, recognising the need for a major resource facility that was designed to serve the professional development of teachers of voice and speech and to contribute to the wider international community in HE actor training, David established the International Centre for Voice at CSSD. During his term as Director of the International Centre for Voice he organised a number of events intended to support and influence colleagues. In July 2001, he was responsible for organising a major international conference on the work of the Roy Hart Theatre under the title of *The Contribution of Alfred Wolfsohn, Roy Hart and the Roy Hart Theatre to Vocal Expression*. Roy Hart was a pioneer of vocal performance art who created the Roy Hart Theatre (RHT), an international theatre research group based in France, in the 1970s. David had come into contact with a number of RHT practitioners and felt that their work deserved to be known more widely in the UK; he therefore organised the conference to enable a reassessment of the work. Participants included UK HE voice teachers and drama practitioners and international visitors from Europe, Australia and the US. As a result, the work of Roy Hart practitioners such as Noah Pikes, Kevin Crawford and Nadine George has entered the mainstream of voice teaching in a number of HE institutions.

David left Central in 2003, returning to the vocal training of actors as Voice Tutor at the Royal Academy of Dramatic Art, where he continues to teach. In 2004 he revisited the RSC to coach their touring productions of *Julius Caesar* and *Two Gentlemen of Verona*, and in 2005 spent two months with the Oregon Shakespeare Festival as Voice and Text Director for productions of *The Philanderer* by George Bernard Shaw and *By the Waters of Babylon* by Robert Schenkkan. He also maintains a relationship with the Stratford Ontario Festival in Canada, where he was vocal coach for the 2007 production of Oscar Wilde's *An Ideal Husband*. He is an Associate Editor for the *Voice and Speech Review*, the journal of the Voice and Speech Trainers Association.

David's pedagogy is an eclectic one which draws on the work of the leading voice teachers of today, such as Cicely Berry, Kristin Linklater and Patsy Rodenburg. His academic interest in linguistics – he has a Masters in Contemporary English Language and Linguistics from Reading University – also informs his practice through a deep understanding of language, vocal anatomy, phonetics and dialects. He also draws actively on his experience of Alexander Technique and T'ai Chi. He places emphasis on exploring and developing the natural potential of the voice, with equal attention paid to physiological function and imaginative intention, so that fundamental work on breathing, alignment, resonance and articulation is integrated with expressive work on text and communication.

David was awarded a prestigious National Teaching Fellowship in 2007 by the UK's Higher Education Academy in recognition of his contribution to vocal pedagogy.

Rebecca Clark Carey

Rebecca Clark Carey trained as an actress at the University of California at Irvine's Master of Fine Arts programme. Her principal voice and speech teacher there was Dudley Knight, and she continues to draw heavily on Dudley's teaching in her own work. Dudley himself studied voice with Kristin Linklater and Catherine Fitzmaurice, both of whom did their initial training in London — Kristin at the London Academy of Music and Dramatic Art with Iris Warren, and Catherine at the Central School of Speech and Drama with Cicely Berry and Gwynneth Thurburn.

Dudley Knight is a Master Teacher of Fitzmaurice Voicework, a method of training that draws on and adapts various disciplines such as hatha yoga and shiatsu to free and strengthen the voice. It also uses the inducement of involuntary muscle tremors to release deep tensions and achieve true spontaneity in breathing and the making of sound. This work is characterised as 'Destructuring'. Fitzmaurice Voicework also includes work in 'Restructuring', which encourages physiologically efficient breathing to support the voice without sacrificing flexibility. It was under Dudley's tutelage that Rebecca came to understand voice work as being largely about getting out of the way of the body's natural ability to produce free, strong, expressive sound.

Dudley is also an internationally respected teacher of speech who regularly conducts workshops on Knight Speechwork. While this book does not address speech as an independent discipline, the chapter on articulation has been greatly informed by Dudley's emphasis on agility and clarity.

While at Irvine, Rebecca further developed her thinking on voice by participating in an intensive, summer-long course in Jerzy Grotowski's Theatre of Sources work led by two of Grotowski's principle associates, James Slowiak and Jairo Cuesta. The experience led her to a deeper understanding of physical and mental discipline and focus, and the nature of working from impulse. Her physical training in the Suzuki method also informed her understanding of the connection between body, breath and voice. In her third year, she was selected to teach an Introduction to Voice class to undergraduate drama students.

After leaving UC Irvine, Rebecca worked as a professional actress, primarily on the west coast of the United States. She gained skills in classical text particularly through her work with the California Shakespeare Festival, Shakespeare Santa Cruz, and the Oregon Shakespeare Festival. While in Los Angeles she also had the good fortune to study

Shakespeare with Dakin Matthews at the Antaeus Company of classical actors. It was during this time that Rebecca was first invited to work as a voice and text coach, at Palomar College in San Diego County. She coached every Shakespeare play produced at the college for a number of years.

When Rebecca decided to make the transition to teaching and coaching full time, she went to London to study at the Central School of Speech and Drama. While working on her MA in Voice Studies there, she had the opportunity to receive instruction from many prominent voice practitioners, including Cicely Berry, Andrew Wade, Joanna Weir-Ouston, Gillyanne Kayes and Meribeth Bunch Dayme. Her dissertation was on speaking Shakespeare's late plays (an edited version was published in *Voice and Speech Review: Film, Broadcast and Electronic Media Coaching,* 2003).

Shortly after completing the course, Rebecca joined the education department at the Oregon Shakespeare Festival and was invited to assist voice and text directors Scott Kaiser and Ursula Meyer on productions of *Handler,* by Pulitzer Prize winner Robert Schenkkan, and *A Winter's Tale.* Their expertise and generosity continue to inform and inspire her coaching work. The following year she served as voice and text director on *Hedda Gabler* and *Wild Oats.* She has since returned regularly to coach Shakespeare plays, including *King Lear, Much Ado About Nothing, The Taming of the Shrew,* and *The Tempest.*

Rebecca currently resides in England where she has taught voice at The Central School of Speech and Drama, The Italia Conti Academy of Theatre Arts, The Oxford School of Drama, and The Royal Academy of Dramatic Art.

Index